Asking Good Questions

Case Studies in Ethics and Critical Thinking

Asking Good Questions
Case Studies in Ethics and Critical Thinking

NANCY A. STANLICK

and

MICHAEL STRAWSER

Hackett Publishing Company
Indianapolis/Cambridge

Copyright © 2015 Hackett Publishing Company

21 20 19 18 17 16 15   1 2 3 4 5 6 7 8

For further information, please address
  Hackett Publishing Company, Inc.
  P.O. Box 44937
  Indianapolis, Indiana 46244-0937
  www.hackettpublishing.com

All concept maps were created using MindManager, Standard Edition © 2001, Mindjet LLC.

Cover image: *School of Athens*, Apostolic Palace, Vatican City. Painted in 1511 by Raphael.

Library of Congress Cataloging-in-Publication Data
Stanlick, Nancy A.
  Asking good questions : case studies in ethics and critical thinking /
Nancy A. Stanlick and Michael Strawser. ~ First [edition].
    pages cm
  Includes bibliographical references and index.
  ISBN 978-1-58510-639-4 (pbk.) ISBN 978-1-58510-731-5 (cloth)
  1. Ethics—Textbooks. 2. Critical thinking—Textbooks. 3.
Questioning—Textbooks. I. Title.
  BJ1012.S64 2014
  170—dc23   2014031283

TO NATHANAEL AND NICHOLAS,
who always ask the best questions.
– MS

TO TRACY AND GLEN,
whose strength of character in the face of adversity humbles me.
I am so proud of both of you.
– NS

Table of Contents

Preface

The study of ethics is both complicated and eminently useful. Perhaps these two characteristics are inseparably connected. There are various approaches to teaching ethics, and one in particular, the one presented in this book, focuses on case studies to teach and learn both theoretical and applied ethics. A benefit of this approach is that it may facilitate the process of learning (and teaching) important concepts, principles, distinctions, and nuances of theories through critical reasoning about "real-life cases." Cases present problems, issues, and the opportunity to apply theories. The most important benefit and aspect of a case study approach to ethics is that it combines theories, reasoning, creativity, and awareness of many varied elements of moral decision-making that are not available simply by reading, analyzing, and writing or speaking about ethical theories as abstractions. Another way to put the case is that often in teaching ethics, peculiar examples are used to illustrate a moral problem or dilemma and a theory or principle is presented to students who are then tasked with "solving" the problem by using that theory or principle. "Real life," however, is not so simple even though it often presents us with peculiar and intractable problems.

A popularly used example in ethics courses and texts is the "trolley problem" which has seen a recent spate of attention in discussing and teaching moral reasoning. Philosophy professor Michael Sandel uses the trolley problem in his massive open online course (MOOC) on justice from Harvard University, and in 2013 at least two books on the trolley problem were popularized in an article in *The New York Times*. While the trolley problem is interesting and often humorous in a macabre way, it does very little to tell us how to solve everyday moral problems.

The trolley problem is simple. We imagine that there is a trolley that has gone out of control, and in at least one variation on the problem, the tracks diverge a short distance from two places onto two separate tracks where innocent people will be severely injured or killed if the trolley is not stopped or diverted. Assume that it is not possible for you to stop the trolley, and to your knowledge the only means at your disposal by which to divert it is to hit the switch that will change its direction. If you are situated such that you have control of the switch (and assuming that you cannot stop the trolley and that you, and you alone, must make the decision what to do), and you know that on the left there are five innocent people who will be killed if the trolley is permitted to go in that direction and on the right there is one innocent person who will be killed if it is permitted to go in that direction, the question is: What should you do?

In some variations of the trolley problem, a contingency is added that is particularly problematic. At the point at which you are trying to determine how or whether to flip the switch to divert the trolley, a very large "fat" man is walking across the bridge where you are standing by the switch. It dawns on you that you could push the fat man over the bridge and into the path of the oncoming trolley, and his girth will, in itself, cause the trolley to stop. What should you do?

In the first case where there is no fat man to push off the bridge, the decision is left to you to determine whether you will save the five people on the left track or save the one person on the right. Alternately put, it is your decision whether to expedite the deaths of the five on the left track or the single person on the right. In the second case where you have a fat man at your disposal to push in front of the trolley and whose size will effectively stop it, you are now put into a position in which you can either ignore the fat man and decide whether to save five people or one, or you can use the fat man by pushing him over the side and save six other innocent people.

While the case is amusing to consider and it allows us to apply theories and principles from theoretical ethics, and perhaps it even tells us each something about ourselves from which decision we make, "real life" problems are generally not trolley problems, and "real life" problems are not usually those in which ordinary people consider minute distinctions between ethical theories such as utilitarian ethics and deontology, or between virtue ethics and contractarianism (these and other ethical theories are discussed specifically in Chapter 1 and utilized in others). Further, trolley problems are ordinarily presented as cases in which a lone person makes a moral decision affecting others and in which those who are affected have no say in the matter, but it is often the case in complex, "real life" cases that we take into consideration—and that we must take into consideration—the reasoning, interests, positions, and concerns of others who may have ideas and points of view different from our own. Moreover, considering the ideas, points of view, counterarguments, and alternate ideas of others may in fact make our own reasoning better and facilitate reaching a conclusion in a more effective and morally mature fashion than deciding and acting as an isolated moral agent.

Because the approach we take in this book is for practical application of ethical theories to cases, and because moral decision-making is more than simply making a decision and acting on it, the method presented in this book of teaching and learning ethics for practice involves both individual reasoning and group consensus building. Another way to put it is that decisions and actions in ethics do not occur as abstractions (i.e., they are not purely theoretical problems) and they do not normally occur in isolation. In other words, real-life problems involve human beings dealing with problems that affect the course of their lives and those of others.

There are many different theories of ethics and approaches to moral reasoning. People disagree on whether we should focus our moral attention on the results of our actions or on considerations of what is "right" without reference to consequences. They disagree on principles. They disagree on how to do the right thing or the good thing, and often they fail to agree even on the nature of the moral problem or problems arising from the situations in which they find themselves. In fact, one of the most difficult and important elements of moral decisions and actions is determining what the questions are, and either finding a way to put them in priority order to answer them or agreeing with others which question to ask to facilitate finding a solution.

In the following chapters we present methods of analyzing ethical problems, asking good questions about them, and formulating good answers to those questions in order to facilitate critical reasoning and decision making in moral contexts. As already suggested, understanding and analyzing moral issues is often exceptionally complicated. You may believe that some particular course of action is simply immoral and ought not to be permitted, while your brother believes that the very same action is neither immoral nor impermissible. Both of you may very well have reasons that you take to be good (that is, at a minimum, well-formulated and supported), but your positions are incompatible with each other. Further, it is possible that other people who have access to and understand your reasoning and that of your brother will see points of agreement (and perhaps of disagreement) in each position. So, how do we come to know which answer is the right one—or which is the good one? This book will provide you with strategies for answering this question and others of its kind.

In this book, we present a way to teach and learn ethical reasoning and decision-making in contexts drawn from case studies based on "real-life" situations in which people find themselves and in which important decisions are to be made that affect the lives of others, that affect the environment in which we live, and that have implications far above and beyond mere knowledge of ethical theories. While we include ethical theories and some nuances and problems of theories, they are presented in this book not as the focus of ethical reasoning, but instead as tools to be used in the analysis and creation of ethical arguments about cases. The point is to use the best judgment of which human beings are capable to propose solutions to problems that are thoughtful, practical, justifiable, and acceptable to reasonable persons concerned to ask good questions and formulate good answers to them.

Students and instructors may expect this book to include cases about the "big" issues such as abortion, euthanasia, capital punishment, gun control, and the like, but we have intentionally omitted such cases in the main text for at least two reasons. First, this is not a traditional sort of textbook on ethics and critical thinking. Second, the "big" issues are more than familiar to everyone likely to use this book and, while they are interesting and important, they are ubiquitous, intensely contentious, and historically intractable. Their contentiousness and resistance to solution (amicable or otherwise) are often associated with their religious and political implications and connections, and these considerations often divert attention from the content and quality of reasoning about the issues. It is not that we wish to avoid these issues, but rather, because our concern is teaching ethical theories, ethical action, and ethical principles through cases, we present cases that are more amenable to the goal. With that said, however, there is no reason that readers of this book could not and should not use its methods and principles in tackling the "big" issues after they have sharpened their moral knowledge and reasoning to devote critical attention to details, facts, arguments, theories, principles, and concepts that are conducive to asking good questions and formulating reasonable approaches to such issues. We think, therefore, that this book may actually aid a discussion of the more highly politicized and culturally sensitive ethical issues of our culture and our time.

Among the features of this book that students and instructors will find particularly useful are a chapter on creative problem solving in ethics, a mind-mapping technique for analyzing arguments and positions, and detailed discussion of ways in which to apply theories and principles of ethics to real life problems drawn from real life cases. Given the attention focused on critical thinking and reasoning in higher education, we believe that application of critical reasoning to ethical issues and dilemmas in the professions, in academic contexts, in business, government, and so on will satisfy the need for development and sharpening critical thinking abilities.

In this book, we put central emphasis on asking good questions rather than seeking a "right" answer to complex, difficult, and often vexing ethical problems and dilemmas. We take the position that recognizing variations in viewpoints, cultural influences, individual preferences and other contingencies of life, reasoning, and experience lead to consensus building and practical application rather than to "closing cases."

The plan of the book is to introduce elements of moral reasoning from a case studies approach, beginning with basic information on major ethical theories and logical reasoning in Chapters 1 and 2. Chapter 3, on conceptualizing ethical cases, introduces the structure and format of "real life cases" and suggestions for critical and careful reading. Chapter 4, "Questioning Cases and Mapping Concepts," focuses on identifying major factual and research elements of moral issues presented in cases, including a method of concept mapping the facts and formulating questions to guide research and argument evaluation. Chapter 5 is on creative case analysis and explores mindsets to be avoided in ethical thinking and methods for cultivating creativity. Chapter 6 introduces the application of ethical theories and principles to moral issues involved in cases, including an extended use of concept mapping to formulate and analyze arguments deriving from the questions asked and answered about ethics case studies. Chapter 7 focuses on answering good questions and includes a detailed analysis of a case study to illustrate the specific methods presented in earlier chapters. Here these methods are synthesized into a comprehensive six-step process. All chapters include questions for further thinking and discussion and references with suggested readings.

It is important to note that we have not included a completely "worked out" case in the book. Instead, cases are presented in relevant chapters to focus attention on the specific method or aspect of case analysis central to that chapter. So, for example, in a section on using mind maps to conceptualize a case, we concentrate on concept mapping and not on, say, actual research in which the reader will become involved in "working out" an answer to the moral problem(s) or dilemma(s) a case presents. Further, however, the text is written such that each chapter's content leads into the next, and it is therefore possible for students and instructors to use cases presented in each chapter not only for the content of the chapter in which a case appears, but also to utilize the case in previous and subsequent chapters as well. This provides, we think, a more rich and complete immersion in the methods and concepts presented in the book, encouraging users of the text to apply their own creative and critical thought to the foundations we have laid for case analysis. Another way to put the case is that what is important is for users of the text to ask and to answer good questions and to engage in critical and creative evaluation of problems and proposed solutions rather than to tie users to questions and solutions determined by the authors of this text.

In addition, we have included an appendix with sample cases, including several originally written for this book, and a glossary of key ethical and logical terms (and the terms listed in the glossary appear in boldface in their first occurrence in the text). Finally, for instructors and other potential users there is an online companion to this book including "A Guide for Instructors" with suggestions for assignments, course organization, and course activities available at http://www.hackettpublishing.com

The goals for students and readers using this textbook are the following:

- to demonstrate an understanding of the ethical dimensions of personal, societal, and professional life.
- to demonstrate knowledge of major ethical concepts and theories and use these concepts and theories where applicable to examine and interpret interdisciplinary cases raising significant ethical issues.
- to apply creative problem-solving strategies to specific ethical dilemmas.
- to engage actively in ethical dialogues by critically discussing and evaluating moral issues.
- to articulate effectively, argue persuasively, and think critically about moral judgments.
- to demonstrate the ability to work towards a consensus in making ethical decisions and show an appreciation of the challenges and complexities of arriving at such decisions.
- to develop skills in research and written and verbal expression.
- to take responsibility for and ownership of their own personal ethical development.

This book is collaboratively written with the authors taking primary responsibility for different chapters while at the same time having edited and commented on each other's individual chapters to create what we intend to be a comprehensive introduction to moral reasoning, theorizing, and decision-making. No book is written in isolation, and there are many people to thank for their help and encouragement in the process. Our teachers and professors had an influence on our academic development, and in turn our students have provided us over the years with commentary and discussion of the methods and principles included in this book. We would like to thank our teachers and professors for what we learned from them, and we thank our students over the past several years in our course at the University of Central Florida, Honors Case Studies in Ethics, for their interest and demonstrated abilities and ideas about moral reasoning and teamwork. We thank the University of Central Florida's College of Arts and Humanities for Michael Strawser's sabbatical in the fall term of 2013 and Dean José B. Fernández for Nancy Stanlick's research leave time every week to be able to devote time away from administrative duties to finish this book. We thank Dean Alvin Wang, Dr. Madi Dogariu, and the staff of the University of Central Florida's Burnett Honors College for providing us with the opportunity to develop and teach Honors Case Studies in Ethics for the past several years. We thank Dr. Stuart Yoak, Director, and the Association of Practical and Professional Ethics for permission to publish three cases from the Intercollegiate Ethics Bowl. Thanks to three anonymous reviewers for their beneficial comments and support for this manuscript and to Ron Pullins and Focus Publishing for their enthusiasm for our project and for seeing our manuscript through to its publication. Lastly, to our families, who have seen us through many long hours spent poring over books and articles and sitting in front of a computer screen, we thank you for your patience and encouragement. With that said, however, we are solely responsible for any errors or infelicities that remain.

Nancy Stanlick and *Michael Strawser*
Orlando, Florida, June 2014
Nancy.Stanlick@ucf.edu
Michael.Strawser@ucf.edu

1 Introduction

FROM GOOD QUESTIONS TO QUESTIONING THE GOOD

Ethics is not only a branch of philosophical inquiry, it is also a human activity affecting all aspects of our individual, group, and social lives. While Aristotle (384–322 BCE) famously defined human beings as "rational animals," it is perhaps more appropriate to consider ourselves as fundamentally "ethical animals," and certainly our capacity to reason plays a central role in conceiving ourselves ethically. For as conscious beings we all seek out the **good** in life, however we may conceive it, and we attempt to justify ourselves and the decisions we make in this endeavor. For example, students choose to attend a college or university because they think it will help them to have a better life. Then they make difficult decisions about what major degree to pursue, and these decisions (for example, to major in business, marine biology, nursing, or philosophy) are ultimately justified in terms of some conception of the good—whether it be for oneself, others, or the environment or world we share. It is easy to see how as ethical animals, and in distinction from non-human animals, we are able to ask ourselves self-reflectively this question: "How *should* I live?" Thinking about this question and its partner, "What is the *right* thing for me to do?", accounts for the intellectual history of ethics.

In this chapter we provide a brief history of philosophical ethics, a general introduction to major ethical theories (**virtue ethics**, **deontology**, **utilitarianism**, and others), and a consideration of the significance and kinds of questions that are the overarching subject of this book.

Socrates and the Art of Questioning

The questions we ask matter, and the kinds of questions we ask make all the difference. This is a book about asking *good* questions, and as you have probably already realized, the expression "*good* questions" has multiple meanings. First, a "good question" is a question that is clear, relevant, and perhaps most significant for the study of **philosophy**, it is a kind of question that leads to further questions, to deeper reflection and extended dia-

1

logue, and thus frequently to personal transformation and growth. Socrates (469–399 BCE), the so-called father of our Western philosophical tradition, is most famous for the particular method of questioning he cultivated, one which can be seen in practice as placing greater significance on the questions than on the answers. Second, a "good question" can be read as a question that asks about "the good." In other words, it is concerned with determining the actions (and we must also consider thinking to be an action) that will lead one to the good life—a life of **happiness**, pleasure, growth and learning, and overall well-being or flourishing. In this case, the answers acquire the greater significance, for of course we have to live and we have to act in order to lead a good life. Thus, there is a dynamic, back-and-forth (which is to say what philosophers call "dialectical") relationship involved in asking *good* questions, and this is most plainly explained by noting that "good" can be understood as both an adjective and a noun. It is our goal to maintain this dual signification and dialectical interplay throughout this book.

Let us consider both the nature of questioning and the nature of the good more carefully, beginning with the former. When we consider the nature of questioning, we can at least initially let Socrates be our guide. Socrates wrote nothing himself, and is thus known only through the writings of others, but one common feature of his philosophical method is the repeated affirmation of his ignorance. Socrates took it as his calling to question all those people who claimed to know something, and the result of these interrogations was *aporia*, the lack of an answer revealing an unresolved perplexity. So, in this regard Socrates' method appears to have a negative result, and this is meant in the logical sense that no positive answer is discovered. In other words, there is *no* final answer to the question. What we must realize when reading Socrates' dialogues in action, as written by his most gifted student Plato (427–347 BCE), is that there is nevertheless something positive to be learned by the process. What we can take away from our readings is not a specific answer to a specific question, but rather a particular practice for asking questions and an affirmation of the importance of continuous questioning. At the end of the *Apology*, which contains the defense speech Socrates gave at his infamous trial, Socrates even imagines that if there is a life after death he will continue his philosophical questioning there! So, we see clearly that there is something specific that Socrates does know and master, and that is the art of questioning.

Consider further that in Plato's *Symposium*, a wonderful dialogue in which the speakers take turns giving speeches on **love**, Socrates says this:

"the only thing I say I know is the art of love." Now, of course, the significance of love in the study of ethics should not be overlooked, although it has surprisingly been much neglected throughout the history of the subject. But is it really the case that Socrates, the master of irony, is truly a master of love as well? How can this be so given that when Socrates has his turn to speak on love in the dialogue he instead presents a speech from someone else, a mysterious woman named Diotima? Instead, it appears that Socrates is playing on the Greek words *erôtika*, which is translated as the "art of love," and *erôtan*, which means "to ask questions." As C. D. C. Reeve explains in his Introduction to *Plato on Love*, what Socrates is thus expressing in his indirect way is that he "knows about the art of love in that—but just insofar as—he knows how to ask questions." So, let us follow Socrates' lead and question the art of questioning. What are we doing in asking questions?

According to Martin Heidegger (1889–1976), one of the major German philosophers of the 20th century, the ability to ask questions lies at the heart of being human, so we can extend our understanding of a human being above to "a questioning ethical animal." Heidegger's student, Hans-Georg Gadamer (1900–2002), who was as much influenced by his teacher as by Plato's dialogues, explains the "priority of the question" in his magnum opus, *Truth and Method*. According to Gadamer, whose work is written to explain **hermeneutics** or the "art of interpretation," the structure of a question is characterized by openness and indeterminacy. When we ask a question we open ourselves to new possibilities in anticipating an answer. Thus every question has a sense and already expresses a kind of knowledge in directing us towards a certain object or state of affairs. This knowledge is exemplified by Socrates' knowing that he does not know. But the openness of a question is not unlimited, and the indeterminacy is not absolute, for it is conditioned by the horizon implicit in the question, which is to say that not just any answer will count as a good answer to any particular question.

We wish to help our readers to see that all experience is subject to ethical questioning, and recognizing this is the first condition for being able to ask good questions. We also realize that asking good questions is not an easy task. As Gadamer explains, "among the greatest insights that Plato's account of Socrates affords us is that, contrary to the general **opinion**, it is more difficult to ask questions than to answer them." From this account we can understand a good question as one that is authentic, which is to say it is genuinely open and leads to further dialogue. In contrast, questions that are closed or slanted (e.g., a question asked solely to prove oneself right) are inauthentic and have no place here. For example, asking "Do you know why X is wrong?" or "Why is X wrong?"—where X could stand for abortion, cheating, using military force, etc.—already presupposes the wrongness of the act in question, whereas asking "Is X wrong?" or "Is X morally justifiable?" does not.

Something else that should be avoided, or at least suspended, as we embark on our journey to ask questions, is opinion. "It is opinion that suppresses questions," Gadamer writes, and "a person skilled in the 'art' of questioning is a person who can prevent questions from being suppressed by the dominant opinion." Thus, we ask that you check your opinions at the door, so to speak, so that we can open up genuine dialogue through asking good questions about perplexing ethical issues.

Although we have not yet addressed the notion "critical thinking" and all that it may entail, we can already begin to realize the significance of "the art of questioning" for critical thinking. Following Gadamer, "the art of questioning is the art of questioning even further—i.e., the art of thinking. It is called dialectic because it is the art of conducting a real dialogue." This, then, is one of the overarching goals of our book: to enable readers to conduct real dialogue on important ethical issues. Our goal is not to tell you how you should think about abortion, gun control, or climate change (to cite but a few of the hot issues today). Given what has been said so far, if we were to do that we would effectively preempt critical thinking. And while we will discuss the central role reason and argumentation play in critical thinking, our goal is not to enable readers to argue effectively for their already fixed opinions. Such argumentation—to seek to defend one's own position at all costs without effectively engaging with alternative positions—was characteristic of the ancient **Sophists**, itinerant paid teachers who were solely concerned with **rhetoric** and had no concern for establishing real dialogue. Our goal is to help you pursue "the art of questioning even further," in which case reasons and conclusions for established positions all become open and are best understood as fluid possibilities. If you can do this, then you will be on your way to thinking critically, and even more, you will also be on your way to thinking creatively by multiplying the possibilities for questioning and thinking.

The Case for Critical Questioning

Although in a certain sense all philosophers are concerned with thinking well, the American philosopher John Dewey (1882–1953) is one of the few to offer a clear and straightforward account of the nature of thought in his work *How We Think*. Initially published in 1910, Dewey substantially re-vised and expanded this work in a second edition which appeared in 1933. Interestingly, in relation to Gadamer's work which belongs to a rather dif-ferent philosophical tradition, we can find parallel considerations of the priority of questioning in the art of thinking in Dewey's *How We Think*. For our purposes, Dewey's work is significant for two major reasons. First, Dewey's effort to approach "the best way of thinking" is helpful in consid-ering what we might mean by "critical thinking," which could be argued to be synonymous with what Dewey designates by the term "**reflective thinking**." Second, Dewey's work significantly equates *thinking* with *questioning*. Let us look at some of the details.

Dewey opens *How We Think* by asking "What is Thinking?" and he calls "the better way of thinking" with which he is concerned "reflective think-ing: the kind of thinking that consists in turning a subject over in the mind and giving it serious and consecutive consideration." Reflective thinking is carefully distinguished from three other common meanings given to think-ing: stream of consciousness, imagination, and believing. The last of these, believing, involves the unconscious acquisition and acceptance of ideas without considering reasons or evidence in support of the ideas, and this can be related to the notion of opinion referred to above. Reflective think-ing, on the other hand, "impels to inquiry" and "aims at a conclusion" that is derived from a method of *"active, persistent, and careful consideration of any belief or supposed form of knowledge in light of the grounds that support it and the further conclusions to which it tends."* This is a fine initial state-ment of the kind of thinking promoted by this book and the way that we should approach any ethical belief, although if we seriously wish to follow Dewey's understanding of "reflective thinking" we cannot simply accept it as a belief based on his authority as a famous philosopher; instead, we must carefully consider what this definition implies and "the further conclusions to which it tends," such as those features that may not be expressly included in his definition. Two features that we wish to make more salient are ques-tioning and creativity.

Towards the end of the revised edition of *How We Think*, Dewey makes an interesting connection between thinking and questioning, and this has the powerful effect of recasting what has thus far been characterized as "reflective thinking" as "the art of questioning." In the context of explain-ing how recitation should be used to promote good study habits, Dewey writes: "Thinking is inquiry, investigation, turning over, probing or delving into, so as to find something new or to see what is already known in a dif-ferent light. In short, it is *questioning*." This adds a dynamic, and we would say dialectical, element to critical thinking in that the goal is never to rest in any firm conclusion, but rather to endeavor continually to question that which is known, or in the context of ethical studies, to seek always and anew to ask good questions about the cases at hand. Given the ambiguity surrounding current discussions of the term "critical thinking," these considerations—specifically of Socrates, Plato, Gadamer, and Dewey—lead us to propose a term that captures what we would like to intend here both by "asking good questions" and "critical thinking": let us call it *critical questioning.*

Critical questioning, perhaps in contrast to certain conceptions of critical thinking, is essentially ethical in that it is guided by a desire for the Good as well as a recognition of our human limitations to know absolutely and with finality what this Good is. Again, we can see how we are basically continuing on a path forged by Socrates and Plato in which the good life, that is to say the only life worth living, is that of the critical questioner, or what Jill Gordon in her recent study of Plato calls the interrogative soul. Gordon demonstrates that Socrates in his life and Plato in his writings make "clear that the interrogative psychic state is best for humans and that the interrogative soul is the well-cultivated erotic soul." Why would such a life be better?

First, as explained above, asking good questions is challenging, and Gordon writes that "one must be resourceful in order to ask a good question." As Socrates showed, there is a certain wisdom involved in questioning, in that one knows that he or she does not know. This knowing one's own limitations is clearly an important form of knowledge that is all too frequently overlooked, and it is arguable that it conditions all true knowledge acquisition. Socrates is aware of his lack of knowledge, and "he understands the nature of desirous searching for fulfillment, of the desire to reach beyond oneself, and of openness. Questioning is all of that." Thus, the critical questioner is marked by resourcefulness and wisdom, and finds herself or himself in the best position to acquire knowledge. Second, as the life and death of Socrates show quite powerfully, the art of questioning involves significant risk, and thus it takes courage to ask good questions. The critical questioner knows, however, that this is required for growth, and for Plato it is the Socratic method of questioning that becomes the bridge from the mortal to the divine life.

Of course, there are many kinds of questions that can be asked, and even similar kinds of questions can be formulated in various ways, so we should inquire more into the method of questioning. One the one hand, the lack and corresponding openness involved in questioning point to a clear problem in any attempt to formulate a specific method of questioning. Gadamer expresses the matter in this way:

> The priority of the question in knowledge shows how fundamentally the idea of method is limited for knowledge. . . . There is no such thing as a method of learning to ask questions, of learning to see what is questionable. On the contrary, the example of Socrates teaches that the important thing is the knowledge that one does not know. Hence the Socratic dialectic—which leads, through its art of confusing the interlocutor, to this knowledge— creates the conditions for the question. All questioning and desire to know presuppose a knowledge that one does not know; so much so, indeed, that a particular lack of knowledge leads to a particular question.

When Dewey focuses his attention on the art of questioning towards the end of *How We Think* he begins with a point that echoes Gadamer's view above: "The art of questioning is so fully the art of guiding learning that hard and fast rules cannot be laid down for its exercise." Nevertheless, Dewey does not stop there, but he goes on to offer helpful suggestions for the art of questioning. Here is a summary of his five suggestions with our comments adapting these suggestions to the context of ethical case studies.

"First, in reference to material already learned, questions should require the student to *use* it in dealing with a new problem rather than to reproduce it literally and directly." In other words, after students have learned about ethical theories and the details of particular ethical cases, good questions will require students to apply their knowledge in a new way and not simply call for a repetition of what has already been learned. As Dewey explains, this "demands the exercise of judgment" and "cultivates originality," which is also an expression of creativity. For example, one could ask questions with the following form: Would X find Y ethically justifiable?— where X designates a particular moral theorist, and Y designates a particular moral problem. For example, would Plato find gay marriage ethically justifiable? Would Immanuel Kant find George Zimmerman's killing of Trayvon Martin ethically defensible?

"Second, questions should direct the mind of students to the subject matter rather than to the teacher's aim. This principle is violated when emphasis falls chiefly on getting the correct answer." This suggestion basically calls for genuine or authentic questions, which is to say open questions that do not have one and only one right answer. The questions given above as examples do not have one right answer in the same sense that "What is 2 + 2?" does, although one may surely argue that the correct interpretation of Kant's moral theory leads to this or that particular view.

Perhaps a better formulated set of questions which draws our attention more closely to the subject matter would be something like this: What reasons can one find in Plato to support gay marriage? What reasons can one find against it? (Interestingly, one can find various kinds of reasons in Plato's works supporting multiple positions on this issue.) Which reasons are stronger and why?

"Third, questions should be such as keep the subject developing. That is, they should be factors in a continuous discussion, not asked as if each one were complete in itself." This fits nicely with the emphasis placed on dialogue, and it calls for a recognition that any significant ethical case study is going to involve a complex situation that can be looked at from multiple angles.

"Fourth, questions should periodically require a survey and review of what has been gone over, in order to extract its *net* meaning, to gather up and hold on to what is significant in the prior discussion and to make it stand out from side issues, from tentative and explorative remarks, etc." This suggestion is particularly helpful for group discussions and drafting positions on specific case studies. In order to progress through an ethical analysis of a case, students must periodically ask such review questions to establish where they are in their understanding and this in turn will create a new horizon for further questions. When analyzing cases with others or in groups, this will involve arriving at a consensus with regard to a certain interpretation in order to see how that interpretation can be developed further.

"Fifth, and finally, . . . the minds of [students] should even more be put on the *qui vive* [lookout] through a sense of some *coming* topic, some problem still in suspense. . . ." This suggestion calls for students to cultivate a desire to conceive new questions and problems in order to continue to grow intellectually. Dewey can be seen here as expressing a point similar to what has already been expressed above, namely that good questioning is forever questioning.

Thus, even though we have recognized that there is no once-and-for-all final method of questioning, Dewey's suggestions offer us a sketch of key steps that can lead us forward, and as you can see, these are easily applied to ethical case studies. Nevertheless, we wonder whether you can think of any other suggestions that should be added to this list.

Plato and Questioning towards the Good

Both Socrates and his most gifted student Plato held that the desire for the Good was the most central and highest task of philosophy. "Philosophy" literally means the "love of wisdom," and we see that the "desire for the Good" maps on neatly here, for it shows that desire, which is to say *eros* or love, is the fundamental human activity, the goal of which is the Good. Although Socrates only points us towards the Good in his endless questioning, Plato presents the Good as the highest and most difficult idea to realize. Thus, for Plato the Good is highly abstract and can only be realized after protracted philosophizing. This is suggested allegorically in the well-known "myth of the cave" from Plato's *Republic*, in which he imagines humans as prisoners bound in a cave and only able to see the reflections of things on the wall. Here is how Plato explains his allegory:

> The realm of the visible should be compared to the prison dwelling, and the fire inside to the power of the sun. If you interpret the upward journey and the contemplation of things above as the upward journey of the soul to the intelligible realm, you will grasp what I surmise. . . . Whether it is true or not only the god knows, but this is how I see it, namely that in the intelligible world the Form of the Good is the last to be seen, and with difficulty; when seen it must be reckoned to be for all the cause of all that is right and beautiful, to have produced in the visible world both light and the fount of light, while in the intelligible world it is itself that which produces and controls truth and intelligence, and he who is to act intelligently in public or in private must see it.

It is difficult to imagine a more powerful expression of the effect of the Good, which is understood here as the cause of all that is right, true, and beautiful. Plato's conception of the Good is metaphysical (i.e., beyond the physical, earthly realm), in that it locates the Good in the "intelligible world," which is the real world for Plato. Thus the Good is conceived as divine and eternal, and although distinct from the "visible world," it is that which produces all that we call good within our lives in this visible world. While we may want to question the dualism implied in Plato's vision (i.e., that there are two separate and distinct worlds), it is nevertheless hard not to be attracted by the priority he gives to the Good and the desire to seek out the source of all the things we call good in our lives. This book is for all readers who share in this attraction and desire.

One more thing. Although we have emphasized the art of questioning and our human limitations, this should not be taken as implying **ethical relativism** or **subjectivism**. None of the philosophers discussed above who recognized the centrality of questioning (i.e., Socrates, Plato, Gadamer, and Dewey) were ethical relativists or subjectivists, and this clearly shows that one can acknowledge human ignorance and finitude without succumbing to one of these views. Ethical relativism is the view that all ethical values lack a solid foundation and are relative to particular individuals or groups such that no one view can be seen as better than another, while ethical subjectivism holds that ethical values are merely an individual's subjective preferences, such that what's right for me need not be right for you. Anthony Weston appropriately calls these views "ethical avoidance disorders," for if you really believe that ethical values are relative or subjective, then there is little reason to read this book and discuss ethical case studies. If critical questioning, research, and dialogue make no difference in understanding ethical values and approximating the good life, then why engage in these sorts of activities? While we may not know whether to agree with Plato that we can have philosophical access to the absolute form of the Good, this still does not imply (let alone demonstrate) that there is no Good. And although we have to accept that as human beings we are limited in our knowledge by our time, place, and status, this does not imply that no movement to limit our limitations is possible.

It is also important to note that accepting the significance of critical questioning, and that all views may lead to new lines of questioning, does not imply that all views are essentially equal. The art of questioning goes together with the art of argumentation, which shows that some views are better than others because of their reasonableness, evidence, and justification, all of which will be the focus of the next chapter.

Euthyphro: The First Case Study in Ethics?

Perhaps the earliest case study in ethics can be found in Plato's *Euthyphro*, one of his first writings, in which Socrates, the philosopher, encounters Euthyphro, the theologian. This encounter provides us with an excellent example of applying critical thinking to a particular case study, and the significance of its implications cannot be understated. The case involves Euthyphro charging his father with murder and trying to determine how one should act in light of this. According to Euthyphro, these are some of the details:

> Now the man who died was a laborer of mine, and when we were farming on Naxos, he was serving us there for hire. So in a drunken fit he gets angry with one of the family servants and cuts his throat. So my father, binding his feet and hands together and throwing him into a ditch, sends a man here [Athens] to ask the exegete [sacred interpreter] what he should do. During this time he paid little attention to the man he had bound and was careless

of him, on the ground that he was a murderer and it was no matter even if he should die, which is just what happened to him. For because of hunger and cold and the bonds, he dies before the messenger returns from the exegete.

Here we have the basic structure of a "case," which in general means a specific situation calling for action and inquiry. Now, what questions can we ask about this? Initially, we could ask questions about the facts of the case in order to get a fuller picture of this situation. This is always useful, as few if any situations are without any complications whatsoever. We might want to know about the relationship between "laborers" and their masters, and perhaps be surprised to learn that slavery was an accepted institution in ancient Athens. We may also be concerned with the conditions of some of the actions (e.g., Does being drunk affect one's responsibility for one's actions? Should one's prior deeds affect how one is treated?). For the supposedly wise Euthyphro, however, the matter is clear; his father should be charged with murder and prosecuted for impiety. This leads Socrates to ask the following question:

But before Zeus, do you, Euthyphro, suppose you have such precise knowledge about how the divine things are disposed, and the pious and the impious things, that assuming that these things were done just as you say, you don't fear that by pursuing a lawsuit against your father, you in turn may happen to be doing an impious act?

In other words, how can we know what makes an action pious and impious? An alternative translation would read "holy and unholy," and while these words may not be used as frequently in our contemporary discourse, they are for all practical purposes equivalent to "right and wrong." The central question of the dialogue then is "What is the pious?" It is crucial, however, to understand that what is at stake in asking this question is the desire to know how the conceptual value of an action can be determined, whether we call that value "piety," or "holiness," or "rightness." Thus, in our pursuit to ask good questions we learn from Socrates that one kind of question that is beneficial is a question regarding a specific definition of the concept involved. Definitional questions are central, and asking such questions will lead us to work towards establishing a consensus regarding the meanings of our words. This is not to say that we come to a final, once-and-for all definition (and of course this has not happened with regards to "the Good"), but that we are open to accepting certain meanings that are reached through reasoned dialogue while knowing that further questioning may lead to revisions in our prior thinking and thus development in our understanding.

In the course of seeking to define the concept of piety and in response to Euthyphro's answer that "the pious" is "what all the gods love," Socrates poses what is surely the most famous question in the entire dialogue: "Is the pious loved by the gods because it is pious, or is it pious because it is loved?" This is followed by a dizzying discussion that has baffled students of philosophy for centuries. For our purposes, the question could be formulated in different ways to get at the same point. For example, if we wished to express the question more generally in a monotheistic, rather than polytheistic, way, we can ask: "Is the good commanded by God because it is good, or is it good because it is commanded by God?" Further, if we wish to avoid the theological context altogether, we can ask: "Do humans like (or approve of) something because it is good, or is it good because humans like (or approve of) it?" What is the common thrust of each of these formulations?

If you reflect carefully on these questions you will discover that in the first part of each formulation the value of the pious (or the good) appears independent to the will of the gods, the God, or humans, while in the second part, the value is dependent upon someone's willing (i.e., loving, commanding, or liking). Thus, the point Socrates and Plato wish to make is that values need to be considered rationally and independent of any arbitrary will or authority. In other words, what is being suggested here is that values have an absolute essence; they are knowable objectively through reason and are not simply subjectively willful expressions relative to those beings who hold them. This point, it is perhaps needless to say, has been the subject of debate since the time of Socrates, and we cannot get into a thorough discussion of **absolutism** versus relativism here. As pointed out previously, however, if one seriously believes that values are essentially relative, willy-nilly expressions of an arbitrary will (e.g., what's good for me isn't necessarily good for you), then there is really no point in discussing ethical issues and attempting to reach an agreement on the good or the right thing to do.

Another important point that follows from Socrates' question, which has come to be referred to as "the **Euthyphro problem**," is that we see clearly how the philosopher (Socrates) and the theologian (Euthyphro) must part ways, at least when the latter holds to a belief that is beyond reason and beyond rational demonstration. Euthyphro expresses a kind of ethical theory characterized as the **divine command theory**, which holds that moral values come from God's divine decree and that we have a duty to follow such commandments (e.g., the acts of Zeus or the Ten Commandments in the Old Testament). Plato raises serious difficulties with this theory through the expression of Socrates' question: "Is the pious loved by the gods because it is pious, or is it pious because it is loved?" Regarding the latter part, if something is pious (or good) because it is loved or because of a divine command, then this implies (1) that the divinity is omnipotent and creates moral values (and, consequently, without the divinity there would be no right and wrong), and (2) that moral values are arbitrary and relative (i.e., they depend on the gods—or a God's—will and preferences). In this case we must face difficult questions such as these: Which God(s)? Do we follow Zeus or Kronos, Jehovah or Allah? And supposing that this could be determined once and for all, how can we then *know* the will of the God(s)? Of course, Plato was operating within a polytheistic framework, but even if one were to accept, say, Christian monotheism, the problem appears no less acute, for there are thousands of different Christian denominations in the world today with their varying interpretations of God's will. Such a conception of ethical values makes morality inaccessible to reason for Plato, and his teacher Socrates, who argue rather that it must be the former case that God loves or commands something because it is pious or good.

There are implications of this view—that "the pious is loved by the gods because it is pious"—as well. First, it implies that the values of pious and impious (or right and wrong) are absolute and lie outside of God's will or command. Second, it suggests that values are determined and can be known through human reason (a line of thinking that has been developed as "**natural law theory**"), with which presumably even God must be in conformity, thus undermining God's omnipotence. Not unexpectedly, the Euthyphro problem has been the subject of intense debate since it was first elaborated, but we cannot go into the history of this debate here. Nevertheless, it is fair to say that the majority of philosophers have followed Socrates and Plato rather than Euthyphro, thus viewing ethics as a viable human activity.

To explain further, the view put forth by Socrates is that we must consider the pious (and by extension all ethical and religious terms) in itself and independently of theological reflections. This is not to suggest that theological and religious reflections are utterly meaningless and without any value, as some philosophers would have it, but rather it is to recognize that faith-based considerations, especially when dogmatically held, often serve to bring to an end rather than to promote critical questioning. Although this is not necessarily be the case, as we can distinguish a healthy religious outlook from an unhealthy one (and there are certainly examples of religious thinkers engaging in critical questioning before God that go back as far as Abraham and Job), it is not uncommonly the case that theologians turn to faith as an answer to or justification for their actions. Plato illustrates this through Euthyphro, as the young theologian expresses a dogmatic assurance that he surely knows the will of the gods and thus his actions cannot be wrong or called into question.

One straightforward difference between philosophy and theology (and the related subject, religion) is that for the latter discipline there are some fundamental ideas (e.g., the nature of God, the value of the scriptures, etc.) that are not subject to question. Philosophy, on the other hand, is constantly stirring things up and its constant questioning has the effect of potentially undermining all beliefs, even those often taken as fundamental to the discipline. In his comedy *The Clouds*, Aristophanes (c. 448 BCE—c. 385 BCE) describes Socrates' activity as an "ethereal vortex," and there can be no doubt that at times philosophizing can be perceived as frustrating and threatening. Perhaps the greatest classic example of this is that Socrates was ultimately sentenced to death for denying the gods of the state and supposedly corrupting the youth. Thus, it may not be possible to teach philosophy without in some way disturbing the peace—as has been noted by the great modern philosopher Baruch Spinoza (1632–1677)—and we must also be aware of this with regards to teaching the art of asking good questions. Of course, we also recognize that this view of philosophical inquiry as an ethereal vortex of constant questioning can also be directed at this very work, and it leads to reflection on the question: Why do we need this book on asking good questions? While we think an answer to this question is developed in the Preface and continually elaborated throughout this work, we must ultimately leave it to our readers to determine the value of this book and of critical questioning, just as we leave it to readers to determine the values that they will utilize, and the reasoning they will employ, in seeking to question and to answer questions about the good, the right, the good life, and the solutions to complex moral problems.

The Big Three: Aristotle, Kant, and Mill

Let us now turn our attention to the history of philosophical ethics. Many major philosophers (e.g., Socrates, Plato, Spinoza, and Immanuel Kant) have viewed ethics as the most important branch of philosophy, and thus it is conceived as a philosophical activity. This means that when you are investigating ethics, as we are doing here, then you are doing philosophy. Colloquially, the word "ethics" is commonly used to refer to a code or set of principles by which people live or work (e.g., Buddhist ethics, business ethics, etc.), but for philosophers, ethics involves the critical study of concepts involved in practical reasoning (e.g., good, right, duty, etc.) and ethical or moral theories. Note that although a few philosophers have tried to distinguish "ethics" from "morality" and "ethical" from "moral," we shall use these as synonymous terms throughout this book. Philosophers also distinguish between theoretical and applied (practical) ethics. **Theoretical ethics** has two branches: (1) **normative ethics**, which asks generally what is the best way to live (i.e., Are there certain norms or rules that will lead to the good life?), and (2) **metaethics,** which is "about" ethics and questions the status of ethical thinking by asking whether ethics itself as a viable intellectual enterprise. In considering the Euthyphro problem above, we touched on an important metaethical question concerning the status of moral values: Are they objective and absolute or subjective and relative? For our purposes, which involve analyzing cases involving ethical issues, we are mainly interested in understanding key components of normative ethical theories in order to apply them to particular cases in an effort to arrive at the good. Thus we will have little to say about metaethics in this work, noting that the study of normative ethics is foundational for further ethical inquiry.

In the history of ethics in the Western world there have emerged three ethical theories that can easily be called "the big three," for they are the theories traditionally and most often turned to when reflecting on ethical questions. These theories are virtue ethics, originally developed by Aristotle (384–322 BCE), Kantian ethics or deontology as developed by the German philosopher Immanuel Kant (1724–1804), and utilitarianism, which was founded by Jeremy Bentham (1748–1832) and most famously defended by John Stuart Mill (1806–1873). Each of these three theories can be read as offering a response to the question: "What determines the value of an action?" Accordingly, the answers given are respectively (1) a virtuous character, (2) the intentional **goodwill** to do one's duty, and (3) the consequences of the action. As we will suggest, all of these aspects are important when considering case studies in ethics, so let us consider a brief overview of these three major ethical theories.

ARISTOTLE'S VIRTUE THEORY

As expressed above, the questions we ask matter, and an authentic question projects an open, indeterminate, but not unlimited horizon of meaning. When considering the question "How should we live?" we can think of this question in terms of rules or laws—in which case we may ask "What is the right thing to do?"—or, we can think of it in terms of character development. Aristotle takes the latter path, and thus for him ethics is not primarily an activity setting out strict rules of behavior to be followed, but rather it involves asking the question "What traits of character make someone a good person?" and then trying to cultivate those traits. It is important to note that there is an etymological connection between the Greek words "ethics," "character" (*ēthos*) and "habit" (*ethos*), and as we shall see, Aristotle understands the traits of character needed for a good life in terms of virtues.

Aristotle's most celebrated ethical text is his *Nicomachean Ethics* (330 BCE), and it is in this work that he develops what has come to be called a virtue theory of ethics. In Section 3 of Book I Aristotle offers readers an important metaethical caveat that addresses the limitations of ethics:

> Precision cannot be expected in the treatment of all subjects alike . . . problems of what is noble and just [and good] . . . present so much variety and irregularity . . . that we must be satisfied to indicate the truth with a rough and general sketch . . . for a well-schooled man is one who searches for that degree of precision in each kind of study which the nature of the subject at hand admits.

In other words, ethics is not like geometry, in which one can expect certain, fixed truths. But this does not mean for Aristotle that ethics is without truth, but rather that we must be realistic about the degree of truth to expect. This description of the subject of ethics fits well with the critical questioning approach developed above, as it suggests a "variety and irregularity" that is best addressed through the art of questioning that leads to genuine dialogue.

Aristotle explains early in the *Nicomachean Ethics* that all human actions are **teleological** or purposive, which is to say that everything we do tends towards some end or goal. For example, why do you go to college? You go to college to achieve the end of getting an education and a degree. Why do you get a college degree? You get a college degree to get a good job, you get a good job to buy a nice house, etc. There is, however, a final, self-sufficing end—the greatest Good-in-itself—that will put an end to this series of questions, and this final end according to Aristotle is *eudaimonia*, which is commonly translated as "happiness." In other words, it makes sense to say that you buy a nice house to be happy, but it hardly seems appropriate to ask "Why do you want to be happy?"

Aristotle then tells us that we must understand happiness in terms of our essential function, and in his view the essential function of humans is to reason. Happiness is the good of a human being, and his rough definition of the good is the exercise of one's faculties (rational soul) in accordance with excellence or virtue. In other words, happiness is an activity of the soul in accord with perfect virtue. Now this is hardly the common meaning of "happiness" in English, as "happiness" is often associated with pleasure and considered to be a state of bliss or excitement arising from a particular experience (e.g., you favorite team wins the championship, or you get married). In Aristotle's understanding happiness is not a passive state resulting from some experience. Instead, it is the activity of exercising one's rational faculty in a virtuous manner, and a more recent translation of *eudaimonia* that avoids the passive connotations of the English word "happiness" is "flourishing." For our purposes, then, asking questions that will help us to achieve a life in which we flourish—which is to say we continue to excel—is the goal of ethical thinking. For Aristotle virtue is central to this pursuit, so the next thing we need to understand is just what he means by this important term.

According to Aristotle, moral virtue is the result of habit, and the meaning of this is that we become virtuous by doing or practicing virtuous acts repeatedly throughout our lives. Aristotle emphasizes that we do not become happy or virtuous within a small period of time, but rather it is something that requires a full life. He writes, "One swallow or one fine day does not make a spring, nor does one day or any small space of time make a blessed or happy man." Related to this view, Aristotle clearly understands the importance of developing good habits early on, as he writes: "The habits of one's youth make all the difference." But how should we act—specifically—in order to achieve happiness? What habits should we seek to cultivate? In answering these questions we arrive at what is famously known as Aristotle's "doctrine of the **golden mean**." We learn that acting virtuously is avoiding extremes and seeking the intermediate, the mean, which is relative to one's needs and the situation. An analogy is helpful here: being happy is like being well-fed. Neither eating too much nor too little reveals a happy activity, but rather by eating moderately, or just the right amount depending on the individual (e.g., a professional heavyweight wrestler requires a greater calorie intake than a beginning sprinter), we will be avoiding extremes and thus analogously acting virtuously and flourishing.

Aristotle defines numerous virtues of moderation in his text. For example, courage is the mean between cowardice and rashness, and pride is the mean between vanity and humility. An important consequence of his theory is that there are various correct ways of living for different people, there are various moral peaks, and one has to find out through trial and error where the actual mean lies. Thus, while cultivating the virtues is of absolute importance in Aristotle's theory, such that the good person needs to be courageous, proud, etc., how these virtues are put into practice will depend on the particular individuals involved and their particular situations.

By expressing a broad range of virtues Aristotle's theory covers both our lives as public and private persons, and this is seen by many as an attractive feature of his theory. For Aristotle it is virtuous to be partial to our friends and family, and he has much to say about the significance of friendship in his treatise. Nevertheless, it is commonly thought that his theory suffers from incompleteness, and sometimes students misunderstand what he intends by his doctrine of the mean, which avoids the extremes of excess and deficiency. In English the words "mean" and "moderation" often refer to objects or states of affairs that are seen as less than enticing, and our culture frequently glorifies the extremes (think of, for example, "extreme sports" or "extreme nachos"). After all, one might think that loving according to the mean or loving moderately is less than desirable, but this would be based on a misunderstanding of Aristotle's theory. If we act according to the mean of friendliness, following Aristotle, this entails that we avoid the extreme of obsequiousness, in which we fully submit to the other person, and also the extreme of cantankerousness, in which we behave in an irritated manner around the other. Or, with regards to love, we could also say that to love moderately is to avoid, on the one hand, the extreme of loving too much to the point of obsession—which would likely involve jealousy or even stalking behavior—and, on the other hand, the extreme of loving too little, in which we subject the other to neglect, should also obviously be avoided. Thus, a better understanding of the virtuous mean in Aristotle is that it refers to what we mean in English by saying that something is "just right," or in other words, it is the excellent or perfect. As Aristotle writes in Book II of the *Nicomachean Ethics*, the characteristic of moral virtue, of "what is both intermediate and best," involves feeling and acting "at the right times, with reference to the right objects, towards the right people, with the right motive, and in the right way." In light of this explanation, we can see that Aristotle's moral theory is an expression of an ethic of **perfectionism**, in which the central goal of human beings is to act continually and completely in every situation in the best way possible.

KANT'S DEONTOLOGY

Whereas Aristotle's central question leads him to focus on character development, Kant's focus on doing the right thing leads him to develop a theory of ethics that is probably more in line with the way most people today conceive of ethics or morality. For Kant, acting ethically involves doing one's duty in following certain fixed ethical rules. This is called a deontological view (from the Greek word for duty, *deontos*), as it highlights the intention or motive to do the right thing specifically because it is one's duty. In Kant's view, the primary focus is one's intention of doing one's duty without direct concern for the consequences, such as pleasure or happiness (although one may still hope for a felicitous result), or for character development.

In one of his major writings on ethics, *Foundations of the Metaphysics of Morals* (1785), Kant initially discusses the significance of goodwill, which he understands as the rational faculty for acting according to principles. According to Kant, goodwill is the only thing that can be understood to be good-in-itself, not talents, gifts of fortune, or moderation (note the contrast to Aristotle here). Related to this is Kant's view of freedom, which he understands as the ability to be governed by reason. If we always acted according to reason—which is to say freely—we would not really need ethics or have to reflect critically about what to do. But humans do not always act rationally (surely we do not have to convince you about this point), and it is because of this state of affairs that duties or obligations are necessary.

The key doctrine in Kant's theory is the **categorical imperative** (or absolute command), which he states in these terms: "Act only on that maxim whereby thou canst at the same time will that it should become a universal law." In other words, Kant's categorical imperative makes clear that when thinking morally one should ask oneself this important question: "What if everyone else did what I am to do?" If you would not be able to accept (or "to will") that your behavior becomes a universal law, then your behavior would not be ethical. In *Foundations of the Metaphysics of Morals* Kant applies the categorical imperative to four examples involving both duties to oneself and duties to others. He argues in effect that neither suicide nor lying is **universalizable** (i.e., capable of becoming a universal law), and consequently both are immoral. He also argues that while neglecting a natural gift and being indifferent to the plight of others are universalizable, they are not actions that a rational being would will. Basically, then, Kant is claiming that we have an absolute duty to preserve our own life and develop our natural talents, to tell the truth and to help others. In Kant's view these and all other moral laws are as absolute and objective as the natural laws of physics.

Let us consider an additional example in more detail. Suppose that you are an "A" student (perhaps this is happily not a point that you have to "suppose"), but due to a family hardship beyond your control, you are unable to find the time to study for an important final exam. If you do not do well on this particular exam you will fail the course, even though you have earned high marks on all the other work throughout the course. Now suppose that you are able to cheat on the final exam in a way that is foolproof, such that neither the instructor nor any of your peers would ever find out what you did. The question that Kant would have you ask is this: Would you be willing that your action becomes a universal law such that everyone in a difficult situation such as yours should cheat on the exam? Well, would you?

The answer that Kant would give is that it would be irrational to will such a universal law, since it would effectively void the purpose of an exam to demonstrate acquired knowledge. If we lived in a world in which anyone in a difficult situation could cheat without being caught, then we would not be able to distinguish who actually has learned the material from who has not based on their grades earned. Thus, cheating behavior cannot be universalized and is unethical.

Kant's ethical theory is complex, and he offers multiple formulations of the categorical imperative throughout his work. His second formulation is important and reads: "So act as to treat humanity, whether in thine own person or in that of any other, in every case as an end withal, never as means only." In general, this formulation states that we should treat others and ourselves as ends and not means to an end. In other words, when considering the ethical thing to do one should be sure not to use other people. For example, one should not be friends with another person solely because one wants to gain something from the friendship, such as help on an exam or an opportunity to date the friend's sibling. This would not be treating the other person as an end, but rather as a means. Further, when considered in the light of the requirement of universalizability, it could not possibly be rationally willed that one should form friendships in this way, as it would effectively undermine the meaning of friendship altogether.

In general, the second formulation of Kant's categorical imperative is based on a profound respect for the dignity of persons, which is to say rational beings who are ends in themselves, and this is doubtlessly a highly significant point. It is more than unfortunate, however, that both Aristotle and Kant had a very limited conception of a rational person, leaving out women and individuals from other races.

Kant's ethical theory is problematic in other ways, and one much debated problem is that Kant provides us with no clear way to resolve a conflict of duties. For example, what if by lying I am able to help someone or save a life? According to Kant one has an absolute duty to tell the truth as well as an absolute duty to help others, so what do we do in situations where these duties are at odds? The most frequently given example of such a situation involves imagining that you live in Europe during World War II and that you know there are Jews hiding in the basement of your building. Now suppose that Nazi guards are patrolling your neighborhood and ask you whether there are any Jews in your building. What would you say? Whether you answer "yes" or "no," from a Kantian perspective you will be violating a formal ethical command. How do you evaluate different duties and determine which have precedence over others?

Another problem of Kantian ethics is that it is at least in principle possible for a moral agent to universalize actions that have no apparent or actual moral import at all. For example, for all people who have two feet, it is entirely possible to will universally that when getting dressed in the morning all such people always put a sock on their left foot first. But under ordinary circumstances there is nothing of moral importance in which foot is first covered with a sock. Despite these difficulties, Kant offers readers many important ethical insights, and his deontological theory remains one of the most frequently discussed and applied to ethical situations today.

MILL'S UTILITARIANISM

The third major ethical theory, utilitarianism, offers a decidedly different focus for us to consider. Whereas Aristotle's central focus was on living the good life by cultivating moral virtues and Kant emphasized our duty to follow rules derived by human reason, Jeremy Bentham (1748–1832) and John Stuart Mill shift the primary focus to the consequences of our actions. They are thus called "**consequentialists**," because on their view what determines the moral value of an action are the consequences or the objective results of our actions. For Mill this theory marks progress in ethics, as it provides a seemingly objective way of determining the value of an action. After all, there is no way to observe directly human intentions and virtues, but we can observe at least to some degree the effects our actions have on others. Further, consequences that have utility are those useful for promoting happiness or pleasure (note this is different from Aristotle's conception of happiness, since it was not equated with pleasure), whereas those leading to pain lack utility. The theory Bentham initiated and Mill defended is therefore known as "utilitarianism," and this is most clearly defined in the first paragraph of Mill's work titled *Utilitarianism*: "The creed which accepts utility as the foundation of morals, or the Greatest Happiness Principle, holds that actions are right in proportion as they tend to promote happiness, wrong as they tend to produce the reverse of happiness."

One benefit of this theory that can be seen right away is that it offers a method for resolving conflicts that may arise in Kantian deontology regarding competing duties. This method is seemingly quite straightforward. In order to determine what the right thing to do is, one must solely consider the consequences of possible actions and perform that action which will produce the greatest happiness for the greatest number of people (or sentient creatures). So, reconsider the World War II example given above. From a utilitarian point of view it appears quite reasonable to argue that when facing the situation in which Nazi guards inquire as to whether there are any Jews in the basement of your building, you should lie and tell them "no," since this will lead to the greatest happiness as the Jews will then not be captured and harmed. With regards to the example of whether one should cheat when facing a difficult situation, in this instance it would appear that the cheating could be morally justified, provided that it leads to the greatest happiness on the supposition that you would not get caught and no one would find out what happened.

Having stated this seemingly simple theory, Mill then goes on in *Utilitarianism* to consider the objection that such a view is no more than a "doctrine of the Swine." Mill's response to this objection is threefold: (1) human pleasures are more elevated than the pleasures of the swine (i.e., merely eating, sleeping, and procreating is not what makes us truly happy), (2) pleasures of the intellect are higher than sensation (i.e., mental pleasures are greater than bodily ones), and (3) the value of pleasures is determined democratically by those who have experienced the pleasures. These points make the utilitarian calculus more complicated, but they also point to a general difficulty of this theory, namely the problem of accurately assessing happiness. Although it is fair to say that we can often have a reasonably good idea of the consequences of our actions, it is certainly not the case that we always know and can predict the effects of an action on all others involved, including those effects that may occur remotely in the future. For example, maybe in the cheating situation you get away with the deceptive act and are happy to have passed the course and earned your degree. But perhaps later in life you come to regret your action and feel considerable anguish remembering what you have done, such that on the whole over a period of years you experience more pain than if you had not cheated on the exam.

Another objection considered by Mill is that many people postpone higher pleasures for the lower ones. His response to this is that it is due to a weakness of character. The "capacity for the nobler feelings is in most natures a very tender plant, easily killed," he writes, and then implies that young people should seriously consider those occupations that will allow them to protect and grow this "plant," which may seem to be related to one's character.

Utilitarianism is a popular view, and most people will likely agree that we should consider the consequences of our actions. It also widens the realm of ethical concern to include "the whole sentient creation" (i.e., all beings that can experience pleasure and pain), which is an obvious improvement. It is not without its problems, however, and one often debated is that utilitarianism requires strict impartiality when weighing the happiness of sentient beings. This is undoubtedly challenging, and for many thinkers it seems contrary to basic human behavior, as it suggests that one should act with the same concern for the happiness of neighbors and strangers as for one's closest family members and friends. But Mill himself recognizes this challenge, and he even suggests that "in the golden rule of Jesus of Nazareth, we read the complete spirit of the ethics of utility."

Another difficulty for utilitarians that is particularly troublesome is that the happiness of the majority might require the unhappiness of the minority (which could include one's own family or friends). This problem is powerfully expressed in *The Brothers Karamazov* by the great Russian novelist Fyodor Dostoevsky (1821–1881). Here is the challenge Ivan Karamazov puts to his brother Alyosha:

> Tell me yourself, I challenge you—answer. Imagine that you are creating a fabric of human destiny with the object of making men happy in the end, giving them peace and rest at last, but that it was essential and inevitable to torture to death only one tiny creature—that baby beating its breast with its fist, for instance—and to found that edifice on its unavenged tears, would you consent to be the architect on those conditions? Tell me, and tell the truth.

Although Alyosha softly says "no," the utilitarian would have to consent based on the greatest happiness for the greatest number of people. Finally, another worry for utilitarianism is that it does not seem sufficient for moral deliberations to consider only consequences and not intentions or motives. So we find again an ethical theory with limitations.

It seems that none of "the big three" presents a wholly adequate ethical theory, which is a strong reason for promoting the view (as we do in Chapter 6 below) that multiple theories should be consulted when analyzing ethical cases. But there are some other important ethical thinkers to consider, so let us now look at those who express a theory known as **contractarianism**.

Rights and Justice in Hobbes, Locke, Mill, Rawls, and Nozick

In addition to the "big three" theories, there are theories affecting moral, social, and political thought that are also important in the development of Western philosophy. Among these are the social contract and "natural law" theories of Thomas Hobbes and John Locke; John Stuart Mill's work in social philosophy, *On Liberty*, in which issues concerning individual rights, **paternalism**, and censorship take center stage; and the 20th century contractarian and rights-based theories of John Rawls and Robert Nozick. These theorists' views are useful in handling many ethical cases, especially those dealing with agreements and facets of agreements people make with each other personally, in business relationships, socially, and politically and in reasoning about the status and nature of individual and group rights. We shall consider each of these theorists and their particular contributions to ethics and social philosophy (ethics conceived through rights, justice, and liberty) in historical order.

HOBBES AND LOCKE:
HUMAN NATURE AND SOCIAL CONTRACT THEORY

Thomas Hobbes (1588–1679) is the theorist who made famous the saying that the "life of man" is "solitary, poor, nasty, brutish, and short." He made this comment in the *Leviathan*, a work published in 1651 on the nature of the commonwealth or political state. What concerned Hobbes was to gain an understanding of the origin, nature, function, and limits of political power. You may wonder what an inquiry about political power has to do with ethics, and that is certainly a legitimate question.

Hobbes held the position that to determine the origin, nature, function, and limits of political power, it was necessary first to understand the nature of the elementary parts of a political structure. Since political activity and political structures are human inventions, and because Hobbes was influenced by the early modern tradition of philosophical inquiry in which knowing the causes and elementary parts of things is essential to knowing the thing itself, it is in turn necessary to understand human nature. Human nature, in turn, is essential to understand human desires, relationships, and conceptions of what is good and right. In other words, human nature affects what Hobbes understood to be the nature of ethics and ethical inquiry.

For Hobbes, human beings are no different in structure from any other living things. Living things strive for survival, and in addition, all natural things (and even artificial things) are composed of parts that contribute to their functioning and to their continued existence. With respect to human beings, we are matter in motion (Hobbes was a mechanistic materialist who believed that all things in the universe are nothing but material things subject to the laws of physics), and we are moved by our desires and aversions. Simply put, those things we desire are those to which we are drawn and we literally or figuratively move toward them; a similar consideration applies to those things to which we have an aversion. We move literally or figuratively away from them. That which we see as likely to contribute to our continued existence and survival are things to which we are drawn (we desire them and "love" them). The things we desire we call "good" and those to which we are averse we call "bad" and "hate" them. This is the beginning of Hobbes' view of ethics. But it is only the beginning.

Since individual human beings differ in various ways from each other with respect to their particular desires and aversions, "deep down," so to speak, there is no absolute way in which to determine what is good and what is bad. If I, for example, do not like peanut butter (I find it unpalatable or I am allergic to it) but you do, I consider peanut butter to be "bad" while you consider it to be "good." It is similar with respect to ethics. Suppose that you and I both desire the same thing, but the thing we both desire is something that only one of us can possess. We both consider that thing, X, to be good. On the other hand, if we cannot share it (or if we are unwilling to share it with each other), then there will be a parting of our ways concerning your pursuit of X and my pursuit of X. If you pursue X and manage to get it, you consider it good that you are now in possession of it. However, I also want X and if you have it and we either cannot or will not share it, from my point of view, it is bad that you are in possession of X. If I had managed to take possession of X instead of you having possession of it, you would consider my possession of it a bad thing while I consider it good. We are now in a position in which we differ with respect to what is good (a specific person's possession of the object, X) even though we agree generally that possessing X is good. There is, therefore, no universal or absolute state of affairs determining, at the most base level of human desire, that your possession or my possession of X is good. This means, then, that there is no universal standard to which to turn to determine what is good and what is not good.

For Hobbes, in conditions of scarcity (such as when X cannot be shared or will not be shared) people compete with each other. Competition for scarce resources leads to quarrels and disagreements which are the state of war where human life becomes "solitary, poor, nasty, brutish, and short." It is important to note that Hobbes did not agree with Aristotle that human beings are naturally social or political animals. Instead, Hobbes' view was that people are essentially self-interested and acquisitive, leading them to be essentially singular and engaged in cooperative enterprises with others only when it is to the individual's benefit to be so engaged. Because of this position, and because of his view of the nature of our understanding of the terms "good" and "bad," there is no external standard of good and bad or right and wrong. Since that is the case, there is also no effective means by which to enforce any rules or procedures that individuals may singly or cooperatively formulate.

Suppose, for example, that you and I decide to share equally in harvesting fruit from a tree growing wild in a forest. We shake hands on it and agree that tomorrow we will begin picking the fruit from the tree and each of us will take half. Unknown to me, however, you stay up all night long and pick all the fruit from the tree. When I awake in the morning, the tree is barren and you are nowhere near it. I go to your residence to tell you about the unfortunate turn of events, and you inform me that you decided to pick all the fruit and keep it for yourself. You will not share it, and from your point of view, since you picked all the fruit and did all the work, the fruit is all yours. I refer you to yesterday's conversation in which we agreed to share in the harvest equally. In response, you slam the door in my face. How do you think I will respond?

If you are a Hobbesian and you believe that I am a Hobbesian, you believe that I will not go off and sulk about the issue, feeling sorry for myself and allowing you, my "friend," to keep all the fruit. Instead, I will want to force you to honor the agreement we made. How, however, will I go about doing that? It's possible that I can remind you again of the agreement. But if you still reject it, I will need to think of a different approach. Perhaps I will wait until night, sneak into your house, and take the fruit that I want (which might be all of it). If I can't get into your house, perhaps I will burn it down, reasoning to myself that if I can't have the fruit, nobody will have it. But whatever I do, insisting that you honor the agreement is bound to lead to further disagreement between us, and perhaps result in unpleasant animosity and violence.

If all human beings were to live the way you and I are now living in the hypothetical fruit-picking example, the world would certainly be unpleasant and unproductive, and we would indeed live solitary, unfulfilled, unpleasant, violent, and short lives. So, something must be done. Hobbes' solution is to recognize laws of nature that, if followed, would more effectively allow us to satisfy desires without, at the same time, leading to quarrel and dissent. It is interesting and important to note that the satisfaction of desire is both the cause of quarrel and war as well as its solution. It is the cause of quarrel without recognition of the laws of nature; it is the solution to quarrel when mediated by the laws of nature.

The laws of nature are rules of reason that Hobbes claims are derivable by any rational person. In other words, and in a way similar to Kant's contention regarding our recognition of the categorical imperative, the laws of nature are obvious to us through the use of reason. Hobbes enumerates no fewer than 19 laws of nature among his moral and political works, but it is the first three that are of importance for our purposes in ethics.

The first law of nature is the obligation each person has to preserve her or his own life. The second law of nature, to give up the right to all things, provides for the ability to satisfy the first law. For Hobbes, outside of social organization, each person would believe himself to be the sole arbiter of all things, including the notion that anything that he possesses belongs to him and anything he wants ought to belong to him. If everyone thinks that everything he wishes to possess is or should be his, conflict is inevitable. So people ought, according to Hobbes, to recognize and follow the third law of nature—to keep agreements made. The problem, however, is that of trust. How will we go about ensuring that everyone honors the promise not to invade the rights and property of others?

The Hobbesian solution is both a political and a moral solution. It is to institute an absolute sovereign power that is the sole arbiter of right, wrong, good, and bad. In short, Hobbes' ethics and politics are absolutist in nature because there is an authority in place part of whose purpose is to dictate the meaning of morality. While being absolutist, it is also interesting and important to note that Hobbes' political thought is the beginning of modern **social contract theory** embodying the notion that governments exist by the consent and agreement of the governed. And in the moral realm, contractarian thought means that morals, too, exist by agreement. Even though Hobbes' view of ethics lends itself immediately and necessarily to absolutism because the ultimate sovereign is the ultimate authority in all realms, it does not mean that all contractarians are absolutists. In fact, other contract theorists often disagree with Hobbes' conception of human nature and the associated ethical views accompanying it.

John Locke (1632–1704) was also a contract theorist whose work forms the backdrop and much of the content of American and other Western political thought. Locke's view, like Hobbes', was that governments exist legitimately only by consent of the governed. While Locke's major work in political theory, *The Second Treatise of Government*, does not focus specifically on ethics, there are elements of his political thought that are congruent with that of Hobbes and, in being so, form part of what C. B. MacPherson called "the political theory of possessive **individualism**."

An important moral and social aspect of the works of Hobbes and Locke is that they both conceived of individual human beings as the atomistic elements of the construction of social and political systems, and that individuals take center stage in determining the appropriate and justifiable processes and formation of governments. Seeing humans as atomistic elements of social and political systems, Hobbes and Locke both presented positions regarding human beings such that they are primarily self-interested. Most commentators on Hobbes recognize **psychological egoism** as the dominant trait of human beings. Psychological egoism is a descriptive view essentially meaning that human beings are self-interested and will do whatever they believe is in their own best interest. This is different from **ethical egoism**, a view that human beings ought to be self-interested.

While Locke is not normally recognized as a psychological egoist, there is reason to believe that his view of the nature of humanity is not wildly different from that of Hobbes. Note, for example, that Locke asserts in *The Second Treatise of Government* that there is one and only one law of nature, and it is that every person is obligated to preserve his own life and, when his own life is reasonably secure and assured, he has an obligation to preserve the rest of mankind. Interestingly enough, the obligation to preserve others manifests itself in each person being required to avoid interfering in the lives, liberties, and property of others. There is no obligation in the theories of either Hobbes or Locke that any person does anything to assist others in the pursuit or protection of life, liberty, or property. The obligation is instead very minimalistic—it is an obligation of non-interference. In fact, the obligation not to interfere in the rights of others as a primary duty is what makes traditional contractarian thought like that of Hobbes and Locke very minimalistic in scope, content, and application. Unlike virtue ethics, which is closely associated with and dependent upon community-oriented concepts to achieve a life of flourishing for individuals (who can flourish as individuals only if the communities of which they are a part are also "flourishing"), traditional social contract theorists tend to think of human beings as grudgingly social rather than as essentially so. In their grudging acceptance of the need to live cooperatively with others, egoistic contractarians set up minimal rules and procedures that make longer and more productive human lives possible. They do this because they see their individual rights as primary in the moral, social, and political realms and that the rights of others ought always to be preserved simply by leaving other people alone to live their lives as they see fit.

MILL AND LIBERTY

Earlier in this chapter, utilitarian moral theory was presented as one of the "big three" ethical theories in Western thought. John Stuart Mill also saw utilitarianism as a means of ensuring appropriate social organization for the realization of the production of the greatest happiness for the greatest number. His book, *On Liberty*, contains three very important concepts for the protection of individual rights that, if followed, are supposed to be conducive to achieving the utilitarian ideal. Those concepts are (1) a rejection of paternalism, (2) a rejection of censorship, and (3) safeguards against the tyranny of the majority and a defense of individualism.

Even though utilitarians concentrate their moral attention on creating the greatest happiness for the greatest number, it does not mean that anything goes. Mill recognized that there are safeguards to be put in place to protect the dignity of the individual over and against the pleasure or lesser interests of the majority. For example, Mill argued that it is important and essential for the individual to be sovereign over his own body and mind. While the individual might engage in behaviors or activities that are dangerous to herself or himself, it is not appropriate for others to attempt to stop him from doing as he wishes to do. There is nothing in this view to stop someone else from trying to convince someone who smokes, drinks, or engages in other risky behaviors to stop doing so, but paternalism, when wielded against rational adults who are capable of making their own decisions, is unjustified.

In addition, there are people who believe that there are movies, video games, books, TV shows, and other forms of media or entertainment that are inappropriate for everyone and that such forms of literature, art, or entertainment ought to be banned or censored. The utilitarian social view, however, rejects this contention. The reason is simple. If we assume that truth is superior to error, censoring or banning works of art, literature, and forms of entertainment is likely to be a means by which truth is stifled rather than promoted. Even if a work of literature, for example, is nothing but fiction and falsehood (or at least the censor's position is that this is the case), there is no person who is infallible, and it very well might be the case that the work contains truth rather than falsehood. Even on the chance that the censor is right that the work is filled with falsehood, however, it is still not justified to ban or censor it because, according to Mill, the truth is likely to be even more clearly revealed when it is compared with falsehood. Finally, works might be likely to contain some combination of truth and falsehood, and all the same liabilities are attended with censorship in any case.

Utilitarians also value individualism, understanding it to be part of personal freedom and creativity as well as beneficial to society generally. Part of what it is for a person to live a good and happy life, and for society to do the same, is for individuals to be free to develop their talents and to engage in forms of amusement and pleasure as they see fit. This does not mean that pedophiles are free to molest children or that people who derive pleasure from causing the suffering of others are free to do as they please. If they were, the general happiness would be decreased rather than increased. Instead, the view of the utilitarian regarding individuality is much like the position on paternalism. It is not justified for those who are capable of making their own decisions and forming a plan of their own lives and whose actions do not violate the "**harm principle**," which is the notion that a person is free to do as she or he sees fit just so long as that person's actions do not harm others.

RAWLS AND NOZICK ON DUTY, PROPERTY, INDIVIDUAL RIGHTS, AND THE SOCIAL CONTRACT

John Rawls (1921–2002) and Robert Nozick (1938–2002), are two prominent 20th-century political theorists taking their lead from works in social contract theory, Kant, and Locke. Rawls and Nozick represent liberal and libertarian views of the nature of social and political agreements, the distribution of property and social goods, and individual rights. Rawls' liberalism is stated in his seminal work, *A Theory of Justice* (1971), and Nozick's libertarianism is expressed in *Anarchy, State, and Utopia* (1974).

Rawls was a social contract theorist whose position was that previous ethical and social theories are not sufficient to explain clearly or to represent adequately the interests of individuals in social organizations. For example, utilitarianism allows for the rights of individuals to be overridden for the benefit of a majority, and Hobbesian and Lockean contract theories rely on a hypothetical and non-historical state of nature and an inadequate conception of human nature. Rawls offers an alternate view of contract theory that may be considered an improvement over those traditional contract theories.

Rawls holds the position that it is best not to consider contract theory as a process, like the traditional theorists, of completely overhauling entire government and social systems. Instead, we should reconfigure the principles upon which existent societies already rest. In other words, instead of imagining ourselves in a hypothetical natural condition from which we completely build an entirely new government and society, what we should do is try to determine what principles of justice should guide the government and society in which we already live. To do this, Rawls proposes that we engage in a process of deliberation about appropriate principles of justice for the proper ordering of society that any rationally self-interested person would agree to accept.

To determine the principles of justice to create "justice as fairness," Rawls proposes that we think of ourselves in abstraction from the contingent details of our lives. In other words, we work from "the original position" under a **"veil of ignorance"** in which we deliberate about principles of justice from the point of view of how we would decide if we did not know our economic condition, our health, sex, gender, educational status, intelligence, and other factors that may make a person decide on principles of justice that would benefit himself or herself to the detriment of others. Instead, if a person does not know the contingent details about his own existence, he will, from a rationally self-interested point of view, decide, with the concurrence of all others, on two principles: the **Equal Liberty Principle** and the **Difference Principle**.

The Equal Liberty Principle is essentially that every person would recognize that everyone should have the same basic right to participate in the social and political process and to have an equal voice in the arrangements and decisions made on a social level. Rights such as voting, freedom of speech and assembly, and privacy are among those involved in the Equal Liberty Principle. The Difference Principle, on the other hand, is that every rationally self-interested person would agree that social and economic inequalities are to be arranged so that they are to the advantage of the least advantaged members of society. So, because it is clear that there will be people who occupy positions in society that are more respected and are attended with higher levels of income and status, it would be in no one's interest to allow such inequalities to exist without at the same time ensuring that those in society who are incapable of participating in or being part of these higher levels of attainment are not oppressed and made worse off by the advantages enjoyed by others. Another way to put the case is that inequalities in income, opportunity, and social standing are to be offset by corresponding gains in the condition of those who are the least well-off members of society.

Further, Rawls argues that the Equal Liberty Principle takes precedence over the Difference Principle such that it would never be in any person's best interest to give up liberty for economic advantage. No reasonable person would give up basic liberties that are part of what it means to be a respected member of society simply to have more money or a higher standing in a community. For example, it would not be in the best interests of a person to give up freedom for security or to give up the right to free speech for some kind of monetary compensation. That would simply set up a person to be oppressed by those who have retained basic rights.

The way that Rawls' system of justice plays itself out, however, is a matter of considerable debate and disagreement. Rawls' principles of justice are redistributional principles that essentially require that the most well-off members of society redistribute some portion of their economic standing to those who are not well off. They require that we look at our social, political, and economic existence on the basis of "end-state principles" (his principles of justice) that tell us how things in the social, political, and economic world ought to turn out. But Rawls' colleague at Harvard University, Robert Nozick, disagreed with Rawlsian justice and offered a different look at what are fair and just arrangements in the moral, social, and political world in which we live.

According to Nozick, we should look at any theory of justice on the basis of historical facts and create corresponding historically-informed principles of justice. For Nozick, this is the pathway to a theory of justice. So rather than produce end-state principles to determine how social and individual goods ought to be distributed, Nozick looks to historical facts.

It is important to note that both Rawls and Nozick look at the distribution and possession of social and individual goods on the model of Kantian ethics, especially with reference to the notion of the dignity and **autonomy** of the individual human being. Where Rawls believed that redistribution of social and individual goods for the benefit of the less well-off members of society would be conducive to maintaining the dignity and autonomy of individuals, Nozick held that this is clearly not the case. To justify this position, Nozick employed also a Lockean view of the nature of one's holdings in property.

For both Locke and Nozick, people have a right to property as a basic fact of existence. For Locke, we are born holding property in our own persons and in our own labor. Further, every person has the same right to her or his own person, labor, and its products. Since this is the case, distributing my property to you, and especially doing so without my consent, is tantamount to disrespecting my autonomy and my right to property. Nozick takes the position farther than Locke, however, in providing principles of justice that he believed any rationally self-interested person would agree to follow. Using a variation on one of Nozick's own examples should be sufficient to introduce those principles.

Suppose that there is a basketball player whose ability and skill lead him in every game to score at least four times the number of points any other individual player on the team can score. Fans are willing when they buy tickets to see basketball games to put an extra dollar or more in a box intended specifically for the star player. Suppose at the end of the season that the star player amasses a total of $250,000 from the extra money put in a box prior to each game. Who is the rightful recipient of the $250,000?

There are those who claim that the funds belong to the entire team since, without other team members, the star player couldn't be a star at all. Or perhaps there is a sense in which there is some percentage of the funds that should go to other team members even if it is not necessary to divide the funds evenly between players or based on their relative salaries as members of the team. Robert Nozick, however, sees things much differently. The player to whom the money was given by the fans is the sole rightful recipient of the funds. This is the case because two principles of justice, the principle of justice in transfer and the principle of justice in holdings, verify and solidify it.

If the fans who put the money in the box had a right to do as they saw fit with the money, and if they saw fit to give it to the star player, then because they had a right to the money (applying the principle of justice in holdings) and to do as they saw fit with it, then the person to whom they transferred the funds has the right to them just as they did when transferring it (applying the principle of justice in transfer). These, for Nozick, are the two principles of justice through which we can properly understand the holdings that people possess and that respect their right to do with their property as they see fit.

Rights-based theories such as those of Hobbes, Locke, Rawls, Nozick, and even Mill are not without problems. For example, Hobbes' view of human nature is rather stark and bleak and not necessarily an accurate representation either of our actual lives or of agreements we make with each other. More specifically, the Hobbesian human being is conceived by Hobbes as an isolated individual who has no necessary social, familial, or friendship connections with others. In point of fact, however, we are born into social groups and have affiliations with others that are not easily and not properly "abstracted away" in thought experiments in a hypothetical state of nature. But more, commentators on Hobbes often note that his version of contract theory (and that of Locke in this respect) is unacceptable because it is unjustified to believe that people will be bound by agreements they would have made if they had been in a natural condition with no social connections to others. In other words, why should we think that people are bound by agreements they never made?

A similar consideration applies to Rawls' theory in that his view of the nature of property distribution is based on the original position under the veil of ignorance in which people reason from the assumption that they do not possess knowledge of the contingent features of their lives, and instead know only that they have a conception of the good and that they are rationally self-interested. It is obvious, however, and as Michael Sandel, a contemporary virtue-theorist and colleague of both Rawls and Nozick has noted, that this view of human nature and decision making portrays us as "unencumbered selves," and that this is an inaccurate representation of who we are as human beings. Further, Sandel notes, one of the problems with abstract theorizing such as that seen in traditional and contemporary contractarian thinking is that having no conception of the good with which to work in formulating principles of justice makes our reasoning abstract and inapplicable to real human lives that are lived, in fact, with specific plans of life and ways of communal living that are not easily or properly separated from us. While it is reasonable to be concerned in our moral and social theorizing with protecting the rights of ourselves and others, it is not clear that these theories necessarily succeed in providing us with a complete or accurate guide to do so.

Further, it is not clear that Mill presented a compelling case regarding reasons to eschew censorship with his claim that the truth shines ever more clearly through its collision with error. He provided no evidence to support the claim, and even if true, it is at least possible that falsehood might cause more harm in allowing its dissemination than the good that truth might engender. In addition, Mill's harm principle may not go far enough when we consider actions that an individual might perform, or behaviors in which a person may engage, that may at first appear to affect only that individual but that could have important social consequences violating the principle of utility. For example, one might argue that Mill's harm principle would not allow a society or government to ban or limit smoking by adults because smoking hurts only the smoker and not others. As we have found over time, however, second-hand smoke is dangerous and often deadly to non-smokers, and the health risks and associated social and monetary costs of diseases and conditions caused by smoking do significant harm to more than just the smoker. Thus we find that contractarian and rights theorists have also been unable to provide a wholly adequate ethical theory.

Critical Questioning and the Other

We have now understood the nature of the art of questioning and its centrality to critical thinking. We have also considered the nature of the good and the right and the major ethical theories that explore these concepts. If we are to follow our own thinking on asking good questions, then we must now seek out questions that will open up alternative possibilities for thinking about ethics. Why are the theories of Aristotle, Kant, and Mill so commonly accepted as the major ethical theories in the Western philosophical traditions? Do these theories and others like those of Hobbes, Locke, and contemporary contractarians, actually stand in fundamental opposition to each other, such that one must choose one over the others? Or, is there a way that they can be reconciled? Additionally, are there any marginalized thinkers who serve to advance the ethical project further? If so, who are these other ethical thinkers that we should introduce here? Let us offer several possibilities of thinkers with profound ethical views who are rarely presented in traditional textbooks on ethical theory.

First, we can mention the Dutch thinker Baruch Spinoza (1632–1677), whose work simply titled *Ethics* is one of the greatest works of Western philosophy. Perhaps one reason that Spinoza's work is rarely included in textbooks on ethical theory is the unusual and difficult style of his writing—his ideas are presented in geometrical order—as well as the fact that this work is often viewed as primarily metaphysical or epistemological. The fact that Spinoza titled his *magnum opus* "Ethics" is significant, however, for it highlights what is most central in Spinoza's vision, and this is not metaphysics or epistemology as commonly interpreted, but rather a practical ethics of life. Had Spinoza wished to highlight something else, he could have titled his greatest work "Truth," "True Knowledge," or "The Way of Reason," but he did not. Nor did he call it "God" or "God and Nature," which would not have been unreasonable. Instead, his work is simply titled *Ethics* (1677). This signifies that the heart of Spinoza's philosophy and the key value of this work lie in communicating the proper way of living or acting in the world (i.e., living the good life).

Two concepts that are central to Spinoza's ethical vision are what he variously calls "love" or "nobility" and the notion of a moral exemplar. Although the concept of love has been important for many religious thinkers, it is perhaps surprising to note that for the most part philosophers—literally "lovers of wisdom"—have neglected this concept, and we would be remiss not to question this neglect, especially in a pursuit of the good life, which many or most of us would commonly believe to include love at its center. Perhaps it is due to the fact that philosophers have long denied love's **rationality** that they have failed to investigate this important concept, but remarkably for his time, Spinoza provided an understanding of the emotions that included active emotions in line with reason. "Nobility" or "love" is one of these emotions and is defined by Spinoza as a desire to help others and join them in friendship based on reason alone (which is to say that it is not based on selfish ends or ulterior motives). Thus Spinoza presents an original way to link emotion and reason, and he provides us with an ethics in which emotions play an active role. Questions about the role of emotion in ethics have become more frequently discussed today, but however important, this complex discussion cannot be explored further here. Suffice it to say that Spinoza was well ahead of his time and his work is still relevant today on this account.

Spinoza also argues that we need a moral exemplar (i.e., a model) to whom to look for guidance in living the good life, and such a person desires the same good for others as for oneself, and acts according to reason (which *nota bene* [note well] does not exclude emotion) in showing fortitude and nobility. Such a person, Spinoza writes, "is angry with no one, envies no one, is indignant with no one, despises no one, and is far from being proud." Perhaps most importantly, a moral exemplar, which for Spinoza is equivalent to a free and wise person, will return hatred with love, as he demonstrates in proposition 43 of Part III that "hatred is increased by reciprocal hatred, and conversely can be destroyed by love." Thus, Spinoza presents readers with a powerful vision of a good life which attempts to unify the concepts of reason, emotion, virtue, and happiness.

Like Spinoza, the German philosopher Arthur Schopenhauer (1788–1860) is known more for his metaphysics than for his ethics, and both philosophers hold that an ethical theory requires a metaphysical grounding. With respect to ethical theory, Schopenhauer is significant for his sharp criticism of Kantian ethics, which as has been indicated is one of the most influential theories of ethics to date. A central question Schopenhauer raised about Kantian ethics was this: Why should we assume that ethics must take the form of a categorical imperative? In other words, where does this idea that we are commanded to follow certain laws come from and is it justifiable? "Preaching morals is easy," Schopenhauer writes, "grounding morals is hard." Thus, instead of offering us a list of ethical rules, which is what Kant's theory does in practice, Schopenhauer seeks to describe what constitutes a genuinely moral life, and this for him is **compassion**. Compassion, Schopenhauer explains, serves as the basis of the virtues of justice and loving kindness, and it is an everyday phenomenon that involves participating in the suffering of another and willing the other's well-being. As Schopenhauer sees it, only actions motivated by compassion have moral worth.

Schopenhauer's moral philosophy shows a connection to Eastern ethical traditions and thus leads us to ask what these traditions have to offer in expanding our ethical thinking. As Schopenhauer points out, in the Western world it was not until the time of Christianity that the virtue of loving kindness became central to the good life, although it had been of central importance a thousand years earlier in ancient Hindu teachings and became the primary ethical virtue in the Buddhist tradition. Perhaps not surprisingly, then, an important feature of Schopenhauer's ethical thinking is his view of the continuity of all life and that non-human animals are also to be shown loving kindness. Schopenhauer forcefully denounces European systems of morality for their lack of concern towards non-human animals, and it seems that Americans also still have much to learn in this regard. As Schopenhauer shows, a morality based on compassion must embrace all life, and this way of thinking is certainly highly relevant today.

Søren Kierkegaard (1813–1855) is a Danish philosopher who has also received marginal treatment in the Western ethical tradition. Kierkegaard is perhaps most well-known for being the so-called "father of **existentialism**," a philosophical view that emphasizes the significance of individual choice. Kierkegaard offers readers a complex assortment of writings with some given under various pseudonyms and others devoted to more religious themes written under his own name. Kierkegaard's philosophy illustrates three main stages or spheres of life: the aesthetic, the ethical, and the religious. The focus on the aesthetic and ethical spheres occurs most prominently in a massive two-volume work titled *Either/Or* (1842), in which the ethical life is characterized by the pseudonymous author Judge William in response to a young aesthete. Judge William's focus is on explaining the essential nature of the ethical life rather than offering ethical prescriptions, and we learn that the key aspects of living an ethical life are conscious choice and a willful commitment to whatever choice one makes. Judge William (the significance of the pseudonym expressing *decision* and *will* should now be plain) goes further in suggesting that it is through our taking responsibility for the choices that we make that we become the individuals that we will become, and this is a guiding idea in the later popularization of existentialism by Jean-Paul Sartre (1905–1980).

Kierkegaard's *Either/Or* is his earliest major work, and he will later suggest in *Works of Love* (1847), a text written under his own name, that the essentially moral life consists in loving one's neighbor. In what is perhaps the most profound analysis of the ethical precept to love one's neighbor as oneself, Kierkegaard provides readers with insightful descriptions of the kinds of works of love that following this precept entails. The neighbor is what philosophers call "the other," which designates that which transcends oneself. The focus on the encounter with the other has become a dominant theme in later continental philosophers' thinking about the ethical, and this marks a movement distinct from the kind of ethical theory that one commonly finds in the multitude of textbooks in circulation today.

Are there are other thinkers relevant to questioning the good life who should be included here? Doubtless there are, but we cannot continue this chapter much further. With continuous questioning and some research, as well as some guidance from your instructor, we are confident that you will be able to expand your thinking on the subject of ethical theories.

Now let us consider the concepts of justice and rights, the significance of which has been shown above. But are these the most central concepts in ethical inquiry? This question leads to the possibility of an alternative conception of ethics in which other concepts may be central. Further, perhaps you have noticed that all of the ethical thinking we have explained so far has been developed by men. Is this not a problem? What if women had had more prominence in the Western philosophical tradition and had been able to give voice to their ethical thinking? What concepts would be central then? Would it still be the concepts of rights and justice?

This line of questioning leads to the final perspective on ethical theory that we will introduce in this chapter—**feminist ethics**. Without a doubt, women have been greatly marginalized throughout the Western philosophical tradition. They have served the role of the other who has not had a voice in questioning the good life, and we can only imagine what our intellectual horizon would be today if they had had a voice from the early beginnings of Western philosophy. Sure, there have been a few female thinkers mentioned throughout Western intellectual history, but their ideas lacked the prominence given to their male counterparts. One such example is the Greek philosopher and mathematician Hypatia (c. 350–415), who is also relevant here for the importance she placed on questioning dogmatic beliefs. For Hypatia all children, both boys and girls, should be given a proper education, one which emphasized rational discourse and philosophical questioning leading to independent thinking. She thought it was tragic for young children to be taught religious dogmas unquestioningly, as she realized how difficult it is to change the beliefs forced upon us in childhood. "Fables should be taught as fables," she said, "myths as myths, and miracles as poetic fancies. To teach superstitions as truth is a most terrible thing. The mind of a child accepts them, and only through great pain, perhaps even tragedy, can the child be relieved of them." Sadly, Hypatia would become a philosophical martyr like Socrates, although her death was much more gruesome, and her writings were also destroyed. One additional surviving remark is pertinent in this context: "Reserve your right to think, for even to think wrongly is better than not to think at all."

Contemporary feminist philosophers have argued that when seen from a female point of view, ethical theory looks quite different from the major theories promoted by men. Much of the work by feminist philosophers is metaethical in nature, in that it deals with questions about the nature of ethical theory (e.g., Do men and women have different moral disposi- tions?). Carol Gilligan has popularized the distinction between an ethics of justice or rights and an **ethics of care**, as she argues that male theorists are more abstractly focused on the former, while female thinkers center their thinking on the latter. Annette Baier follows Gilligan in suggesting that if there were a distinctive moral theory of women, it would be an ethic of love. While it is interesting to consider whether fundamentally different moral perspectives attach themselves with one's sex, a more modest **argu- ment** can be found in Claudia Card, who argues that the responsibilities of different kinds of relationships result in a significant difference of ethical orientation for men and women (thus avoiding the strong claim that there is a fundamental, innate difference), and understanding the nature of these relationships can improve our ethical theory.

In "One Feminist View of Ethics" Card accepts a more modest version of Carol Gilligan's view, which states that the responsibilities of different kinds of relationships yield different ethical preoccupations, methods, priorities, and even concepts. Basically, women have had more personal and informal relationships (e.g., in the home with children), whereas men have had more impersonal and formal relationships (e.g., on the job). The distinction is one of the public versus the private spheres, and generally speaking in the history of Western ethics, the public sphere has been con- sidered the more important one while the private sphere, that of the home and of personal relationships, ties, and love, does not belong in the realm of the rational and logical. These personal relationships, it seems, have led women to develop an ethics of attachment and caring, while men have developed an ethics of control and justice. A question that remains is whether these alternative views can be reconciled in a way that will lead to the good life for all persons regardless of their sex or gender.

The concept map on p. 34 (Figure 1.1) contains an overview of some primary features of major ethical theories presented in this chapter.

In this chapter, we have seen that the history of Western ethics is char- acterized largely by competing points of view. There are distinctions be- tween virtue ethics and contractarian ethics, between the public and the

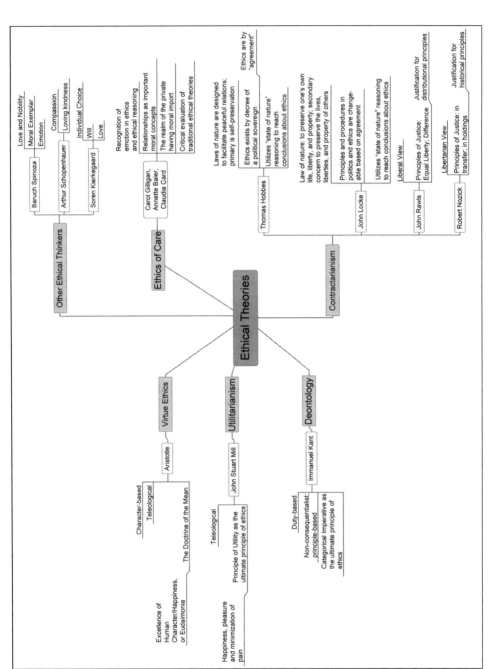

Figure 1.1

private spheres, between consequentialist and non-consequentialist theories, and between the interests of groups and the rights of individuals. Traditional textbooks on moral theory tend either simply to present various theories of ethics in historical order or they present them as incompatible opposites that cannot be reconciled or used with each other. In this text, however, we think differently, since our purpose is to employ ethical theories and to engage in ethical theorizing to attempt to find workable and acceptable solutions to real problems affecting our lives, families, professions, happiness, and social existence. To do this, we do not present ethical theories as incompatible, but instead we focus attention on the ways in which moral argumentation may be constructed to yield practical results that will tend toward formulating good answers to good ethical questions. To begin that task, the next chapter, on **logic** and persuasion, is a look at some principles and problems in reasoning that will be helpful in formulating your own arguments and in evaluating the arguments of others.

Questions for Further Thinking and Discussion

1. Can you illustrate how being a "questioning ethical animal" is woven into your daily life?
2. What do you understand by the notion of "critical questioning"? How can this be further developed or can you think of additional suggestions to contribute to Dewey's list?
3. Consider the case from Plato's *Euthyphro*. What would you advise Euthyphro to do and why? What is the "Euthyphro Problem" and how would you respond to it?
4. Read the full dialogue *Euthyphro* and answer the following questions: What is the central question of the dialogue and what possible answers are proposed? What questions does Socrates raise concerning these answers? What should we conclude from this dialogue? (See the references below for electronic editions of Plato's *Euthyphro*.)
5. With regards to Aristotle's virtue theory, do you think virtues are the same for everyone? Is "character" a plausible notion? How responsible is one for his/her character?
6. Explain either the cheating example or the World War II example in this chapter from both a Kantian and utilitarian perspective. Which perspective do you favor and why?
7. Take the Ivan Karamazov challenge! Explain how you would respond

to Dostoevsky's character Ivan regarding sacrificing one child for the eternal happiness of all others. Can you think of any real-life situations in which the happiness of the few has been sacrificed for the happiness of the many?

8. Do you think that morals are created "by agreement," as seems to be indicated in contract theory? What are the major differences, in your view, between the conceptions of human nature of Hobbes and Locke? Do you find the views on distribution of wealth and opportunity more convincing from the point of view of Rawls or of Nozick? Why? If you were to try to apply contractarian thinking to the World War II case study, how would it be different from an application of Kantian or utilitarian theory?

9. Which ethical theory (or theories) do you find most compelling and why?

10. Are there any other concepts that you think are central to the good life that have not been mentioned in this chapter? Are there any other thinkers whose ethical views should be considered as offering further possibilities for ethical thinking?

References and Suggestions for Further Reading

Aristotle. *Nicomachean Ethics*. Books I & II. There are numerous translations of this classic text and it can be accessed online at http://classics .mit.edu/Aristotle/nicomachaen.1.i.html. The first quotation from Aristotle above is from Martin Ostwald's translation (Pearson, 1999), and the remaining quotations are from F. H. Peters' translation (1881).

Aristotle. *Eudemian Ethics*. Trans. Anthony Kenny. Oxford University Press, 2011.

Card, Claudia. "Gender and Moral Luck." In *Identity, Character and Morality Essays in Moral Psychology*. Eds. Owen Flanagan and Amélie Oksenberg Rorty. MIT Press, 1990, pp. 199–218.

Card, Claudia, ed. *Feminist Ethics*. University Press of Kansas, 1991.

Dewey, John. *How We Think*. Revised Edition. In *The Collected Works of John Dewey: The Later Works, 1925–1953*, Volume 8: 1933. Southern Illinois University Press, 2008. See Chapter 1: "What Is Thinking?" for Dewey's account of "reflective thinking," and see Chapter 18: "The Recitation and the Training of Thought" for Dewey's discussion of the art of questioning.

Donovan, Sandy. *Hypatia: Mathematician, Inventor, and Philosopher*. Compass Point Books, 2008. The quotations above are from page 43.

Dostoevsky, Fyodor. *The Brothers Karamozov*. Trans. Constance Garnett. Macmillan, 1912. The quotation is from the section titled "Rebellion" in Book 5.

Gadamer, Hans-Georg. *Truth and Method*, 2nd ed. Trans. Joel Weinsheimer and Donald G. Marshall. Continuum, 2004. In the central section "Elements of a Theory of Hermeneutic Experience" Gadamer discusses "The Hermeneutic Priority of the Question," which includes the subsections "The Model of Platonic Dialectic" and "The Logic of Question and Answer" (pp. 356–371).

Gordon, Jill. *Plato's Erotic World: From Cosmic Origins to Human Death*. Cambridge University Press, 2012. See especially Chapter 2: "Questioning," from which all of the above quotations are taken.

Hobbes, Thomas. *Leviathan: with selected variants from the Latin edition of 1668*. Ed. E. M. Curley. Hackett Publishing Company, 1994. Parts I and II are most closely associated with ethical issues.

Kant, Immanuel. *Foundations of the Metaphysics of Morals*. The quotations are from Thomas K. Abbot's translation first published in 1873. For a more recent translation, see *Grounding for the Metaphysics of Morals with On a Supposed Right to Lie Because of Philanthropic Concerns*. Third Edition. Trans. James W. Ellington. Hackett Publishing Company, 1993.

Kierkegaard, Søren. *Either/Or*, Part II. (Kierkegaard's Writings 4). Ed. and Trans. by Howard V. Hong and Edna H. Hong. Princeton University Press, 1987. Part Two contains the letters of Judge William on the ethical sphere of existence.

Locke, John. *Second Treatise of Government*. Ed. C. B. MacPherson. Hackett Publishing Company, 1980. This is a classic statement of the notion that government exists by the consent of the governed.

MacPherson, C. B. *The Political Theory of Possessive Individualism*. Oxford University Press, 1965.

Mill, John Stuart. *Utilitarianism*. Ed. John Sher. Hackett Publishing Company, 2001. In this classic work, Mill writes the standard historical text to present the major elements of utilitarian moral theory in which the greatest happiness for the greatest number is offered as the moral ideal.

Nozick, Robert. *Anarchy, State, and Utopia*. Basic Books, 1974. In this work, Nozick provides a libertarian theory of justice that critically evaluates Rawlsian distributional principles of justice and argues instead for a historical right to holdings.

Plato, *Euthyphro*. This short dialogue from Plato's early writings is a common starting point for many students of philosophy and ethics. The quotations above are from the following translation: *Four Texts on Socrates*. Trans. Thomas G. West and Grace Starry West. Cornell University Press, 1998. However, as with many classic philosophical texts, it is easy to find online versions of this dialogue, and a recommended version with numerous helpful hyperlinks can be found at http://socrates.clarke.edu and an audio version is available at http://librivox.org/euthyphro-by-plato/. Additional electronic additions are available through Project Gutenberg (www.gutenberg.org) and several college and university websites such as The Internet Classics Archive at MIT (classics.mit.edu).

Plato. *The Republic*. Available online at http://classics.mit.edu/Plato/republic.html. "The Myth of the Cave" is in Book VII.

Plato, *Symposium*. The quotations above are from the following edition: *Plato on Love*. Ed. C. D. C. Reeve. Hackett Publishing Company, Inc., 2006. The quotation from Reeve's Introduction is from page xx.

Rawls, John. *A Theory of Justice*. Harvard University Press, 1970. Rawls presents a version of Kantian contract theory in which he offers two principles of justice for the reorganization of existing societies to achieve "justice as fairness."

Sandel, Michael. "The Procedural Republic and the Unencumbered Self." *Political Theory*. Vol. 12, No. 1 (Febuary, 1984): 81–96. This paper presents a critical evaluation of traditional ethical theories and offers an alternative recognizing human beings as encumbered selves rather than isolated individuals.

Schopenhauer, Arthur. *The Two Fundamental Problems of Ethics*. Trans. David E. Cartwright and Edward E. Erdmann. Oxford University Press, 2010. The second essay, "On the Basis of Morals," includes Schopenhauer's view of compassion and the virtues of justice and loving kindness.

Spinoza, Baruch. *Ethics*. Ed. and Trans. G. H. R. Parkinson. Oxford University Press, 2000. Books III, IV, and the first half of V contain Spinoza's essential ethical philosophy.

2 Logic and Persuasion

Stating an opinion on an ethical (or any other) issue is easy. All it takes is to assert it. Justifying the position that is embedded in your opinion, on the other hand, is not always so easy and it takes both care and time. To justify a position is to argue for it. Arguments are the subject-matter of the specialized area of philosophical inquiry that is logic. In this chapter, primary concerns are distinctions between types of arguments, understanding argument forms and the quality of argumentation, and identifying and avoiding errors in reasoning.

Arguments are reasoned discourse. They are ordinarily divided into two categories: **deductive arguments** and **inductive arguments**. Deductive arguments are formulated such that their conclusions are true if the information provided in support of the conclusions is true. Inductive arguments are formulated such that their conclusions are likely to be true if the information provided in support of the conclusions is true.

Arguments can be of any size, from one sentence in length to a position justified in a multi-volume set of books. No matter the length of an argument, the most important consideration about an argument is whether it is cogent. **Cogency** is a characteristic of arguments of any kind, whether deductive or inductive. If an argument is well-formulated and the information provided in support of its conclusion is true or likely to be true and makes the conclusion true or likely to be true, the argument is cogent; if the argument is not well-formulated or if the argument contains information that is false or is likely to be false, then it is instead fallacious.

Arguments are composed of three main parts. First, **premises** are the reasons offered in support of the point at issue. Second, the point at issue is the conclusion. Third, the intellectual move (the thought process) involved in moving from the reasons (premises) to the conclusion is an **inference**. Arguments can go right—and they can also go wrong—in any one or more of their three parts. For now, however, it is important to note that whether we consider the premise(s) of an argument or its conclusion(s), premises and conclusions are composed of statements.

Statements (sometimes also called "propositions," and in this book we will use "statement" and "proposition" interchangeably) are different from mere sentences. All statements are sentences or parts of sentences, but not all sentences are statements or propositions. Statements or propositions are declarative sentences that are either true or false. The sentence: "What time is it?" is not a proposition because a question is neither true nor false. The answer to the question, however, is a proposition. Even if I ask you what time it is and you reply that it is 3:00 P.M. when in fact it is actually 2:30, the statement "It is 3:00 P.M." is a proposition, and it happens to be false. Exclamations such as "Ouch!" are also not propositions. "Ouch" is an expression of pain, and an exclamation is neither true nor false. On the other hand, a person may exclaim "Ouch!" when he is not in pain. The exclamation, however, is still not truth functional.

Remember that propositions are statements that are either true or false. If we seek truth or some approximations to truth in our investigations and inquiries, then false information provided in the form of false propositions is not acceptable. It is not only other people, however, who might provide you with false information. You may inadvertently (or perhaps intentionally) manipulate information that is true, and through manipulation render it false or questionable. Alternately, one may manipulate claims that are false to make them seem to be true or acceptable. There are many ways in which the quality of statements may be analyzed and manipulated. Sometimes, information presented to you, or that you find on the Internet, in magazines, books, and on TV or radio, is false or questionable. Other times, you may repeat information in a way that changes its quality. There are ways in which to identify and to avoid such problems. Because statements are the most elemental parts of an argument, we turn first to an analysis of statements and some ways in which statements may "go wrong" before embarking on an analysis of arguments and their inferential quality.

Statement Transformations, Equivalences, and Inferences

It is not possible to summarize or to consider all possible forms of statement transformation or inferences that could be made from statements either in this book or in any other venue, but it is possible to present some common and useful methods of determining whether any two statements are equivalent to each other or whether one follows from another. We will consider some basics from Aristotle's logic and some common forms of statement equivalence from propositional logic.

BASICS FROM ARISTOTLE'S LOGIC

Suppose that you are presented with the following claim in an ethical dilemma regarding the process for securing organ donors: "Some organ donors are required to undergo testing for communicable diseases." The statement is simple enough, but what does it mean and imply? If you know that some organ donors are required to undergo testing for communicable diseases, is it also true that all organ donors are required to undergo testing, too?

The simple answer is "no," logically speaking. In the logic of class relationships and simply as a matter of common sense, if something is true of some things in a class or category, it does not automatically follow that the same consideration is true of all things in that class. The more complicated answer, however, is that the logical implications may be muddied, so to speak, by what you know or think you know, or by what you believe or prefer. Suppose, for example, that there is a policy that only those who have been tattooed in the past year are required to undergo testing for communicable diseases. If that is in fact the policy, it does not follow that every organ donor must undergo testing. On the other hand, you may *believe* that every organ donor, without qualification, must undergo testing for communicable diseases. If that is the case, it is easy to be distracted from what actually follows from a piece of information by what you *think* ought to be the case. It is important, therefore, to be careful not to interject what you believe or what you prefer when trying to determine what follows from any given piece of information. This does not mean that you cannot argue for the claim that all organ donors ought to be tested, but it does not follow from the policy statement alone that this is the case.

Consider the following statement: "All veterans are entitled to healthcare benefits." If this statement is true, what follows from it? It clearly does not mean that no veterans are entitled to healthcare benefits since the two statements are contrary to each other. That is, it is not possible for both of them to be true. But what about this? "Some veterans are entitled to healthcare benefits." This statement is obviously true since, in the logic of classes, whatever is true of an entire class of things is also true of the individuals constituting that class. The statement "some veterans are not entitled to healthcare benefits," however, is clearly false given the truth of the original statement that all veterans are entitled to such benefits.

There are legitimate inferences that you can make from some particular piece of information, but there are also inferences you may make that are mistaken and erroneous. Do not assume more than the information you have received warrants and do not confuse what you prefer or wish to be the case with the facts. In ethics, what ought to be the case is the primary concern, but this does not detract from factual information regarding policies, procedures, events, and occurrences in the world.

Some basic facts about the logic of classes and their relationships should be helpful in taking care not to assume anything that is not warranted by the facts and meanings of statements. In traditional logic, there are four forms of propositions. An A form statement is a universal affirmative; E form is universal negative; I form is particular affirmative; and O form is particular negative. Examples of each type, using "S" and "P" as place-markers for the "subject" and "predicate" of the propositions, are below:

A: All S is P

E: No S is P

I: Some S is P

O: Some S is not P

In the traditional "square of opposition," which is used to determine whether a statement is true based on some given fact, it is possible quickly and accurately to make such judgment to determine what follows from some given fact. The square of opposition appears below (Figure 2.1).

Succinctly stated, if you know that an A form proposition is true, its corresponding E form must be false; its corresponding I form must be true; and its corresponding O form must be false. If you know that an E form proposition is true, the corresponding A form is false; the corresponding O form is true; and the corresponding I form is false. If you know that an I form proposition is true, its corresponding O form is unknown; the corresponding E form is false; and the corresponding A form is unknown. If you know that an O form is true, its corresponding I form is unknown; the corresponding E form is unknown; and the corresponding A form is false.

In cases in which you are given factual information in statements like the traditional A, E, I, and O form propositions that is false, it is easy to determine whether corresponding statements in the other three forms are true, false, or unknown by immediately moving to the contradictory statement of the one given. For example, suppose that you know that "Some A is B" is false. You know immediately that "No A is B" is true since the I form (Some A is B) contradicts the E form (No A is B). When statements are contradictory in traditional logic (that is, when they are related diago-

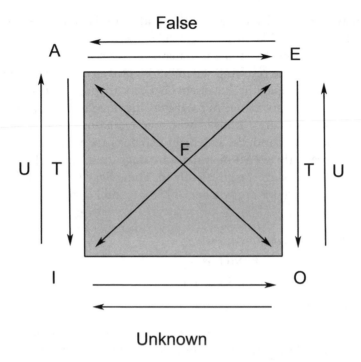

Figure 2.1

nally across the square of opposition), if the given statement is true, its contradictory is false; and if the given is false, its contradictory must be true. So, if you know that an A form is false, the corresponding O form must be true; if you know that an E form is false, the corresponding I form must be true; if you know that an I form is false, the corresponding E form must be true; and if you know that an O form is false, the corresponding A form statement must be true.

Beyond the determination of simple truth values of statements in traditional logic, there are also ways in which statements may be made more (or less) clear in ordinary language through the use of additional forms of immediate (that is, unmediated, instantaneous) inference. There are three basic forms of immediate inference from traditional logic. They are **conversion**, **obversion**, and **contraposition**. Knowing these forms of immediate inference may prove very useful in being able to clarify language in arguments.

Remember that statements in traditional logic are composed of a subject and a predicate. There are times when the position of subject and predicate terms may be reversed and the meaning and quality of the statement does not change. In a case like this, the statement has undergone conversion. In traditional logic, only two types of statement (E and I forms) may undergo conversion where the resulting statement is equivalent to its original formulation. For example, the statement "No cats are dogs" converts to "No dogs are cats" with no change in meaning. The same is true for the I form such as "Some cars are Hondas," which converts to "Some Hondas are cars." On the other hand, the statement "All dogs are mammals" does not convert equivalently to "All mammals are dogs" and "Some dogs are not Beagles" does not convert equivalently to "Some Beagles are not dogs."

Equivalent converses are possible only for E and I form propositions, as shown below:

A: No equivalent converse

E: No A is B = E: No B is A

I: Some A is B = I: Some B is A

O: No equivalent converse

Another form of immediate inference and transformation of statements is called obversion. Every A, E, I, or O form statement transforms to its obverse with no change in meaning. An obverse is formed by changing the quality of the statement (i.e., an affirmative becomes a negative and a negative becomes an affirmative) and adding the prefix "non-" or its equivalent to the predicate term of the statement. For example, the statement "No cats are dogs" becomes "All cats are non-dogs" by obversion. Further, "All humans are mammals" becomes "No humans are non-mammals." The statement "All non-bachelors are non-single males" becomes "No non-bachelors are single males." Here, it is important to note that the statement "No non-bachelors are single males" can also be converted to "No single males are non-bachelors." In addition, "No single males are non-bachelors" can undergo obversion and be rendered simply as "All single males are bachelors."

The example in the previous paragraph of the obversion, the conversion, and the subsequent second obversion of the statement "All non-bachelors are non-single males" illustrates an essential point in speaking, writing, and arguing for a position. Clarity is preferable to confusing language. Speaking and writing in "negatives" is sometimes unavoidable and it is sometimes desirable even if avoidable; but it is normally the case that simple, straightforward language and statement construction will allow your arguments to be understood more quickly and clearly.

The obversion of statements in A, E, I, and O forms is below:

A: All A is B = E: No A is non-B

E: No A is B = A: All A is non-B

I: Some A is B = O: Some A is not non-B

O: Some A is not B = I: Some A is non-B

Another form of immediate inference, contraposition, is simply a combination of conversion and obversion. You saw this in the example of the statement "All non-bachelors are non-single males." Obversion yields "No non-bachelors are single males." Conversion of "No non-bachelors are single males" yields "No single males are non-bachelors," and further obversion of "No single males are non-bachelors" yields "All single males are bachelors." In other words, a contrapositive is formed by the obverse of the converse of the obverse of a statement. The following chart shows equivalent contrapositives (applicable only to A form and O form propositions).

A: All A is B = A: All non-B is non-A

E: No equivalent contrapositive

I: No equivalent contrapositive

O: Some A is not B = O: Some non-B is not non-A

These forms of immediate inference are related to the analysis of arguments in traditional logic that is discussed later in this chapter.

THE LOGIC OF STATEMENTS CONTINUED: CONJUNCTIONS, DISJUNCTIONS, NEGATIONS, IMPLICATIONS, AND BICONDITIONALS

In addition to statement transformation and equivalence in traditional logic, the logic of propositions (propositional, or sentence, logic) is important in stating and evaluating positions in arguments. All of the forms of statements in propositional logic are very familiar since they are part of ordinary language that is used in ordinary conversations, writing, and argumentation.

Statements in propositional logic are either atomic or compound. Atomic statements express one concept at a time. Compound statements are composed of atomic statements and express more than one concept. For example, "It is raining" is an atomic statement while "It is raining and windy today" is a compound statement. The compound nature of the statement is obvious by considering the fact that it can be taken apart and expressed as two separate, declarative, atomic sentences like this: "It is raining. It is windy today." Combining the two atomic statements into one compound in this case is a **conjunction**, like this: "It is raining today and it is windy today." Other compound statements are formed as **disjunctions** (using "or" or any of its equivalents), negations (denying a claim made in an atomic or compound statement), implications (statements in "if-then" or "hypothetical" form), and **biconditionals** (statements using the phrase "if and only if" between two atomic sentences).

Basic propositional logic is "two-valued"—i.e., statements are either true or false. For compound statements, there are variations in determination of the truth of statements depending on the quality of each of its atomic components. For example, the statement "I will go to the doctor and to the grocery store today" is true depending on the truth values of the atomic statement components. Being joined by the word "and," this statement is a conjunction. If you do, in fact, go both to the doctor and to the grocery store, the compound statement is true because both of the conjuncts are true. But if you go to the doctor but not to the grocery store, the compound statement indicating that you would do both is false. If you go to the grocery store but not to the doctor, the compound statement is false; and if you do neither, the statement is false. In other words, conjunctions are true only when all the atomic statements composing them are true.

The statement, "My car is either green or blue," is a disjunction. Disjunctions are of two kinds. One kind of disjunction is a weak, or inclusive, disjunction. The other is a strong, or exclusive, disjunction. We begin with the weak disjunction such as that given in the statement regarding the color of my car. Assuming that my car is one and only one color, the statement that "My car is either green or blue" is true if either of the disjuncts is true. It is false, however, if neither of them is true. For the exclusive disjunction, however, things are a bit different. Exclusive disjunctions are actually complex compound statements that are often stated like this: "Either A or B, but not both A and B."

Suppose, for example, that you are buying a new car and you can get either a low interest rate or a rebate on the price of the car, but the deal is that you cannot have both. In a case like this, the statement "You can have a low interest rate or a rebate, but you cannot have both a low interest rate and a rebate" is not true when both disjuncts are true because, in fact, it is impossible for both disjuncts to be true. This statement, then, is true when one and only one of the conditions (disjunctions) is satisfied.

Implications (hypothetical statements) are "if-then" statements. There are many kinds of "if-then" statements, but the common shared meaning among all of them is that they are false only when the antecedent (the part of the sentence following "if" and preceding "then") is true and the consequent (the part of the sentence following "then") is false. Otherwise, the statement is true. Interestingly, then, a hypothetical (implicational) statement beginning with a false antecedent is true regardless of whether the consequent is true (or false).

Negations change the value of the statement to its opposite. So, for example, the atomic statement "It is raining" is negated by asserting that "It is not raining" or "It is false that it is raining." If it is true that it is raining, then the statement "It is not raining" must be false; and if it is false that "It is raining," it must be true that "It is not raining."

Biconditionals are what their name indicates: they are double conditionals or double hypotheticals. Biconditionals are often identified by the use of the phrase "if and only if" between two atomic statements. For example, "You will be charged a fee if and only if you accept the service on this website" means essentially that "If you are charged a fee you have accepted the service" and "If you accept the service, you will be charged a fee." Another way to put it is that the antecedent and consequent are interchangeable in position in a biconditional statement, and both must be true or both must be false for the statement to express a truth.

Finally, much more complicated statements are ones in which several atomic statements are combined, as illustrated by this: "Neither John nor Mary will go on vacation but both Ann and Carol will go on vacation if they have sufficient funds in savings." This statement combines a negated disjunction with a conjunction that is part of a larger hypothetical statement. In a statement like this, it is imperative to determine the type of statement it is (i.e., is its general format a negation, a conjunction, a disjunction, or a hypothetical?). Knowing this determines the conditions under which the statement is true. In this example, the compound statement is a conjunction. This is the case because John and Mary not going on vacation is separate from the conditions under which Ann and Carol will go. Their ability to go is conditional (i.e., it depends on their funding). Nothing about funding is given in the statement regarding John and Mary. So if it turns out that John and Mary go on vacation after all, since the compound statement is a conjunction and it is true only when both conjuncts are true, it makes no difference whether Ann and Carol go on vacation. The statement is known to be false because its first conjunct is false. The important point is that care must be taken in speaking and in writing to ensure that the intended meaning of a statement is what is conveyed and that clarity in the formulation of statements is carefully guarded.

STATEMENT TRANSFORMATIONS IN PROPOSITIONAL LOGIC

Some considerations applying to statements from traditional logic also apply to statements in propositional logic. Just as some statements can reverse their subject and predicate terms and retain the same meaning, so also conjunctions and disjunctions can reverse the positions of the first and second and any other conjuncts or disjuncts without changing the meaning or truth of the statements. For example, "Jeff and Margaret will go to the islands on vacation but Ann and Greg will go to Alaska" is a conjunction (the major connective of the statement is the word "but," a synonym of "and") and it makes no difference whether the statement is reformulated to state that "Ann and Greg will go to Alaska but Jeff and Margaret will go to the Islands" or "Ann will go to Alaska and Jeff will go to the islands and Greg will go to Alaska and Margaret will go to the islands." Because the statement is not only a conjunction given its major connective, all the statements in the larger compound are joined with conjunctions. Since conjunctions are true only when all the conjuncts are true, and any conjunct is replaceable with any other, any rearrangement of atomic statements in the compound yields the same ultimate compound statement value.

"Chile or Venezuela will raise the price of goods" is equivalently stated as "Venezuela or Chile will raise the price of goods," with it making no difference which of the country names appears first (or second). Disjunctions are therefore like conjunctions in that it is possible to move the disjuncts without changing the meaning or the truth value of the statements in which they appear. On the other hand, however, disjunctions are quite different from conjunctions because disjunctions are false only when both or all of the disjuncts are false.

Negations, as you have already seen, are denials of any atomic or compound statement. If a statement is true and a negation is added to it, the statement is rendered false. If a statement is false and a negation is added to it, the statement is rendered true. It is often the case that statements composed of negations are confusing not only when written, but also when spoken, especially in conditions in which you must think quickly. For example, "It is not the case that neither John nor Robert will not attend the football game." Take the statement one part at a time. The beginning is a negation ("it is not the case that"), but so is the word "neither." "Neither" negates "either." So if a statement is "Neither A nor B," it is the negation of "Either A or B." Think of the statement as though it did not contain the word "neither" and that it did not contain the negation at the very beginning of the sentence. If it did not contain these, it would be "Either John or Robert will not attend the football game." This means that one or the other of them, and perhaps both of them, will not go to the game. However, the statement asserts that "neither" of them will not go to the game, which means that both of them will go. But in addition, the statement begins by negating everything else that the statement asserts. This means, in short, that one or the other, and perhaps both of them, will go. Even simpler is to consider the negation at the beginning of the sentence as negating the negation in the word "neither," which renders the statement as "Either John or Robert will not attend the football game." In essence, it is very important to think through negations to be sure that you have understood the statement correctly.

Even more, however, are potentially confusing statement constructions and their purported equivalents.

Consider these:

> Is the statement "Neither A nor B" equivalent to "Not A or not B" or is it equivalent to "Not A and not B"?
>
> Is the statement "Not both A and B" equivalent to "Not A and not B" or is it equivalent to "Not A or not B"?

The first, "Neither A nor B," is equivalent to "Not A and not B." The second, "Not both A and B" is equivalent to "Either not A or not B."

While there are some people who see these equivalent statements as equivalent immediately, others do not. It is important to know the difference in either case.

Hypothetical statements sometimes pose difficulties because there are people who take them to be "factual" when they actually express things "hypothetically." If you know that "If it rains, then I will take my umbrella," it does not automatically mean that it is in fact raining. A person could assert that this hypothetical claim is true even in the absence of rain. But more important is that which is equivalent to the statement, "If A, then B," and what is not. "If A, then B" is equivalent to "If not B, then not A," but it is not equivalent to "If not A, then not B." Using an analogy for clarification should make this clear.

Suppose you know that "If you take an aspirin, your headache will subside." If this statement is true, then if your headache does not subside, it is clear that you did not take an aspirin. On the other hand, if you do not take an aspirin and your headache does not subside, it does not necessarily mean that the reason your headache is not gone is because you did not take an aspirin, since it is possible that taking an aspirin wouldn't have made it subside in any case.

In a course in **formal logic**, you would learn a symbol system and the use of truth tables to determine the equivalence of statements to each other, as well as to determine when statements contradict each other and when they may be true given the truth of some other. The scope of this text does not include the use of truth tables and other methods of the analysis of formal reasoning, nor does the ability to analyze the meanings of statements necessarily require such formalization. What it does require, however, is careful attention to the content and form of the statements made by yourself or by others, and to be careful not to make quick or careless judgments about statements. In making judgments about the meanings of statements and what they imply, there are four considerations to take into account regarding claims of statement equivalence or lack of equivalence: Two statements may be equivalent to each other, they may contradict each other, one may imply the other, or they may be completely unrelated to each other. We will take each of these distinctions in turn.

When statements are equivalent to each other, they "say" or "mean" exactly the same thing. So, for example, (1) "I will go to the grocery store or to the gas station" is equivalent to (1a) "I will go to the gas station or to the grocery store." But (1) "I will go to the grocery store or to the gas station" is not equivalent to (2) "I will go to the grocery store and to the gas station," even though it might be the case, given that "or" in this context may be meant in the weak, inclusive sense, that I will go to both of these places. In this case, they could both be true, but that fact does not make them equivalent to each other. On the other hand, the statement (3) "I will go neither to the grocery store nor to the gas station" contradicts the original claim (1). In other words, (1) means exactly the same thing as (1a); (2) could be true at the same time that (1) is true; and (3) cannot be true if (1) is true. Another way to put it is that given (1), (1a) is necessarily true while (2) and (1) are related contingently to each other and (3) is necessarily false if (1) is true.

Finally, if you know that statement (1) is true, what do you know about the statement that (4) "I will go to the bank and to a restaurant for lunch"? While there may be some contingent relationship between going to the gas station or the grocery store and to the bank and to a restaurant, for all you can know in these statements without a context, (4) may be true or it may be false; it is not possible without a context to know which is the case. In other words, there are conditions in the world that would render (4) true if

(1) is true, but there is no necessary connection between them (absent further information about their relationship) allowing us to know whether (4) is true, false, or indeterminate.

Knowing how statements are related (or unrelated) to each other can be helpful in clarifying points in an argument, it can help to avoid stepping into a logical trap, and it is essential in ensuring that you know what is—and what is not—implied by any given statement.

Evaluating Deductive Arguments

The discussion of statements and statement types in the previous section applies to deductive arguments in basic traditional (Aristotelian) logic and in propositional logic, but they also apply to inductive and natural language arguments that are discussed later in this chapter. All arguments are composed of statements, and as you have seen in the previous section on the analysis of statements, what is said or written may be modified in various ways that sometimes render statements unclear or ambiguous, and it is up to you, the person evaluating or creating an argument, to ensure that the information in the argument is clear and complete.

Traditional logic is the logic of classes and it is probably familiar to you in the use of Venn Diagrams (three-circle diagrams indicating class inclusion and exclusion). While Venn Diagrams are not within the scope of discussion in this book, a brief overview of some useful features of Aristotle's logic to evaluate arguments in general should be helpful in constructing and analyzing arguments in ethics.

In traditional logic, arguments have a rigid structure requiring that there be two and only two premises, one conclusion, and all the propositions in the argument must be categorical statements (some or any combination of A, E, I, and O forms that were introduced earlier in this chapter). Out of a total of 256 forms of argument in traditional logic, at most only 24 of them are **valid** (i.e., they follow appropriate form such that if their premises are true, their conclusions must also be true, or better, the falsehood of their conclusions is inconsistent with the truth of their premises). It is clear that at least 232 of the 256 forms of argument in traditional logic are invalid (i.e., their premises do not guarantee the truth of their conclusions), so there is plenty of room for error commission and identification.

The general format of arguments in traditional logic should be familiar to you. A common example from this type of logic is the following:

> All Men are mortal.
>
> Socrates is a man.
>
> Therefore, Socrates is mortal.

The argument presented here is valid. If its premises are true, its conclusion must be true as well. But consider this argument:

> All Greek philosophers are wealthy.
>
> Brad Pitt is wealthy.
>
> Therefore, Brad Pitt is a Greek philosopher.

This is clearly invalid. The truth of the premises (if indeed they are true) does not guarantee the truth of the conclusion. In addition, it is actually false that "All Greek philosophers are wealthy" and with respect to the second premise ("Brad Pitt is wealthy") the claim's truth depends, perhaps, on one's interpretation of the term "wealthy." But more, the conclusion itself is false (i.e., Brad Pitt is not a Greek philosopher). This argument is therefore invalid.

But consider this:

> All Greek philosophers are wealthy.
>
> Brad Pitt is a Greek philosopher.
>
> Therefore, Brad Pitt is wealthy.

This argument is valid. If its premises were true, its conclusion would be true as well. But it is not a **sound** argument because it contains false (or at least highly doubtful) information, rendering parts of it, at least, false. In this example, even if it is true under some or all interpretations that Brad Pitt is wealthy, the claim that he is wealthy does not follow from the information presented in the argument.

In evaluating ethics cases in ordinary reasoning, an efficient method of determining whether the reasoning presented is plausible or acceptable is to formulate analogies to the argument you are considering. Consider the example given previously:

> All Greek philosophers are wealthy.
>
> Brad Pitt is wealthy.
>
> Therefore, Brad Pitt is a Greek philosopher.

It is straightforward how to determine whether the argument is acceptable. Replace the two premises with information you know to be true. So, for example, consider this:

All dogs are mammals.

All cats are mammals.

Following the exact format of the argument regarding Brad Pitt, you can immediately see that "all cats are dogs" is both false and does not follow from the information in the premises.

To construct an analogy, simply replace each of the premises in the format in which they appear in the original argument with statements you know to be true, and if the argument is invalid, the conclusion will be false. Similarly, if you replace premises in an argument that is valid, your analogical reasoning will yield all true premises necessitating a true conclusion—the mark of a valid argument.

Another type of deductive reasoning is from propositional logic. There are some common forms of valid (and invalid) deductive arguments that it is useful to know and to apply, whether in the creation of one's own arguments or in evaluating those of others.

Modus Ponens takes the following form:

If A, then B.

A.

Therefore, B.

To see that this form of argument is valid, again it can be useful to use an analogy such as the following: If you work hard and understand all the concepts in this course, you will pass. You work hard and understand all the concepts. Therefore, you will pass.

On the other hand, an argument form that is sometimes thought to be valid but that is not valid looks much like Modus Ponens, but instead commits a **fallacy** called "The Fallacy of Affirming the Consequent." It takes this form:

If A, then B

B.

Therefore A.

By analogy, consider this:

If you were born in Florida, then you are an American citizen.

You are an American citizen.

Therefore, you were born in Florida.

Clearly, this argument form is invalid because, as shown in the analogy, it is possible for the premises to be true while the conclusion is false, and that is the mark of an invalid argument.

Another form of valid argument is **Modus Tollens**. It has this format:

> If A, then B.
>
> Not B.
>
> Therefore, not A.

Using an analogy, replace A and B by statements you know are true and you will see that when you do so, it is impossible for the premises to be true while the conclusion is false.

Like Modus Ponens, there is a form of argument similar to Modus Tollens that is sometimes mistakenly thought to be valid. It is called "Denying the Antecedent." It has this format:

> If A, then B.
>
> Not A.
>
> Therefore, not B.

Replacing A and B in the premises with statements known to be true, it is clear that it is possible for the conclusion to be false while the premises are true, which again is the mark of an invalid argument. For example:

> If you were born in Florida, then you are an American citizen.
>
> You were not born in Florida.
>
> Therefore, you are not an American citizen.

From this analogy, it is clear that one may not be born in Florida and still be an American citizen, and even though the first premise is true and the second premise is true of those not born in Florida, the conclusion does not follow.

Other forms of valid deductive arguments are the following:

Hypothetical syllogism, having this format:

> If A, then B.
>
> If B, then C.
>
> Therefore, if A, then C.

Disjunctive syllogism, a valid argument form, takes this general format:

Either A or B.

Not A.

Therefore, B.

There are many other forms of valid deductive argumentation that are too numerous to list here, but those already mentioned are commonly encountered in ordinary and in formal reasoning. Knowing them can help you to avoid errors in your own reasoning and to identify them in the reasoning of others.

Evaluating Inductive Arguments

Another form of argumentation is inductive. Inductive arguments are structured such that the truth of the premises offered in support of the conclusion make the conclusion, at best, likely to be true but they can never guarantee the truth of the conclusion. Inductive arguments are, by their very nature, invalid deductive arguments. The reason for this is simple. Since deductive arguments are valid only when the falsehood of the conclusion is inconsistent with the truth of the premises, and since inductive reasoning cannot guarantee the truth of conclusions (that is, it is possible for the conclusion to be false even when the premises are true), there is no means by which inductive reasoning can reach the level of certainty that deductive reasoning meets. This fact does not mean, however, that inductive arguments are to be considered suspect or that only deductive reasoning yields reliable information and conclusions. It is instead the case that inductive reasoning is common, useful, and essential in most of our ordinary and scientific inquiries.

Inductive arguments do not have a specific format such as those found in deductive reasoning in traditional logic or in propositional logic. There are no limitations on the ways in which statements may be formulated and there are no specific formulations of arguments guaranteeing that the conclusions reached will be better than some others. Instead, inductive reasoning depends on facts and their veracity, not on form of argumentation. With that said, however, the *general* structure of an inductive argument is this: The information provided in support of a conclusion is offered as evidence that the conclusion is more likely to be true than to be false.

Inductive arguments may be inductions by enumeration, simple generalizations, informal analogical reasoning, causal claims, and others. For all of them, care must be taken to ensure that the argument is as strong as you can make it, and the construction of the argument is important in giving the best reading to the premises that it is possible to present.

Induction by enumeration is the simplest and most basic form of inductive argumentation. It is a form of reasoning in which one finds, for example, that all observed Xs are Ys, and concludes from this fact that all Xs are Ys, regardless of whether those additional things or objects are observed. This type of reasoning may be illustrated in the following example:

> All observed Cocker Spaniels have quiet dispositions.
> Therefore, all Cocker Spaniels have quiet dispositions.

This argument as it stands may appear to be strong, but such evaluation depends upon how many Cocker Spaniels the speaker has actually observed. If one were to take the premise to mean that every Cocker Spaniel that has ever existed has been observed to have a quiet disposition, a fairly strong argument is present. But suppose the speaker has had contact with or information about only fifteen Cocker Spaniels. Now is it safe to assume that all of them have quiet dispositions? Even if the sample was of every Cocker Spaniel that now exists or has existed in the past, can we infer that every future Cocker Spaniel will have a quiet disposition? The answer is "no." A person making such an argument reasons into the future, making a claim about those things not yet observed. This makes the conclusion of the argument only probable, but in a case such as this, the conclusion is less likely to be true simply due to the sheer number of subjects under consideration.

It is clear that induction by enumeration has merit as an argumentative device, but it is also clear that the larger the sample, the more confidence you justifiably put in the conclusion's veracity. Furthermore, if only one Cocker Spaniel is found to have any disposition other than quiet, then the conclusion is completely falsified since it asserted that the characteristic applies to all Cocker Spaniels. Perhaps it is safer and more justifiable to assert something less than the universal claim about every Cocker Spaniel, such as "Cocker Spaniels generally have quiet dispositions."

Another consideration in evaluating induction by enumeration is whether the sample used to draw the conclusion is representative of an entire population. If one were to claim that every observed Cocker Spaniel that was reared in a kennel had a quiet disposition, and then came to the conclusion that all Cocker Spaniels have quiet dispositions based on that sample (only of Cocker Spaniels reared in kennels), the conclusion is less reliable than "Every Cocker Spaniel reared in a kennel has a quiet disposition" would be. Thus, the more representative the sample, the more confidence you justifiably have that it is likely the conclusion is true.

Causal connections are arguments concerned with supposed causes between events, and are very often used in the physical, natural, and social sciences. When attempting to determine the cause of juvenile delinquency, for example, various factors are considered to determine which factors or group of factors is the cause. The factor or factors that occur most often, or the ones occurring immediately before overt acts of juvenile delinquency, may be taken as the "cause." It is not as simple as this, however, since one cannot simply look to the number of times some action precedes another to find a causal connection. There may be other explanations for the actions or occurrences.

As David Hume famously noted, what we identify as causal connections are accepted by us as matters of belief (and often very strongly held belief), but they fall short of knowledge. Hume distinguished between two types of knowledge, which he called "relations of ideas" and "matters of fact." Relations of ideas are conceptions such as those from mathematics and other mathematically based subject matters (such as theoretical physics) in which conclusions reached are certain based not on any observations or empirical facts, but instead on the format of the statements alone. So, for example, the statement "The blue car is blue" is necessarily true (that is, it falls in the category of "relations of ideas") and because this is so, there are no observations or facts to which anyone must refer to verify the truth of the statement. Matters of fact, on the other hand, are based in experience and observation, and by their very nature the information or conclusion reached from experience and observation is at best only probable. Causal connections, however, fall into neither of these categories of knowledge. The reasons are simple.

Suppose that you observe an event, X, and immediately thereafter another event, Y, occurs. The first time you observe this, you may not think that there is a connection between them. But let's say that you observe X and Y occurring one immediately after the other a dozen times. Perhaps at this point you begin to think that X and Y are causally connected such that because X occurs prior to Y, and Y always (in your experience) occurs not long after X, that X must cause Y. For the sake of explanatory clarity, consider this example:

> During years of the plague in Europe, people noticed that monks who retreated to mountaintop monasteries tended not to contract the plague. Monks spend considerable time praying and paying pious tribute to God.

So, many people concluded, it must be the case that praying and praising God keep people from contracting the plague. And, in addition, those who do not pray and praise God are likely to suffer from plague.

While it may be comforting to the faithful to believe that prayer kept monks from contracting the plague, scientific investigation into the matter later in human history revealed what we take to be likely causal factors in contraction (or lack of contraction) of the plague: it is spread by fleas of infected rats. So while we may believe wholeheartedly that prayer and praise of God kept monks from contracting the plague, their retreat to the mountains, where conditions are too cold for the survival of fleas and where rats are not likely to be in abundant supply, created conditions in which contracting the plague was not favorable.

Even with the advance of science, however, there is still nothing in the concept of fleas and being bitten by fleas that necessitates contracting the plague (that is, there is not the relationship between these occurrences that would exist between concepts in the category of "relations of ideas") and, in fact, there are people who have been and who are bitten by fleas who do not contract the plague at all, which indicates that we do not have strict knowledge of the claim that being bitten by fleas causes the plague.

For all of Hume's careful reasoning on the matter of causation, however, and his conclusion that we do not have strict knowledge of cause and effect relationships, he explains in *An Inquiry Concerning Human Understanding* (1748) that custom or habit "is the great guide of human life" and that it would be foolish not to take notice of events that occur regularly together or that are associated with each other in our minds through repeated occurrence. In other words, even if we do not have strict knowledge of cause and effect relationships, this does not mean that we should throw all caution to the wind and act in ways that common sense tells us are dangerous, ignoring evidence of the senses. Hume's warning about the limits of our knowledge of cause and effect relationships is especially applicable, by analogy, to the study of ethics in Aristotle's acknowledgment that ethics is not an area of inquiry that admits of certainty. Human behavior—and the conditions of our lives on the whole—are variable and contingent, amenable to habitual behavior and often to reasonable expectations, but not always predictable.

Analogical arguments take two different forms. The first is exemplified when one reasons from the similarities of two or more things to their similarity in an as yet unobserved way. For example, one may reason (rather badly) that since cats and dogs are both members of the animal kingdom, both are mammals, both are quadrupeds, and both are domestic animals, that since dogs bark, so do cats. It is clear from this argument that conclusions from analogies can be very weak. Analogies do, however, have significant strengths. The more similarities there are between two or more analogized items, the purported connection between them is more likely than if only one or two common characteristics are noted. If we find, for example, that Congressman X and Congresswoman Y both come from upper middle class families, both have conservative political views, and both have come from the Deep South, and we know that X voted in favor of legislation to ban dumping nuclear waste in the South, we can tentatively assume that Y may vote in the same way. These members of Congress have several relevant characteristics in common and this leads us to believe that they will likely vote in the same way on the bill. It is, however, not certain that they will do so, and enumerating similarities between them, while perhaps helpful in building confidence that they will both vote against dumping nuclear waste in the South, does not guarantee the truth of our belief that they will do so.

The second form of argument by analogy does not involve the comparison of Xs and Ys, but employs a process of reasoning into the future on the basis of Xs now existing or reasoning from observed Xs to some, as yet, unobserved X. We may, for example, conclude that since all shirts purchased at store X have stood up well after hundreds of washings that the next shirt purchased from that store will fare as well. In addition, one may argue that since all observed tablet computers from company Z have broken within two months of purchase under normal use, to buy another tablet from that company would not be a wise move. On the other hand, however, we know that stores often change suppliers of products and there may be a software upgrade that would solve the problem with the tablet, thus the conclusion reached would be rendered false.

Statistical induction is a process of reasoning in which samples of populations are taken, percentages are reported on the basis of those samples, and the results are generalized to the entire population under consideration. It should be clear at this point that statistical induction is very similar to induction by enumeration. The difference between them is the fact that statistical induction concerns the use of percentages while enumeration employs the use of generalizations normally indicated by terms such as "all," "no," "most," and so on. Statistical induction, as evidenced by interviews, questionnaires, opinion polls, and similar information gathering techniques, employs the use of actual numerical values both in the premises and in the conclusion. Induction by enumeration can utilize statistical information or evidence in premises, but rather than generalizing to that particular numerical value or percentage, the conclusion uses terms such as "all," "no," and "some," rendering it a more general inductive method.

There are many arguments that do not fit into a single category. The examples presented above were designed to fit specifically into particular types (enumeration, generalization, analogy, etc.), but it is often the case that arguments in ordinary language have elements of more than one type of inductive argumentation and it may also be the case that some element of deductive argumentation is embedded in reasoning as well. It is possible, for example, that a statistical induction can also lead later in the argument to an analogical inference or any other combination. And even though there is a distinction between deductive and inductive arguments, it is important also to realize that not all arguments are either completely inductive or completely deductive. Some argument may contain elements of both.

Whether the conclusion of an inductive (or any) argument is more likely true than false is a matter of a significant variety of factors impinging on the argument, including issues such as the reliability of the information offered in the premises, the source of the information (whether the source of information is reliable), the meaning of the statements in the premises and in the conclusion, and how much information is provided or required to justify the conclusion. These issues are part of the next section of this chapter on ordinary or natural language argumentation.

Ordinary Language Arguments

"Ordinary Language" encompasses arguments and an analysis of arguments that are not necessarily strictly deductive or strictly inductive. Examples of natural language argumentation come from the news media, politics, textbooks, common conversation, and beyond. The subject matter of such arguments, and the ways in which the arguments are formulated and presented, is unlimited. Further, however, natural language is "messy" in that ordinary conversations and even some specialized discourses contain unnecessary words and phrases, repetitive statements, ambiguous meanings, and complicated and convoluted structure. The evaluator of such arguments may be in a position to interpret meanings of terms and phrases, to guess about the intentions and meanings provided by an author or speaker, and may have to deal with colloquial words and phrases that muddy the waters of reasoning.

No matter the construction of an argument, whether it is purely deductive, inductive, or some combination, there are additional considerations to take into account in determining the quality of argumentation provided. While many texts in formal and informal reasoning provide a list of various "informal" fallacies to look out for and to avoid, our approach is a bit different. Instead of a list of fallacies, it is useful to know that there are three primary ways in which ordinary argumentation may go wrong—they are problems of relevance, problems of strength, and problems of "truth."

Ordinary language arguments in everyday contexts are not always presented in a clear and concise manner or format. Most arguments that we hear or read are composed of peripheral issues, confusing or emotionally charged language, and in such cases, conclusions probably do not reflect exactly the statements made in the premises.

Remember that every subject of which we may speak or in which we are interested is composed of arguments. John Stuart Mill noted in *A System of Logic* that "by far the greatest portion of our knowledge, whether of general truths or of particular facts, being avowedly matter of inferences, nearly the whole, not only of science *but of human conduct*, is amenable to the authority of logic" (emphasis added). Historians present arguments to try to prove something about historical trends or events. Physicians use reasoning in their evaluation of illnesses based on symptoms and through specialized analyses of the structure and function of bodily processes and organs. A news reporter uses reasoning to derive or determine a course of events or to state an opinion in an editorial. Mechanics use complex reasoning to determine the likely causes of problems with automobile engines, and computer programmers reason about probable causes of glitches or bugs in programs and how to correct them. In everything we do, reasoning plays a very important part, and an analysis of "everyday" or "ordinary language" argumentation is essential.

When an entering freshman in college tries to choose a major, the decision is probably not made by closing her eyes, turning the pages in a catalog, randomly stopping at a page, and then proclaiming, "I will major in physics." People normally choose majors based on interests, aptitudes, preferences, future earning potential, and so on. Sometimes, their decisions are based on something entirely different. Suppose that a person chooses a major in physics on the basis of her parents' claim that if she does not, they will provide no funding or other support for her to continue in school. She may then reason that if she wants to go to college, the only course of action is to major in physics. If she refuses to major in physics, she will not be able to go to college at all or she will have to work, apply for a loan, or apply for a scholarship. She either wants to go to college, not work and major in physics, or she cannot go to college until she finds an alternate means to pay—in which case she does not have to major in physics after all. So her decision will be based on the facts at her disposal, and the reasoning is not very complicated since the choice will be clear if we know, for example, that she despises working and searching for funding more than she dislikes physics.

The language employed in the reasoning in the example about one's major and ability to continue in college is not formulaic and deductive. There may be factors relevant to the chain of reasoning in which the student engages that are omitted, and that an evaluator of the argument may know, that will affect the quality of the argument and the veracity of the conclusion. In other words, to determine the quality of an ordinary language argument, it is necessary to look to the premises to determine whether they provide sufficient support and reasons to believe that the conclusion is true. If the premises provide sufficient support and relevant reasons for believing that the conclusion is true, then the argument is cogent. If not, the argument is fallacious. Here, in an inductive or ordinary language argument, the terms "valid" and "invalid" do not strictly apply, and instead this alternate characterization applicable to all forms of reasoning will be sufficient.

Fallacies are problems in reasoning arising in inferences between the premises and the conclusion. An inference is simply the intellectual move from a premise purporting to provide support for a conclusion to the conclusion itself. Fallacies fall under two general headings, irrelevant reason and hasty conclusion, or more generally, fallacious forms of inference are either problems of relevance or problems of the sufficiency of information. An argument is cogent on condition that there are no inferences containing fallacious or erroneous reasoning. Specifically, there are three conditions to be met for an inductive or natural language argument to be cogent. They are: (1) true premises, (2) relevant information, and (3) sufficient information.

An argument must contain true premises in order to be cogent since, although the truth or falsehood of premises is generally independent of inference quality, a false premise lends less support to a conclusion than a true premise, and it thus makes the conclusion less likely to be true. Furthermore, information provided in the premises must be relevant to the conclusion. This condition may seem obvious, but many arguments go wrong in exactly this way. Many people are persuaded by arguments whose premises are completely irrelevant to or only marginally relevant to the conclusion. For example, one might claim that Senator Smith should not be elected for a second term because it was found that he omitted information on his income tax return for the previous year. Even though this finding may be less than advantageous to the senator's standings in the polls, it has nothing to do with his performance as a senator. The premise that he omitted information on his income tax return may not be irrelevant to whether he should be elected to a second term, and it may be that the omission was not his fault or done intentionally.

Finally, the premises of an argument must contain enough evidence to make the conclusion reasonably considered more likely to be true than false. The fallacy "hasty conclusion" often occurs when an insufficient amount of evidence is presented in support of a conclusion. Consider the following example:

> Professor Smith noticed that most of his students (75%) failed the midterm examination in his ethics class this term. Professor Smith concluded that the reason was his absence from class for a week while recovering from the flu. During his absence, a teaching assistant conducted the class and provided review information for the midterm examination. In no other case in over 25 years of teaching have most students failed the midterm examination in ethics (the largest number of failures in the past has been no more than 20%), and the term in which most of the students failed the midterm was the only time Professor Smith had not been present to conduct the class the week prior to the midterm examination.

Has Professor Smith considered all the alternatives? And is he justified in believing that it is the fault of the teaching assistant (or Professor Smith's fault for not being in class for a week) that 75% of the students failed the midterm examination? Are there other reasons that could account for the failure of such a large percentage of students in the class? Has Professor Smith violated the strength requirement in the creation of his argument?

It is at least possible that the reason so many students failed the midterm examination is that Professor Smith is using a new text this term that is not as well suited to the course as the ones he has used in the past, or that he has been feeling unwell all semester and hasn't conducted class with the level of care and completeness that he normally would. There are other possible explanations for the failure of a large percentage of the students, but more information is surely needed to be able to justify (or to discount) the conclusion reached by Professor Smith.

The three conditions that an argument must meet to be considered cogent are an integral part of evaluating inductive and natural language reasoning. These considerations must be a reference point in identifying problematic premises, irrelevant reasons, and hasty conclusions. There is, however, more to the construction, presentation, and evaluation of arguments than the three criteria of cogent reasoning.

Distinguishing between formal argumentation and "rhetorical tricks" is important to determine the quality of an argument. If the purpose of a speaker is simply to win an "argument" (that is, to try to ensure that other people agree with his claims), the use of emotionally charged words and phrases, ambiguous statements, and the presentation of incomplete inferences and irrelevant but appealing information may deflect attention away from an argument and lead to the acceptance of a conclusion that is not in fact warranted by the (mis)information presented. It is easy to be swayed by a speaker or writer, and not be swayed by what is spoken or written. In other words, it is possible to be drawn toward accepting a conclusion because you like the way the information is presented, you are attracted to the speaker or writer, the speaker or writer has presented a position with which you already agree, or any number of potential drawbacks in the construction and evaluation of reasoning.

The means by which to combat the appeal to emotions such as fear or popularity, to guard against irrelevance parading as relevance, and to spot suspect information being presented as though it is sufficient to warrant the statement of a conclusion is to be aware of the pitfalls of reasoning. Being aware (and wary) of such pitfalls in reasoning is to be willing to take the time to verify facts and seek out additional information, not to be persuaded by the appeal of the speaker or writer rather than the content of her or his speech or writings, and to exercise diligence in ensuring that the arguments you write or present and the written or spoken arguments of others satisfy the general requirements of truth, relevance and strength before you accept or act on them.

Even when you are properly persuaded by an argument that satisfies the conditions of cogent reasoning and you accept the conclusion made, there is still value in intellectual humility. The number and types of issues encountered in practical ethics is potentially limitless, and as there is no person who can claim specialization or expertise in every area of human inquiry or interest, it is best, overall, to admit one's potential or actual limitations and adopt a fallibilistic stance. In his *Autobiography*, Benjamin Franklin noted the value of fallibilism in his admonition not to use words such as "certainly," "undoubtedly," "or any others that give the Air of Positiveness to an Opinion; but rather say, I conceive, or I apprehend a Thing to be so or so, It appears to me . . ., or it is so if I am not mistaken."

Just as it is appropriate in evaluating the arguments of others to apply the **principle of charity** (giving the strongest possible reading and rendering of the positions of others so that you can provide the strongest possible evaluations of them), it is also appropriate to apply a conservative principle in the acceptance of your own conclusions or those presented by others with which you agree. Simply put, one's conviction that a statement or group of statements is true is not evidence of truth in fact, just as disliking a person is not evidence against his arguments. Furthermore, the wide variety and range of issues encountered in ordinary language reasoning can go well beyond the abilities, knowledge, and expertise of those who are in a position to evaluate and act on conclusions presented in arguments.

The most reasonable approach to the conclusions we make and the conclusions of others with which we agree and those with whom we do not agree is to take them all as tentative, as the best information available to us at the time, and that we understand our conclusions and the arguments from which they spring to be open to criticism and alteration over time and with the addition of new information. Not to adopt a fallibilistic attitude toward our own researches, interests, preferences, conclusions, and claims is to assume what is clearly unjustified: that the conclusions we reach are true for all time, for everyone everywhere, and that facts and positions do not change with the times, with the addition of new information, and with alternative points of view. Perhaps Richard Rorty's view of the nature of inquiry is instructive in this regard. Rorty notes in *Philosophy and Social Hope* that:

> We cannot regard truth as a goal of inquiry. The purpose of inquiry is to achieve agreement among human beings about what to do, to bring about consensus on the ends to be achieved and the means to be used to achieve those ends. Inquiry that does not achieve coordination of behaviour is not inquiry but simply wordplay. To argue for a certain theory about the microstructure of material bodies, or about the proper balance of powers between branches of government, is to argue about what we should do: how we should use the tools at our disposal in order to make technological, or political, progress.

We think the same holds true in ethics. Mill, in *A System of Logic*, noted that logic is not the same as knowledge; but "logic is the common judge and arbiter of all particular investigations. It does not undertake to find evidence, but to determine whether it has been found. Logic neither observes nor invents nor discovers, but judges.... [L]ogic sits in judgment on the sufficiency of ... observation and experience to justify ... rules and on the sufficiency of ... rules to justify ... conduct." Human beings are not omniscient, and while there may be some ultimate truth in the universe, truth in itself is not the goal of ethics or of ethical action. The goal of reasoning and inquiry in ethics is action—and it is the kind of good reasoning and reasonable inquiry that is intended to find *good* solutions to pressing problems. Among the most pressing problems we encounter are those in ethics.

Questions and Problems for Further Thinking and Discussion

1. Compose an argument of your own to try to justify a position you believe is true on an issue of importance to you. Once you have done so, identify the parts of the argument (premises, conclusion, inferences) and evaluate your own reasoning using the three criteria of cogent reasoning.

2. Suppose you know that the following statement is true: "All non-members must pay an additional fee for use of the facilities at the gym." What is the status of the following statements based on this information?
   a. No members must pay an additional fee for use of the facilities at the gym.
   b. Some members must pay an additional fee for use of the facilities at the gym.
   c. No one who must pay an additional fee for use of the facilities at the gym is a non-member.
   d. No non-members are those who are not required to pay an additional fee for use of the facilities at the gym.
   e. Some members must pay an additional fee for parking at the gym.

3. For each of the following statements, provide the equivalent transformation as indicated:
   a. The contrapositive of "Some non-veterans are not eligible for benefits."
   b. The converse of "No weapons are permitted on this property."
   c. The obverse of "Some non-sporting goods are available in the store."
   d. The converse of the obverse of "All employees are permitted entry at this door."
   e. The obverse of the converse of "Some materials used in production are synthetic."

4. For each of the following statements, indicate whether its form is a conjunction, a disjunction, an implication, a biconditional, or a negation.
    a. If either A or B but not C, then it is not the case that both D and E.
    b. Neither the bill nor the itemized statement is accurate; but both indicate that the cost is over $1000.
    c. It is not the case that both capital punishment and revenge are morally acceptable.
    d. Forgiveness is a virtue; however, if forgiveness is a virtue, then vengeance is ethically suspect.
    e. We can justify the cost of the materials if and only if there is a guarantee provided for the work done.
    f. It is not the case that if the employee is laid off he will find new employment within a month.

5. If you know that A, B, and C are true, that X and Y are false, and that Z is unknown, what is the status of each of the following?
    a. Either A or B, but not both X and Y.
    b. If X then Z.
    c. If either X or C, then not B.
    d. If not either A or B, then it is not the case that both C and Z.
    e. X and B are the case; but neither Y nor not C.
    f. Z and not Z.

6. State which of the following characterizes the following statements (contingent, necessarily true, or necessarily false), and explain how you know that this is the case.
    a. John has been promoted to Captain.
    b. Mike and Peter are both here.
    c. Mary is 54 years old; her brother Bob is 52; and these facts imply that Bob is younger than Mary.
    d. If Ed will attend the party, then Frank will not attend the party, which means that if Frank will attend the party, then Ed will not attend the party.
    e. "It is not the case that neither George nor Henry have been informed of the plan" if and only if it is also the case that "If George has been informed of the plan then so also has Henry been informed of the plan."

7. Based on a topic of interest and importance to you, construct valid arguments about that topic using the following argument forms: Modus Ponens, Modus Tollens, Disjunctive Syllogism, and Hypothetical Syllogism.

8. Search through an editorial page in your local newspaper or in an online news source such as *The New York Times* and identify the conclusion of the argument made by the author. Next, identify and isolate the premises used. In your considered view, is the argument a good one? Why or why not? Defend your answer.

9. What are the three criteria of cogent reasoning? In your considered view, should you check the veracity of claims in an argument before analyzing the quality of the inferences, or the reverse? Why?

10. For the following passages containing ethical problems or dilemmas, evaluate the quality of the arguments, being careful also to identify factors in the reasoning such as the use of deductive forms of argumentation, commission of fallacious forms of reasoning, and the veracity of claims made.

   a. Non-believers and skeptics are incapable of acting morally because they have no foundation on which to base their actions. In addition, non-believers and skeptics cannot have good character because only believers possess the requisite guides to virtue. It follows that non-believers and skeptics cannot satisfy the requirements of either consequentialist or deontological ethical theories.

   b. Giving to charities is a moral requirement of individuals who have the funds and resources to be able to do so. Not to provide for the needy when one is capable of doing so is the same as preventing the needy from being able to exercise their rights to life, liberty, and the pursuit of happiness. We all have an obligation to ensure that every citizen is able to exercise these most basic rights; not to provide them the ability to exercise those rights is dereliction of duty on the part of both individuals and governments. Alternately put, individuals and governments satisfy their duties when they do not interfere in the ability of others to exercise their rights.

   c. Students for a Moral Society (SMS), a student club at our University, has organized a rally to protest the University foundation's investments in business and industry that have a history of violating human rights. One of their planned activities at the rally is a non-violent protest in which members of the group will lie down in front of the Administration building to block access to the main entrance door. The University police notified the faculty advisor to SMS that if the students block access to the building, they will be arrested and detained. The police spokesperson told a news crew covering the story that while students have a right to freedom of speech and expression, their form of protest is unacceptable and will not be tolerated. The faculty advisor for SMS told the news crew that the University administration is essentially bullying the students, using scare tactics, to deflect attention away from the important issues the students wish to address.

d. In response to a charge of sexual harassment against a student, a high school teacher defended her actions by saying that sexual harassment occurs only in cases in which the person to whom sexual references and advances are made does not welcome such references and advances. But her student, she contends, is 18 years old, and therefore an adult. As an adult, and because he enjoys the playfulness of her comments toward him, there is no imbalanced power relationship between them, so it is impossible that her comments to him constitute sexual harassment.

e. A child protection officer in the state recently removed three children from the custody of their parents, citing abuse and neglect of the children because the parents' religious beliefs do not allow vaccinations of the children. The child protection agency, acting on court order, provided the following statement: "The parents are acting contrary to the interests of the children in not having them vaccinated against childhood diseases. While the State respects the rights of the parents to practice their religious beliefs as they see fit, it is also the case that the parents' rights to practice their religion stop at harm to the children. It is the position of the State that the parents failing to have their children vaccinated is tantamount to abuse and neglect not only of their own children, but also of those with whom those children come into contact. The State therefore concludes that removal of the children from the home, and subsequent vaccination of the children, is justified." The parents' lawyer, however, contends that the issue of vaccination is a matter of privacy as well as exercise of freedom of religion and there is no harm caused to the children in not having them vaccinated, since they interact with other children who have been vaccinated, which in turn protects the three unvaccinated children from disease. In addition, the lawyer notes, children who have been vaccinated are in no danger of contracting a disease from the unvaccinated children.

References and Suggestions for Further Reading

Copi, Irving M., Carl Cohen, and Kenneth McMahon. *Introduction to Logic*. 14th ed. Pearson, 2010.

Flew, Anthony. *How to Think Straight: An Introduction to Critical Reasoning*. 2nd ed. Prometheus Books, 1998.

Franklin, Benjamin. *The Autobiography of Benjamin Franklin*. Ed. Leonard W. Larabee, Ralph L. Ketcham, Helen Boatfield, and Helen H. Fineman. Yale University Press, 1964.

Hurley, Patrick J. *A Concise Introduction to Logic*. 11th ed. Cengage Learning, 2011.

Hume, David. *An Enquiry Concerning Human Understanding*, 2nd ed. Eric Steinberg, Ed. Hackett Publishing Company, 1993.

Mill, John Stuart. *A System of Logic*. Ed., Ernest Nagel. In *John Stuart Mill's Philosophy of Scientific Method*. Hafner Publishing Company, 1950.

Rorty, Richard. *Philosophy and Social Hope*. Penguin Books, 1999.

Sinnott-Armstrong, Walter and Robert J. Fogelin. *Understanding Arguments: An Introduction to Informal Logic*. 9th ed. Cengage Learning, 2014.

Van Vleet, Jacob E. *Informal Logical Fallacies: A Brief Guide*. University Press of America, 2011.

Weston, Anthony. *A Rulebook for Arguments*. 4th Revised Ed. Hackett Publishing Company, 2008.

3   Conceptualizing Ethical Cases

Now that we have the necessary logical and theoretical tools, we are ready to begin looking at specific ethical cases. This chapter will deal with the steps involved in conceptualizing cases, including reading techniques and researching the case.

A Day in the Life of a College Student

Cases for ethical reflection, study, and action permeate our personal and social existence. Consider the movement through the day of a college student. You wake up and shower, while recalling the "Global Water Shortage" news story that had caught your attention when you were surfing the Internet yesterday afternoon. You get dressed, putting on your favorite cotton t-shirt, which you now know required hundreds of gallons of water to be made. You then pop a sausage and cheese biscuit into the microwave, and as you unwrap your steaming breakfast you try to forget the "Holocaust on your plate" chants by animal rights activists you had heard outside of the fast food restaurant closest to campus. Usually you lock your front door without pause, but today you vaguely wonder to yourself "what *should* I try to accomplish today?" The sun is shining and you are happy that you live close enough to campus so that you can ride your bike and don't have to rely on a car for transportation. On your way to school you remember that your afternoon class has been cancelled in order to prepare for the evening's football game, and you wonder momentarily about the relationship between athletics and education and how this likely wouldn't happen in any other country. After your first class you see your good friend who asks you why you hadn't told her about "that other student" after seeing his Facebook profile, and you shrug your shoulders. The day's not even halfway over and you can feel the mounting uncertainty and need to question the meaning of life.

You get the point, right? This is not an unusual or exaggerated narrative, and yet you can begin to see the many ethical situations leading to reflection that emerge throughout one's everyday existence. How many ethical issues can you identify that are either directly or indirectly present in this brief narrative? Give it a try and compare your questions with another person.

We think that if you come up with a dozen or more that you have done a good job and have a good understanding of the ethical dimensions of everyday life. What's more, you will have begun to conceptualize ethical cases that can then become the subject of research and critical questioning.

Let's consider an example from the narrative above. Perhaps the most striking phrase is "Holocaust on your plate," which in an arguably controversial way calls us to think about the ethical dimensions of something the vast majority of Americans do every day: eat meat. Why is this an issue and what makes the Holocaust metaphor possible? In order to approach this we would need to research the conditions of non-human animals in the production of meat-based consumables, the extent of these modes of production, and the reasons for eating meat. We could also examine the philosophical and religious texts that present arguments for or against certain meat-eating practices. Health issues and environmental issues could also be considered in answering the ethical question "Should I eat meat?"

But another issue that can be considered here is whether the use of the Holocaust metaphor is morally justifiable. With a little research you will discover that this slogan was part of a campaign by People for the Ethical Treatment of Animals (PETA) in 2004 that juxtaposed images from animal slaughterhouses with ones from Nazi concentration camps. Not surprisingly, this campaign proved to be highly controversial and offended many people, especially the Jewish community, and it was banned in Germany and apologized for, sort of, by the President of PETA, Ingrid Newkirk. What reasons were there for running the campaign and what reasons were there for finding it offensive? Was it mainly the graphic images that caused pain or the metaphor itself? Would one's answer to this question be different upon realizing after deeper research that the Holocaust metaphor was initially used in a short story by the Nobel Prize laureate Isaac Bashevis Singer (1902–1991), a Jewish supporter of showing compassion towards animals, who in his short story "The Letter Writer" writes: "In relation to [animals], all people are Nazis; for the animals, it is an eternal Treblinka"?

What Is a Case and Why Case Studies?

Before proceeding further it is important to consider what is meant by the word "case" and how a "case study" approach to ethics and critical thinking may differ from other approaches. "Case" has the meaning of "a particular instance" and is related to the Latin *casus*, which means "a fall" and the Latin *cadere* meaning "to fall." This etymology is particularly suggestive in expressing the involuntary loss of footing or difficulty that we may experience in encountering new and unique situations throughout life and then attempting to figure out how to deal with them. Thus an approach to ethical thinking that is oriented by case studies views the cases as primary and the theories as secondary. We do not begin with preconceived theoretical notions about how we are "to see" (note that the word "theory" derived from the Greek is originally connected with "seeing") such situations. Instead, we desire to grasp the situation in all its particularity and peculiarity, and through the kinds of questions we ask we begin to cast light on the case. Thus, we will try to reason towards theory, rather than from it.

This point of view has been considered the "end of ethics" by some academics, but we see it as marking the beginning of ethical thinking and providing an opening for ethical creativity. What is meant by the "end of ethics" is explained nicely by John Caputo, professor of philosophy and religion:

> The end of ethics does not mean that all hell has broken loose. It does not mean that the philosophers have decided to lend their voice to the general anarchy, to unchecked greed, the free flow of drugs, and widespread violence. The end of ethics does not mean that "anything goes," which can now be taken to be official, because even the philosophers concur. The end of ethics means instead that for certain philosophers . . . the business as usual of ethics has given out and the ethical verities that we all like to think are true, the beliefs and practices we all cherish, are now seen to be in a more difficult spot than we liked to think. The end of ethics is thus a moment of unvarnished honesty in which we are forced to concede that in ethics we are more likely to begin with the conclusions, with the "ends" or triumphant ethical finales we had in mind all along, and worry about the premises later. The end of ethics means that the premises invoked in ethical theory always come too late, after the fact. So if there are "cases" in the end of ethics, the cases are casualties, "falls" (*casus*), stumbling over unforeseen difficulties and obstacles, the "accidents" that strikes at us in daily life, that sometimes strike us down.

The end of ethics means that we cannot expect a single ethical theory or perhaps any single ethical perspective to encapsulate all the complexities of existence, nor can we expect that a particular human situation can be best understood as a straightforward dilemma between two ethical theories. But this is often how the study of ethics is approached, and it is often how ethically charged situations are reported in the media. This kind of view, which you might say takes "ethics" first and the "cases" second, ultimately narrows perspectives, limiting critical questioning and creativity.

So, we may now consider a "case" to be a particular real-life situation in which we find ourselves somewhat off-balance and have difficulty knowing what we should do. One goal of this book is to help us recognize such situations and to embrace them as opportunities for personal growth, rather than to wish to avoid them or resolve them right away with a preconceived opinion. You might consider it this way: just as when riding a bike and one starts to lose one's balance and wobble, the way to prevent seriously falling flat on your face is to increase the speed of your pedaling, so when confronted with challenging ethical case studies the mechanism for increasing one's speed and avoiding disaster is critical questioning. Of course, in real life cases do not appear as clearly and well-defined as in any textbook, but instead are frequently related to other situations that crisscross and overlap in a complex way. Thus, when we begin to conceptualize ethical cases we seek to isolate a particular situation and only consider the essential facts, which is to say, those facts that define the difficult situation and make it what it is. Then we attribute particular views to the situation based on the individuals involved. These aspects would comprise in the simplest way an ethical case. As Jessica Pierce observes, "a case study plucks a moral problem out of the teeming chaos of life and isolates it in a fishbowl—behind glass, apart from relatives and friends—so that we can examine it up close." Can you think of a situation in your life or one with which you are familiar that could become a case study in ethics? We think it is helpful for students not only to know how to analyze clearly defined case studies, but also be able to create their own case studies for discussion, but we will return to this point in Chapter 6 after having analyzed various cases.

Working with case studies is a significant way of developing one's skills in ethical reasoning and critical thinking, and we are confident that students who do this will be in a better position to face real-life ethical challenges in the future. Here Pierce neatly suggests how intellectual case study exercises may be analogous to physical exercise:

> Moral judgment is shaped by disciplined thought and fostered by repeated practice. We might liken morality to physical fitness. To maintain a level of health, we must exercise regularly; to improve involves even more sweat and tears and some time on the track or in the gym. Similarly, we can do strengthening exercises to keep moral muscles limber and strong. One such exercise is the case study.

Not only will you strengthen your "moral muscles," but when working on ethical case studies in groups you will also improve your social and interpersonal skills as you all work together to build a consensus for how a case should best be approached. As we suggested above, someone with an interrogative disposition who is well-cultivated in critical questioning is a fundamentally open and undogmatic person. We are sure that you will agree that such a person is more frequently sought out when dealing with difficult ethically-sensitive projects than the opposite, a dogmatic, narrow-minded individual who can only see things in one particular way. This is not to say, however, that the open person is uncommitted or unprincipled when it comes time to make an ethical judgment, but he or she knows that such judgments never come with a stamp of 100% certainty given the nature of finite human existence. He or she knows that we must reason the best we can and take into account as many facts and perspectives as possible in order to arrive at the truth (i.e., the ethical perspective that demonstrates the most complete understanding of the situation). Such a person thus welcomes and respects different views, in agreement with Thomas Jefferson's statement that "difference of opinion leads to enquiry, and enquiry to truth." In this regard, when we take a case studies approach to ethics we realize that truth is not where we start, but where we hope to arrive.

One more benefit that can be added to the moral and interpersonal benefits just explained is that in dealing with ethical case studies one will also strengthen one's "academic muscles" (of course, all of these "muscles" are really only metaphorical ways of referring to the one complex human organ that is the brain). In other words, you will develop skills in reading analytically and researching in order to conceptualize the cases to the fullest extent possible. Further, since ethical cases are never simple enough to be relevant to only one academic discipline, you will need to be able to cross over into different branches of knowledge and do interdisciplinary work, which is also highly valued today in our rapidly-changing world.

Beyond the ethical issues that arise in our everyday practices, there are others that we encounter in the larger world around us. Sometimes they are close to home, and sometimes they are thrust upon us through the forces of global mass communication. Consider these recent occurrences in our own home state of Florida that have become major national news stories: How should we regard the killing of Trayvon Martin by George Zimmerman? How should we regard the captivity of Orcas at theme parks such as SeaWorld? How should we regard Alex Rodriguez's visits to the Biogenesis Labs in southern Florida? Opening any daily local or national newspaper will undoubtedly present readers with possibilities for many more ethical cases to analyze and evaluate.

Be that as it may, excellent examples of case studies for ethics are presented at the beginning of every fall and spring semester by the Association for Practical and Professional Ethics (APPE). The APPE is responsible for providing cases for their annual ethics bowl competitions, and they put out fifteen cases in early September for the regional ethics bowl competitions and fifteen additional cases in early January for the national Intercollegiate Ethics Bowl (IEB). These well-crafted cases provide more than enough material with which to work in a semester-long course, regardless of whether one is preparing to compete in an ethics bowl (although we would certainly encourage you to do so!), and the only major difference between the regional cases and the national cases is that references are provided with the former but not the latter. These cases are available through the APPE website, where one can also find information about the ethics bowl. Here is a brief description of the ethics bowl:

> The Intercollegiate Ethics Bowl (IEB) is a team competition that combines the excitement and fun of a competitive tournament with an innovative approach to education in practical and professional ethics for undergraduate students. Recognized widely by educators, the IEB has received special commendation for excellence and innovation from the American Philosophical Association . . . for Excellence and Innovation in Philosophy Programs. The format, rules, and procedures of the IEB all have been developed to model widely acknowledged best methods of reasoning in practical and professional ethics.
>
> In the IEB, each team receives a set of cases which raise issues in practical and professional ethics in advance of the competition and prepare an analysis of each case [we would also say a creative analysis]. At the competition, a moderator poses questions, based on a case taken from that set, to teams of three to five students. Questions may concern ethical problems on wide-ranging topics, such as the classroom (e.g. cheating or plagiarism), personal relationships (e.g. dating or friendship), professional ethics (e.g. engineering, law, medicine), or social and political ethics (e.g. free speech, gun control, etc.) A panel of judges may probe the teams for further justifications and evaluates answers. Rating criteria are intelligibility, focus on ethically relevant considerations, avoidance of ethical irrelevance, and deliberative thoughtfulness [and here we would also add creativity].

It is obvious from this brief description of the ethics bowl that it serves very well in stimulating critical thinking on contemporary ethical issues. We see it also as an opening for the application of creativity (see Chapter 5 below for more explanation), and taken out of the competitive context (in which it is the moderator and judges who ask the questions) there is also a clear opportunity for readers to ask good questions. Thus, whether you are preparing for an event such as the ethics bowl or not, the two sets of cases written annually provide students (and instructors) with a great resource for academic study. It is not our purpose here to replace this invaluable resource, but rather to offer a method for using these and similar cases.

Reading Cases

Obviously, if you have made it this far in the book you are able to read, but more often than not it is assumed that students know what is involved in reading a text well. We want to suspend that assumption by asking how does one get the most out of a text, and although we are focused on particular case studies, which by their nature are shorter texts with incomplete information, our suggestions here nevertheless apply to any material written to increase the understanding of its readers. Further, we expect that readers will also become deeply engaged in reading philosophical texts on theoretical and **applied ethics** as they research the cases studies, and the reading method explained here is most highly suited for these kinds of texts.

When initially approaching a case study or philosophical text, it is very important to read through the text quickly in order to get a sense of the main ideas and the gist of the reading. This applies equally to a longer text, although such a text should be broken up into chapters or sections and one should focus on understanding these parts one at a time. When you perform this "quick reading" you do not stop to look up every new or unclear term or every complicated fact, but you simply read the text straight through to get a general sense of what the text is about. After a quick reading, you should pause and ask yourself what the text was about and spend a minute or two summarizing this in your own words in your mind, or on paper, or in conversation with another. Doing this will naturally lead you to raise questions about your understanding of the text, such as "What ideas am I unable to recall well?" and "How do the ideas and facts fit together coherently?" These kinds of questions will thus enable you to check your initial understanding and thus be better prepared for a closer reading of the text which allows for more learning and understanding to occur. A quick reading and summarizing may also be significant in identifying prejudgments (which is another word for "prejudice" without the negative connotation) or interpretive biases regarding a particular case, especially when these case summaries are presented in discussion with others. When reflecting on these summaries consider whether they are entirely descriptive of the case content or whether they subtly incorporate value judgments. We all bring our own value judgments into play in interpreting our world, but being aware of one's initial judgments which occur pre-reflectively will provide an excellent opportunity for questioning one's own values and ethical perspectives and how they have been formed.

Next, here is perhaps a somewhat surprising claim that we believe is true: reading well requires readers to read with pen or pencil (a writing instrument) in hand. Of course, this doesn't mean that you simply twiddle your pen while reading, but that you use it to mark up and write on the text in various ways. For example, if you have not been reading this text with pen in hand, then it is likely that you have not been reading it as well as possible, which is to say that you have not been understanding as much as possible.

This claim points to a couple of interesting corollaries (a "**corollary**" is a proposition that follows logically from another one). First, it suggests that reading and writing are reciprocal actions such that each activity improves the other. In other words, we become better readers by writing, and we become better writers by reading. Leo Strauss expressed this nicely in *Persecution and the Art of Writing*:

> It is a general observation that people write as they read. As a rule, careful writers are careful readers and vice versa. A careful writer wants to be read carefully. He cannot know what it means to be read carefully but by having done careful reading himself. Reading precedes writing. We read before we write. We learn to write by reading. A man learns to write well by reading well good books, by reading most carefully books which are most carefully written.

At present our focus is on reading case studies well, but it will be helpful to keep this in mind when it comes time to write a position paper on a case. Second, the claim that reading well requires a pen in hand suggests that it may be more challenging to read electronic texts well, although sometimes our concern is not to extend our understanding (as it is here) but simply to acquire information, so a deeper level of reading is not needed. In spite of the fact that writing in the margins of a printed page to develop your understanding is clearly beneficial, technological advances may already make this a less common practice. Some of the apps for tablets that have so far been developed are those for annotating and highlighting text in PDF files. These come with the ability to write or print using a stylus or another input device, including one's finger. In addition, Kindle users have access to storage space for highlights and notes taken on books or documents as well as the ability to see the popular highlights made by other users and readers of the same books and documents. Further technological and software developments will likely augment the ability to imitate the work of pens, pencils, and paper in reading, writing, and research, but whether this will improve our ability to read and write well remains an open question.

There are numerous techniques for marking up a text, and we do not think that there is one common technique that should be prescribed for everyone. But any helpful technique will be consistent in identifying key concepts or terms, important facts, and central propositions. Often, the key sentences are underlined or highlighted, and one could use different colors to identify different kinds of key sentences, such as empirical statements (i.e., sentences that express a fact that can be verified by experience) or logical propositions (i.e., sentences that express a claim that can be either true or false). Readers could also identify key terms by circling them, underlining them several times, or using another colored highlighter. Again, different readers will have different preferences here, as some will prefer to use only pencil, others pen, and others will prefer a more elaborate color-coding system using various highlighters. The important point here is for readers to engage concretely with the written material and in essence "make the text their own" by employing one of these practical methods.

Perhaps more important than marking up a text with lines, circles, and highlights, is for readers actually to write on the text, using the space in the margins and at the top and bottom of the page to formulate questions, comments, reactions, examples, or other thoughts related to the reading content. The most well-read text will consequently be the one with the most markings and commentary.

In your closer reading of the cases you should be able to identify key facts and ideas that are central to the case. These can be understood as the most important details, which make the case what it is and without which we would have a different case. It is useful to identify at most three to five of these key facts and ideas by underlining or highlighting them in the text, and then you should ask yourself what other facts are needed in order to better understand this case and where can these facts be found?

Let us now consider a particular case for study, one which is likely to be relevant to all students paying for their higher education.

Case: Student Loan Forgiveness

As higher education becomes an increasingly essential qualification for jobs and the price of higher education rises, many middle and lower class students have turned to low-interest student loans to finance higher education. Lately, however, student loan debt has soared to $1 trillion dollars and many recent graduates report having trouble finding a job in a slowly recovering economy. Faced with large amounts of student loan debt and no way to repay those debts, default rates are on the rise, with 8.8% of borrowers defaulting two years into repayment in 2009.[1] Many recent graduates believe they were not properly informed of the risks of taking out large loans to finance an education, especially with news that interest rates are set to rise to 6.8% in 2012 (absent action from Congress).[2]

Troubled economic patterns make up a perfect storm for a bill like the Student Loan Forgiveness Act of 2012, which was submitted to Congress earlier this year by Michigan Congressman Hansen Clarke. The bill is intended to lessen the crippling amount of debt that some students have incurred by pursuing higher education in a tough job market. The bill would go a long way towards lessening the burden on borrowers: capping interest rates at 3.4%, offering forgiveness of loans after 10 years of payments, and strengthening programs that trade loan forgiveness for public work. But relief for borrowers is not the only goal of the bill. Supporters of the bill cite the overall economic benefits of loan forgiveness as well. Billions of dollars that are now going into paying off student loans could presumably find their ways into the pockets of business owners, large and small, causing demand for products and services to rise and creating a cascade of new jobs to fulfill that demand.

However not everyone is thrilled with the idea of bailing out struggling students and criticism comes from some surprising sources.

Although the goal of attending the college of one's dreams frequently over-shadows it, those who took on student loans are required to be informed of the risks of carrying debt into uncertain times. While no one could predict an economic collapse, students who started college in 2008 should have known they were entering college during a financial crisis. And there are many ways that students could avoid paying more money for loans such as attending less expensive state schools or working while earning credit at community colleges. Students were, by and

---

1. Tanar Lewin, "Student Loan Default Rates Rise Sharply in Last Year," *The New York Times*, September 12, 2011, http://www.nytimes.com/2011/09/13/education/13loans.html.

2. Jennifer Liberto, "Student loan rate hike: what you need to know," *CNN: Money*, April 24, 2012, http://money.cnn.com/2012/04/24/pf/college/student_loans/index.htm.

large, consenting adults who signed papers promising to repay. Further-more, no relief is extended to students who worked to pay for their edu-cations without taking out student loans. So the act seems to punish those whose ambitions caused them to work harder during college than some of their peers.

But perhaps more importantly, while no one is saying that debt-burdened college graduates don't encounter hardships when they can't find a job after college, these people are, statistically speaking, nowhere close to the least well-off in society. College graduates in 2011 overall are half as likely to be unemployed as those with just a high school diploma, but are almost three times as likely to be employed versus someone without a high school diploma.[3] Even unemployed college graduates still have a college education—no small qualification in the job market. Those without higher education are suffering even more in the poor economy, since they do not even have the entry requirements to higher-paying jobs. Funds that would go toward relieving student loan debt could be targeted at programs that serve the poor and under-educated by offering job training or welfare assistance. Perhaps funds would be better directed at improving the plight of the least well-off rather than younger, college-educated people in the prime of their lives.

The first step in conceptualizing this case involves determining the key facts that define the problem. Usually, there are two or three central facts that are essential to the case and point to the ethical issues involved. When reading any text students should know that the opening paragraphs are most important in presenting a case, and when looking at individual para-graphs they will find that each well-constructed paragraph will have one or two key sentences, frequently called the point sentence(s), and that these are commonly found at the beginning or end of a paragraph. Knowing this al-lows readers methodically to scan a text and quickly locate the important factual information. So, when we read the "Student Loan Forgiveness Case," we find that the first two sentences introduce the topic of student loans, but that it is the second sentence that expresses the key factual information that "student loan debt has soared to $1 trillion dollars." While the second part of this sentence—"many recent graduates report having trouble finding a

---

3. Bureau of Labor Statistics, "Education pays in higher earnings and lower unemploy-ment rates," March 23, 2012. http://www.bls.gov/emp/ep_chart_001.htm.

job in a slowly recovering economy"—makes a transition to explaining what is problematic with the increased debt, it is not factually clear and careful readers would want to know more here. For example, first, the phrase "many recent graduates," which occurs twice in the first paragraph, is vague and gives us no clear sense of the number of graduates involved. Second, the factual information that is conveyed by "reporting" something is not necessarily the thing that is reported, but rather *that* it has been reported. So, we are justified in asking specifically how many graduates have reported this and what percentage of all college graduates does this represent. Next, "having trouble finding a job" is also vague, as we do not know exactly what kind of "trouble" they are having—presumably there could be different kinds—and what someone perceives as "trouble" may be conditioned by certain false presumptions, such as "finding a job after graduation is easy." But more importantly than this, "having trouble finding a job" does not imply that they have not found jobs, so much more research into the specific facts is needed here.

In addition to the $1 trillion student loan debt, another important fact in the first paragraph is the 8.8% default rate for which a reference is provided to a website for CNN: Money. In reading and researching a case we must always consider the credibility of the sources of information, which will be discussed below, but we consider that given that it is a nationally recognized news source, that CNN qualifies as a credible source of information, although this does not mean that they never present inaccurate information. Still, without further research into the facts surrounding the default rate, we do not know how much of a rise this percentage represents when compared with past years, and we have not identified all the conditions that are associated with this increase. In general, proving a factual causal relationship between certain conditions and certain outcomes can be extremely difficult, so we must always be wary of causal claims in others' positions on ethical cases and recognize in our own positions that at best we may claim that the two factors are associated, but not necessarily causally connected.

Nevertheless, the facts that student loan debts are high and that students default more than they have in the past, which is what is referred to as "troubled economic patterns," are not enough to define an ethical case study. What we also need is a perspective on this factual situation that reflects a value judgment. This is what we find in the first sentence of the second paragraph, which expresses the main point of the paragraph as well as a key fact for the case—that Michigan Congressman Hansen Clarke has submitted a Student Loan Forgiveness Act. So, expressing the central facts of the case as concisely as possible, we can say that, first, student loan debt is $1 trillion, and second, a Student Loan Forgiveness Act has been proposed. By initially defining the case and concisely using two or three key facts we are able to focus our consideration on the most basic aspects of the case in order to then work towards agreeing on what research is needed to better understand the case, what moral issues are involved, and ultimately how the moral issues may best be resolved. Obviously, if we cannot agree on the most basic facts of the case, then our later discussions on additional details and moral issues will be much more difficult. Given these two central facts we can then speak of the sub-facts that relate to these, such as the 8.8% default rate related to the first fact and the capping of interest rates at 3.4% related to the second fact.

Researching the Case

What specific research is needed to move forward here? We have already mentioned that it would be helpful to know the number of "many" recent graduates who have incurred debt and have reported trouble in finding a job. Although there may be many students who face difficulty, it is certainly not all students, so we should be interested in knowing which recent graduates have been successful and why? Does the kind of college (e.g., public or private, rural or metropolitan) play a role in student success in finding employment? Are specific majors associated with higher rates of student post-graduate employment? And what about the "many recent graduates" who "believe they were not properly informed of the risks of taking out large loans to finance an education"—again, exactly how many are there and why do they "believe" they were not properly informed? What is the meaning of being "properly informed," as opposed to, say, simply being informed, and what actions are required of informants and informees for proper information to be communicated? As we have suggested earlier, a belief that something is the case does not count as actual evidence that it is the case, and we are justified in asking whether there are equally "many" recent graduates who believe they were properly informed and knew about the risks of incurring student debt. Thus you can see that a lot of factual research into recent college graduates and data on student loans will provide us with a much fuller picture of the actual situation.

Next, we will need to research the Student Loan Forgiveness Act of 2012, and carefully read the actual bill in order to understand better the meaning of this act, the reasons for it, and the intended consequences. Independent of the bill, it is clearly central to our understanding to research the notion of "forgiveness" and inquire into its moral status and applicability to student loan economics. Before beginning this research, we should start the process of asking good questions by considering what moral issues are involved in this case. In this way, our research will be given some direction, although we should expect that while in the process of researching the issues, our critical questions will be refined and often lead us to asking deeper questions. As we see it, there is a back and forth movement between the questions that we are asking and the research (reading) we are doing on the case. Naturally, as we read new material our understanding grows and the initial interpretation of the situation will be modified to lead to new questions.

We must start the process of critical questioning from our understanding of the case itself. We have now identified the essential factual elements, but what moral issues are suggested from within the case? What are the central ethical concepts involved in thinking about the case and how can we best formulate the questions that will guide our research?

Initially, the troubled economic situation coupled with the submission of the Student Loan Forgiveness Act suggests that recent college graduates have been unfairly burdened. Thus, there is an implicit perception of the wrongness of the situation facing these many students, which is suggested through the language that students have not been "properly informed of the risks" and that they are subject to a "crippling amount of debt." Obviously, such **"loaded language"** (i.e., words used to provoke an emotional effect, such as "crippling") is used to convey the severity of the wrongness of the situation facing students today, although it is difficult to find a clear suggestion of who would be directly responsible for wronging the students. So, put simply, one moral issue is whether students are being wronged or treated unfairly through the practices involved in paying for a college education. Further, in order to better understand this issue, we need to ask who (or what) is responsible for this wrongdoing? Are the colleges at fault for charging high tuition and fees that force students deep into debt? Should there be no tuition for higher education, as in many European countries? Is the American government at fault for allowing this situation to have gotten out of control? (The fact that Congress is considering a remedy seems to implicate them of at least some responsibility for the situation.) Can the complex economic situation be blamed for the problem, in which case assigning a responsible agent to the wrongdoing will prove very difficult, if not impossible. What about employers who seek employees with a college education—are they part of the problem as well? And what about the bankers who distribute student loans with supposedly limited information—what role do they play in the problem?

The last two paragraphs of the case shift the focus to the responsibility of the students for being well-informed and knowing the risks associated with student loans. After all, aren't the students themselves responsible for choosing which colleges they attend and for actually taking out a student loan? Involved in incurring any formal debt will be a signed promise to repay the debt, so considered from this perspective would it not be unfair to "forgive" the debts of those students who cannot repay their student loans, while other students, perhaps more resourceful, hard-working, or fortunate, continue to repay their student loans? If some student loans are going to be "forgiven"—and we must still be wary of this concept—then doesn't fairness imply that such forgiveness is granted equally and impartially to all students? Put simply, isn't it unfair to forgive some and not others (which must equally be a problem for divine being!)? Finally, the last paragraph suggests that we consider an even broader perspective of society as a whole and ask whether it is right to direct resources to help bright, young college graduates, when those resources could be used to improve the lives of those who are much worse off in society today. Thus, we can see that a central overarching question for this case is this: Is student loan forgiveness morally justified?—and that this question breaks off into many other questions as indicated above. Finally, we can also see that the central ethical concepts involved include justice or fairness (remember that John Rawls argues that justice *is* fairness), responsibility, promising, and forgiveness.

Now that we have identified the central moral concepts and issues, at least in a preliminary way, we have established a moral problem that is ripe for fruitful research. The etymology of "research" suggests "an intensive seeking," and this is precisely what we need to do. While it is clear that we need to gather information about current economic conditions, numbers of recent graduates, and the details of the Student Forgiveness Act, this information must be contextualized as addressing aspects of the case that lend themselves to the formation of arguments about what we should do. For example, if our research shows that 90% of recent graduates claim that they are not being informed about the risks of their student loans, then this would lend itself to being a reason in an argument that financial institutions that grant student loans need to make changes to inform borrowers properly of the risks involved.

What are the sources of information to which we should turn when researching this case and how should we evaluate these sources? The case itself already includes electronic references to *The New York Times* and

CNN, major news sources with a national reputation, although these would be considered tertiary sources, in that they most frequently report on secondary sources for a large, general audience. For example, a *New York Times* article may be written by a journalist (tertiary source) who reviews someone else's analysis (secondary source) of Congressman Clarke's bill (primary source). While news articles such as these provide a good place to start in gathering information for the case study, it is crucial that we explore the primary and secondary sources as much as possible in our research.

Why is this? The answer is that when we start with primary sources unaided by secondary interpretations, we will be at our freest in forming our own understanding of the text. For example, if you read a secondary source's analysis of the Student Forgiveness Act before reading the act itself, when you do start to read the primary source you will already have formed a preconceived understanding of the act based on the secondary source which may or may not be entirely accurate. Philosophy instructors will be quite familiar with frequent misunderstandings of major philosophical texts occasioned by students reading secondary sources, such as a scholarly work on Plato, or worse tertiary sources, such as *Wikipedia*, and basing an understanding of the philosopher's views on these texts, rather than the primary text itself. For example, if you truly want to know what Plato says about justice you should first read his *Republic* for yourself before turning to secondary sources for commentary that will be based on someone else's own particular background and ideas. The point is not to disparage secondary literature, but rather to emphasize that it is best read after having struggled with the primary text first. Of course, we cannot be experts in all fields and cannot read all primary sources, so we often need to have ideas broken down in terms that a non-specialist can understand, which may help us to be better prepared to approach the primary sources (a purpose we hope this work will serve). But we must still acknowledge that nothing can serve as a substitute for reading the primary sources themselves, and from an ethical perspective, this allows students to take responsibility for their own learning and interpretations (thus we have provided primary sources in the reference lists).

We will all readily agree that nationally recognized news sources and a governmental website will provide credible information. But why is this? What makes these sites credible? The fact that they are nationally recognized sources reflects that the community trusts the information reported on these sites. Given that CNN provides television coverage to a large number of viewers worldwide and that *The New York Times* provides a printed daily publication with a large number of subscribers, this demonstrates further the level of trust that the public grants to these sources. Further, that fact that they provide printed and broadcasted information for millions of people suggests that there must be a large organization of people involved who can verify the information reported, even if we do not know anything about their organizations. Further, we count those sources as credible that demonstrate expertise in a specific area based on their education or employment, and even a cursory look at either source will show that this is evident. In contrast, perhaps we come across an electronic source that seems relevant to the case from a blog entitled "Student Loans Suck," and we can find no information on the blogger's education or occupation, other than the mention that he is the parent of a college student. This would give us good reason to question the authoritativeness of such a site, and it is for precisely this reason that information found on blogs and social media such as Facebook and Twitter would not usually be considered reliable evidence for an ethical argument. In other words, when we evaluate sources we look for an author's reputation as an authoritative expert on the issue, and when we cannot find such information we must deem the author as unreliable. If, however, a blogger's credentials are given and the blogger is a reputable scholar who has published work in the field, then we are justified in considering the information on the blog more reliable, although it would still not have the same status as a published academic article that has undergone a rigorous peer-review process. Nevertheless, when we consider our case analyses from the point of view of applying creativity (see Chapter 5 below), we will want to maximize the number of perspectives on an issue, so in this regard it will be valuable to read opinions and arguments expressed in discussions in blogs, as well as the "Letters to the Editor" sections of newspapers.

When writing an argumentative essay in which you provide an ethical analysis of a case study you will want to base your argument as much as possible on primary sources and peer-reviewed secondary sources. A peer-reviewed source is one that has been read and approved by experts in the field, making it an authoritative resource. While Google searches can be useful for turning up factual information quickly, they do not sort out the peer-reviewed from the non-peer reviewed sources, and thus students will find more valuable resources by turning to specific databases provided via college and university library websites. In philosophy the main database is *The Philosopher's Index*, and here you will find an abundance of articles on ethical theories and moral issues, so this is always a good place to start. Still, you may not find resources here for all contemporary issues, in which case a more general search may be necessary. This is the case for "student loan forgiveness," although if you search "debt" and "forgiveness" you will find numerous sources. A more general search at a major university library website for "student loan forgiveness" turns up hundreds of articles, with the majority of them focused on legal issues involved in the legislation as it relates to business, taxes, and bankruptcy. When faced with this kind of result students will need to understand the difference between ethical and legal issues, as well as how far to consider the legal issues involved.

Although ethics and the law may both be viewed as providing rules for human behavior, they do not express identical concerns or perspectives. Consider, for example, lying, an action that is considered unethical on almost all accounts since it undermines trust and, as Kant suggests, the possibility of successful communication. Still, if you lie to your best friend about your whereabouts last Saturday night you will not have committed any crime. Legal matters pertain to the actual laws that are in place within a certain community, and many of these arise from social traditions and taboos that are not necessarily ethical, whereas ethical ones go beyond questions of legality to questions of the good, and right and wrong. Of course, we all hope that our legal institutions are created from a concern for the good of society and its citizens, but we know from past history that it is always possible to consider whether a particular legal statute is ethical—and that it is thus precisely ethical concerns that motivate changes in our legal system. Just consider the abolition of slavery, desegregation, and women's suffrage, all of which involved changes to our legal system based on a deeper consideration of the moral rights of individuals. Today we question new legal issues from a moral perspective, such as abortion, physician-assisted euthanasia, and the "stand your ground law," knowing fully well that what may be legal or defensible in court is not always what is good and right. For these reasons, it is important when analyzing ethical case studies that one separates the legal issues from the moral ones and focuses on the latter. Thus, knowing the legal status of student loan forgiveness programs and when it is permissible for banks to "forgive" or discharge student loan debt does not help us get very far in determining the moral value of forgiveness.

Consequently, a deeper analysis of the Student Loan Forgiveness Case will involve questioning the nature of forgiveness in order to determine, first, whether discharging student debt may seriously be held to be an act of forgiveness. Second, as just mentioned, we will need to determine the moral value of forgiveness, which is to say whether it is right and just to forgive others' debts and who determines whether forgiveness be granted. Research into the notion of forgiveness will reveal a wealth of religious sources, which may not always be relevant in so far as they may be based on religious doctrines rather than argumentation and evidence, but it will also reveal philosophical discussions that provide arguments from multiple perspectives on whether forgiveness can be rationally justified. As suggested in the case, students who work hard to pay for their educations and pay off their student loan debt seem to be punished by forgiving those who are less diligent, which surely seems less than fair.

Our discussion of conceptualizing cases has already led us to start wondering about asking good questions, which is the central focus of the next chapter.

Questions for Further Thinking and Discussion

1. List as many ethical issues as you can identify in the "Day in the Life of a College Student" narrative. Compare your list with another person. What ethical issue do you find most important and why?

2. Think about your own day today. What situations did you encounter that involved ethical issues? List them and compare your list with another person. Did you confront any of the ethical issues in a deliberative way? Why or why not?

3. What do you understand about the "end of ethics"? How is this significant for a case-studies approach to ethical thinking?

4. Think about your reading habits. How do you get the most out of your reading? What changes could you make to improve these habits?

5. What do you think: Is student loan forgiveness morally justified? If so, why, and under what conditions? If not, why not?

6. Adding a twist to a "Day in the Life of a College Student," suppose that your friend, Cynthia, a 17-year-old freshman, has just told you that she was raped at a party three months ago on campus and that she has just been to the student health center. She is pregnant. Cynthia tells you that she doesn't want to press charges, and in fact was drunk at the party and doesn't remember who attacked her. Because she is embarrassed and ashamed, she doesn't want to tell her parents and instead asks you to lend her half the money she will need for an abortion. What are the moral issues involved in the case of your friend Cynthia? What are your moral responsibilities in this case? How do you know? What should you do?

References and Suggestions for Further Reading

Adler, Mortimer J. and Charles Van Doren. *How to Read a Book: The Classic Guide to Intelligent Reading.* Simon & Schuster, Inc., 1972. This is a helpful source for thinking about what it means to be an active reader. It includes detailed strategies for the major levels of readings that will benefit all students. The information on "Inspectional Reading" in Chapter 4 has informed our discussion of the "quick reading" strategy above, and the section "How to Make a Book Your Own" (pp. 48–51) has informed our discussion of marking up a text.

American Physics Society. The ethics case study topics available at http://www.aps.org/programs/education/ethics/ are conflicts of interest, data acquisition, educational concerns, health and safety, human subjects research, issues of bias, mentoring, publication practices, and responsible conduct of research.

Booth, Wayne C., Gregory G. Colomb, and Joseph M. Williams. *The Craft of Research.* 3rd edition. University of Chicago Press, 2008. This text provides an excellent overview of the research process in general. Although the authors do not discuss researching ethical cases specifically, they do offer an insightful section on "The Ethics of Research" (pp. 273–276), which explains that research is "a profoundly *social* activity" that connects you with "a community in a search for some common good."

Caputo, John D. "The End of Ethics." In *The Blackwell Guide to Ethical Theory.* Ed. Hugh LaFollette. Blackwell, 2000. The quotation above is from page 111.

Ethics Bowl. Association for Practical and Professional Ethics. Cases from 2001 to present are available at: http://appe.indiana.edu/ethics-bowl/previous-cases/. This site also includes detailed information about the Intercollegiate Ethics Bowl (IEB) competitions, including rules, guidelines and past winners. The Center for the Study of Ethics in the Professions at Illinois Institute of Technology also has detailed information at their website, including a case archive with some additional cases, and a link to ethics bowl resources. See http://ethics.iit.edu/teaching/ethics-bowl.

Institute for Global Ethics. This site includes links to many cases, called "dilemmas," available at: http://www.globalethics.org/dilemmas.php. The cases cover business, education, family, medical, philanthropy, personal, and military dilemmas. The institute also offers a free *Ethics*

Newsline: A Weekly Digest of Worldwide Ethics News, which can be signed up for at the site.

Online Ethics Center. This site includes a large number of cases for engineering and research available at: http://www.onlineethics.org/Resources/Cases.aspx. The site is managed by The Center for Engineering, Ethics and Society (CEES) at the National Academy of Engineering (NAE).

Pierce, Jessica. *Morality Play: Case Studies in Ethics*. McGraw Hill, 2005. The quotations above are from page 3. This text provides many recent case studies on a large variety of topics.

Society of Professional Journalists. This site includes a list of short case studies related to journalism: http://www.spj.org/ethicscasestudies.asp.

"Student Loan Forgiveness Case." The Intercollegiate Ethics Bowl℠ cases are published by and may be used only with permission of The Association for Practical and Professional Ethics. (APPE, 618 East Third Street, Bloomington, Indiana 47405; Tel: (812) 855-6450; E-mail: appe@indiana.edu.)

4 Questioning Cases and Mapping Concepts

The student loan forgiveness case seems to lend itself immediately to the general question of whether student loan forgiveness is morally justifiable. That may be a primary question or even *the* primary question, but it is not all that could be asked, or that might be asked by yourself or others, about the case. In this chapter, the focus is on asking good questions about conditions presented and information embedded in cases illustrating or containing moral problems or dilemmas.

Rather than continue with the student loan forgiveness case, we will consider a different one. Doing so will give you the opportunity to engage independently in questioning, investigation, and research regarding the student loan case. With this new case study, on the ubiquitous use of cameras in public and private spaces, we shall continue to develop techniques and processes involved in thorough analysis of issues in ethical cases.

Case: Granny Cams

Traffic light cameras, security cameras in department stores, surveillance in airports, security system cameras in doctors' and veterinarians' offices, and even cameras in private homes are commonplace in many countries in the 21st century. Recently, the use of "spy cams" in nursing homes has revealed instances of abuse of the elderly. Relatives of elderly residents of nursing homes and rehabilitation facilities sometimes place hidden cameras in their loved one's rooms without the knowledge or consent of the owners or management of such facilities, and often without the knowledge or consent of residents. Suspected cases of neglect or abuse are exposed with the use of hidden cameras, but so also are private moments of residents, visitors, and employees of nursing home and rehabilitation facilities.

Proponents of the use of cameras may claim that the benefit of having hidden cameras in residents' rooms far outweighs privacy issues since it is often the case that elderly and disabled residents are not able to communicate to others information about substandard or inappropriate care or ill-treatment they receive in care facilities. Many such nursing homes and rehabilitation facilities have semi-private rooms, which means that cameras meant to record activities and events pertaining to one resident may inadvertently capture private information about a roommate or the roommate's visitors. Employees of the facilities may claim that their privacy is being breached, and that the use of cameras creates an atmosphere of distrust and interferes with proper care of residents.

As we have seen in Chapter 3, it is important to consider issues arising in a case study, and in the process of doing so, your research will often reveal information that you did not anticipate. Your research, however, is not to be limited to the "facts" about the use of security cameras, conditions in nursing homes, and the care of residents of nursing and rehabilitation facilities. Your research also includes consideration of ethical theories and principles to be applied in formulating questions about the case and in creating and justifying your own position.

Generally speaking, all cases fit this question format: "Is it morally justifiable. . . ?" In the student loan forgiveness case, the question "Is student loan forgiveness morally justifiable?" covers a wide variety of potential subsidiary questions. Similarly, the "granny cam" case lends itself nicely to the question of whether it is morally justifiable for family members to put hidden cameras in the rooms of residents of nursing and rehabilitation center facilities, and this in turn might lead you to wonder whether it is morally justifiable for the owners of such facilities to install cameras if it is (or is not) justifiable for family members to do so. The generic nature of these questions is both a benefit and a liability. The benefit is that the questions are general, leading to a wide variety of avenues for research. The liability is that questions with such general applicability may not lend themselves to careful analysis of specific issues that the general question might include or imply.

It is therefore important to consider analogous cases, extensions of the case in question, and issues that arise from considering the primary moral issue and question that you formulate. More specifically, when considering whether it is morally justifiable for there to be hidden cameras in the rooms of residents of nursing and rehabilitation center facilities, it may be beneficial to your argument to attend to related issues such as whether it is justifiable for department stores to hide cameras to catch shoplifters and employees in the act of stealing, whether traffic cameras are morally or legally justified since they can at least sometimes inaccurately represent actual events that occurred, and other such instances of the use of hidden or even visible security-related cameras in a wide variety of conditions and places. Thinking of these analogous and related instances, in turn, should direct your reasoning toward ethical and social issues such as invasions of privacy, misuse of information, curtailing freedom, and so on.

The process of asking good questions, then, is more than simply finding the question that you think is the overriding one for any given case. There are other questions to take into account, and those questions, in turn, can and usually do provide richer and more expansive sets of related cases, theories, and principles to use in the process of reasoning about the case study in question.

On the other hand, one of the most important points to recognize regarding research and reasoning about ethical issues is that ethical issues are complex and dynamic, and it is possible that an individual thinker may not, for whatever reasons—whether they are personal bias, lack of information, or lack of complete understanding of problems and facts—take into account as many or as wide a variety of potential issues that might be considered in conversation with others. The collaborative and communal nature of moral (and many other types of) reasoning is highlighted when, for example, we find that another person engaged in discussion with us notes that a related but very different example of the use of hidden security cameras to observe the care and treatment of infants and children in day care and babysitting contexts does not have the same implications for privacy of the person purportedly being protected by the use of cameras that we see in the case of the elderly. More specifically, infants and small children, while possessors of rights, are incapable of speaking for and taking care of themselves, and paternalism, while justifiable for their benefit, is not always justifiable for the supposed benefit to be gained from the surveillance of elderly adults. Another person—or you—may then note that there are cases in which the elderly are sometimes much like children (for example, in cases of dementia or other cognitive impairments) and that paternalism toward them is justified when they are little or no more able to take care of or to speak for themselves than a small child would be.

Critical reading and listening to the ideas and concerns of others is, in short, valuable for sharpening one's own understanding of a case, for identifying issues that may be unidentified on a first reading, and for compiling information that will be useful in the creation or analysis of an argument about a case.

In the absence of opportunity to speak to others about the facts and issues in an ethics case, critical reading and writing on one's own are valuable and essential as well. While we present in this book the position that understanding ethical issues, identifying them, and arguing about them is most efficacious in a community setting, it is no less important for each person involved in discussing and deciding actions arising from an ethics case study to engage in independent research and to formulate a position of her or his own.

Critical reading and listening to the ideas of others is, in short, valuable for sharpening one's own position, for considering alternatives to one's own argument and position, for expanding the scope of argumentation, and for dealing with weaknesses in and being able to correct errors in reasoning. We see that the communal nature of reasoning may take place in public spaces, such as newspaper and online media websites, where the general public may comment on an article and engage in discussion with others about issues in an editorial or an article. While some of the comments may be irrelevant, mean-spirited, or otherwise unrelated to or related improperly to the issue at hand, there are ideas presented in comments on television and video media, radio, newspapers, magazines, and blogs and blog posts that may be of some value in sharpening one's own position.

Care must be taken, however, when using a source from the media, online or using a traditional print version of information. Recently (2013), for example, a FaceBook post circulated about the purported use of RFID chips in the city of Hanna, Wyoming, as part of "ObamaCare" (i.e., Afford-able Care Act) requirements. The Casper, Wyoming, *Star Tribune* newspa-per reported on the spoof on July 29, 2013, at billingsgazette.com. An article in a website called "National Report" indicated that the mayor of the city, Ted Howell, was fully in favor of the use of the RFID chips because they can be used to deter terrorism. Some people who commented on the article in FaceBook noted, too, that the use of the chips might deter or diminish welfare fraud. Others claimed that the use of the RFID chips is yet another indication of "end-times" and quoted biblical sources to make their points.

While interesting, the source from which the article came is a quasi-journalistic site meant as satire and it is not actually a news source. Unfor-tunately, there are many people who, for reasons of their own or out of sheer ignorance, do not bother to do any background research on an article to determine the veracity of the claims in it and swallow whole, so to speak, the (mis)information that is fed to them. An example like this is a warning to anyone who wishes to take the proffered positions seriously not to be swayed by something you wish to believe is true (for example, if you wish to believe that ObamaCare is unjustified and you think that this is one more instance proving that this is the case) and not realizing that wishing certainly does not make it so. If you seriously and sincerely believe that ObamaCare is unjustified, the way to support your position is not to do so with false, misleading, or otherwise tainted information, but instead to get the best information it is possible to obtain and argue for your position using that. Not necessarily only for this case, but also for others, you may be surprised to find that the information you have gathered leads you to change your position or your attitude when you realize, for example, that while you still are not in favor of the Affordable Care Act, you are not in favor of it for justifiable reasons rather than due to fictions that are very easily refuted and discounted. For example, "Ted Howell" referenced above is not the name of the mayor of Hanna, Wyoming!

Another way to put the case is that just as the principle of charity (discussed in Chapter 2) is used in responding to and critically evaluating the claims and arguments of others, your own reasoning should be subjected to a more conservative principle by which you require of yourself that the arguments you put forth are as strong as they can be. Applying the principle of charity to one's own arguments is dangerous, since you are already in favor of your own case. On the other hand, applying it to the reasoning of others is justified, because even if their argument is weak, there may very well be claims that could have been used to justify the position that were stronger than those actually presented.

A fallacy in ordinary reasoning violating the relevance requirement and often the strength requirement of arguments, **straw man**, is closely related to misuse or lack of use of the principle of charity. To represent falsely or misleadingly, in a weak or weakened form, the ideas or arguments of another person with the express purpose of discrediting the argument does nothing to strengthen one's own position. Just as it is easy even for the weakest human being to knock down a straw man, so it is easy even for those whose intellectual capacities are limited or not adequately sharpened to "knock down" an argument that is intentionally presented in a weak and unjustifiable form. This does not mean that you ought to try to argue for another person's position or to attribute to that person something that she or he did not actually say or write or intend to say or write, but it does mean that you have an obligation, and perhaps even more strongly an epistemic responsibility, to present the case in the best way possible. This, whether to represent the arguments of others or to create arguments for positions of your own, can be done using concept mapping.

Concept Mapping

Concept maps are visual, conceptual representations of reasoning and information that are organized in ways suiting the preferences and chains of thought of the person creating them. While there are some specific formats that may be used for different types of concept maps, there is no compelling reason to insist that any particular type be used for any particular purpose. Maps are creative representations of facts and reasoning used to enhance and check arguments, to identify needed research, and to create arguments. Some of the purposes for which concept maps are useful are identifying central and other elements of a case study, determining the points in the presentation of a case or of an argument that require more information and research, understanding the applicability of ethical theories or principles to aspects of a case, creating an argument, and laying out the parts of an argument for analysis of inferences.

Think of concept mapping for case analysis and argument on the basis of the mapping process shown below, in Figure 4.1.

The left side of the map is the first level containing the preliminary central issue, problem, or main question for the case study. The second level is to identify the main or major facts or ideas presented in the case. While the generic concept map shown here contains only five such fact or idea nodes, there could be any number of these depending on the facts of the case study.

The third level is the process of identifying additional information needed that will be provided by your background research. Associated with this process may be a sub-level of fact-finding that may include the derivation of additional questions, whether for simple fact-finding or for identifying moral issues. The fourth level is preliminary application of ethical theories or principles to help to determine whether they apply to attempt to solve the problem or problems identified. Finally, the fifth level of concept mapping for case organization and presentation is the creation or analysis of arguments presented.

It is important to note that you may approach research on a case study either before or after formulating a preliminary central issue or problem question that applies to it. It is also possible that you will formulate a general question which may, in turn, help to sharpen and focus your research. Much of this depends on the nature of the case, your preference, the clarity of the presentation of the case, and many other issues. Part of the creative element of case analysis is determining for yourself the way in which you will proceed with your research and the development of your position.

The concept map above is only one among many potential abstract representations applying to any ethics case or problem you may encounter. Some people prefer to put the main idea in the center of the map, and then create nodes out from the central or main idea. Others prefer maps that look much like flowcharts, while others prefer maps that look like trees. Whatever your preference for the construction of a concept map, the point

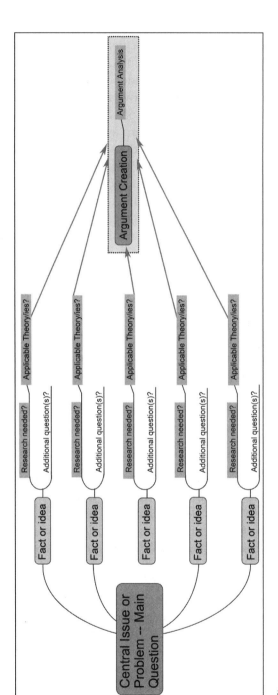

Figure 4.1

is to help to guide your investigations and research into the case study on which you are working, and in ideal cases to reveal ideas and possibilities that may go unrecognized otherwise. Below (Figure 4.2) is a differently configured general concept map with the main problem or idea in the center, with other levels in nodes moving outward from the center, and in which all lead to argument creation.

Because the creation and analysis of arguments is likely to contain just as much, or even more, information than identification of case facts, background research, and preliminary application of theories, it is most likely helpful to construct a separate map for argument creation and analysis. Whether you are creating your own argument or evaluating an argument presented to you, using a concept map to represent the essential features of the argument (premises, inferences, conclusion(s)) is essentially the same. Basic concept mapping for arguments is presented later in this chapter, but because in this chapter we are at the stage of "asking good questions" in case study analysis, we will leave concept mapping for argument creation and analysis for specific ethical case studies in Chapters 5 and 6.

For now, let's take the case of "granny cams" and map out the information presented in it (Figure 4.3). Doing so will lead to some interesting possibilities for research on the case. It will also help to identify relevant moral, factual, and perhaps legal questions to ask, and it will be a starting point for development of your own position regarding all these factors so that you can construct your own argument.

In concept map 4.3, we have set out what may be the primary general ethical question of the case in the center, and from there we have identified in expanded map nodes several facts presented in the case. Associated with those facts are additional nodes in the map indicating what other areas of potential research should be explored (these are moral issues), along with the potential for additional questions that may arise in the case. A listing of some concepts or theories that we think might be associated with the facts and research needs we have identified are also shown.

Because it is important for you to construct your own concept map, or if you wish you could expand on or change in various ways the map of the "granny cam" case above, we have not provided sources of information to answer the questions, nor have we indicated the way or ways in which we think the "granny cam" case might be conceptualized from the point of view of theories of ethics. Further, you may conceive of the case differently, or find that we have not asked enough questions about the case. For example, you may believe that it is important to know what the rates of abuse for children in day care facilities are, because you intend to use day care

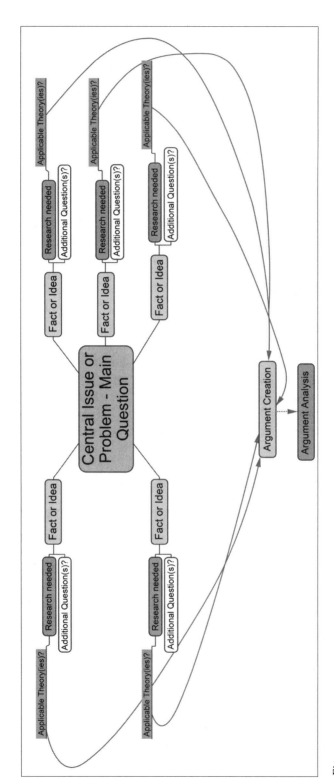

Figure 4.2

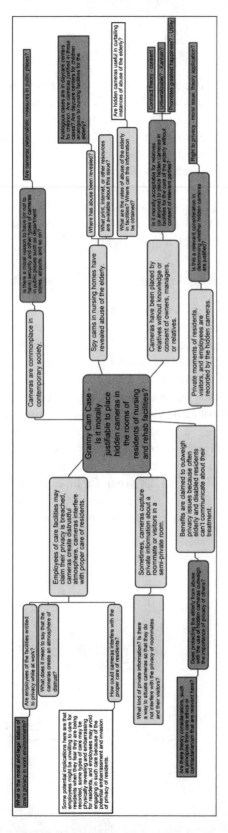

Figure 4.3

facility information with information you find about nursing facilities for the elderly to make a more complete analogy between the two.

Again, it is up to you how you wish to construct a concept map. The fact that we have used a central-idea map for the "granny cam" case does not mean that you must do so. You might, instead, prefer a flow-chart style map or some other. The important point is to be sure that you find a way with which you are comfortable to conceive of the case study and its elements that will lead you to ask the right questions—and the *good* questions—necessary to gain the information you need and to begin the process of developing your position on the moral issue or issues from the case study.

Constructing and Evaluating Arguments Using Concept Maps

As we have seen in Chapter 2, arguments are sometimes simple and straightforward. Other times, arguments are complicated because they contain multiple inferences, numerous premises that may need further justification or clarification, and any of a plethora of elements and problems that may arise as part of creating your own argument and in evaluating the arguments of others. No matter the complexity of an argument, it is necessary to concentrate attention on the veracity of claims made (the "truth" requirement) and the quality of inferences (the relevance and strength requirements) to determine whether an argument's conclusion is adequately established.

Concept mapping is useful in creating and evaluating arguments. One effective method of constructing a concept map for an argument is to put the main conclusion of an argument in the middle of the map with supporting information (premises) leading to the conclusion, as illustrated below (Figure 4.4):

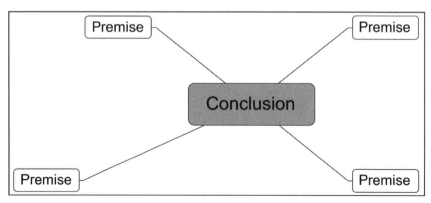

Figure 4.4

Here, unlike concept mapping for organizing and gathering information on a case study, the nodes of the map lead to the center rather than from it. It is also sometimes useful, especially for very complicated arguments, to organize the concepts in the map with the conclusion at the bottom of the map such that the premises lead to the conclusion in a more linear fashion, as shown below (Figure 4.5):

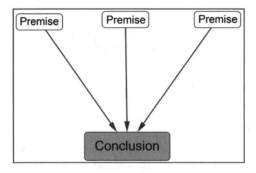

Figure 4.5

Arguments are usually not so simply formulated as the generic mapping formats shown above. There are, however, some ways in which you might find an argument to be organized that are helpful in constructing and evaluating inferences.

SERIAL INFERENCE

The simplest type of inferential structure is illustrated in both of the argument maps above. In these, all the inferences are called "serial" inferences because they are simple, serially arranged pieces of information that each independently lead to the conclusion. In Figure 4.4, there are four serial inferences; in Figure 4.5, there are three serial inferences. A serial inference is formed simply by any premise leading directly to a conclusion, like this (Figure 4.6):

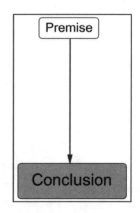

Figure 4.6

CONVERGENT INFERENCE

A convergent inference is formed when two or more premises lead to the same conclusion, as shown below (Figure 4.7):

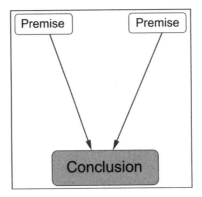

Figure 4.7

DIVERGENT INFERENCE

A divergent inference is formed when one premise leads to two or more independent conclusions (see Figure 4.8). It is often the case that one premise is used to support completely different conclusions. Think, for example, of a statement like this as a premise: "Mary left work early." It is possible to make numerous inferences from it, such as "Mary is not feeling well," in which case you would have the statement "Mary left work early" provided as support for the conclusion that "Mary is not feeling well." Further, however, there may be information you have at your disposal regarding Mary that would lead you also to conclude that because she left work early, someone else will have to attend the meeting that is scheduled at 4:00 P.M.

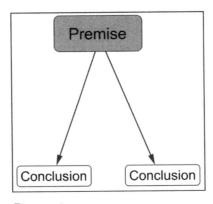

Figure 4.8

DEPENDENT PREMISE INFERENCE

An additive—or dependent—premise inference is one in which premises depend upon each other to reach a conclusion. Or, alternately put, there are instances in which premises must be combined with each other to lead to a conclusion. For example, suppose that you are trying to justify the claim that (1) "The board member has a conflict of interest concerning the matter." Let's say that the reasons offered in support of the claim are that (2) the board member is a voting member and (3) the company proposing to do business with the board is owned by the board member's brother.

If you put these statements together in concept mapped argument structure, the conflict of interest is illustrated in the following dependent premise inference where statement (1) is the conclusion and (2) and (3) are the premises (Figure 4.9):

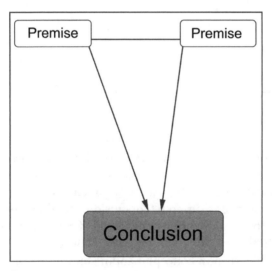

Figure 4.9

COMPLEX INFERENCE

Because complex issues are rarely attended with simplistic arguments, it is likely that argument structure maps or diagrams on ethical case studies will be composed of some combination of the inference types noted above, resulting in a complex inference map, illustrated below (Figure 4.10) in a generic format.

There is an important factor of multifaceted argumentation that appears in the complex inference map above. It is that there are some state-

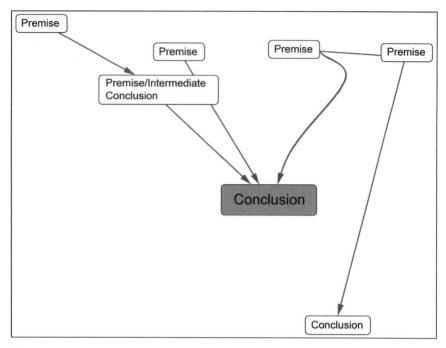

Figure 4.10

ments in an argument that may serve a dual purpose such that they are both premises and conclusions at the same time. Such statements are "intermediate conclusions" that serve as conclusions of another premise but also as premises of a different conclusion. In other words, it is sometimes the case that arguments are composed of combined serial inferences as illustrated in the left side of the argument concept map, above.

To see more clearly how concept mapping for arguments works, we will consider two ways in which they can be used. The first is for analyzing and evaluating an argument; the second is for creating an argument.

Analyzing Arguments with Concept Maps

In the following excerpt from *On Liberty*, John Stuart Mill argues against censorship:

> The peculiar evil of silencing the expression of an opinion is that it is robbing the human race, posterity as well as the existing generation—those who dissent from the opinion, still more than those who hold it. If the opinion is

right, they are deprived of the opportunity of exchanging error for truth; if wrong, they lose, what is almost as great a benefit, the clearer perception and livelier impression of truth produced by its collision with error.

This argument illustrates another important element of the analysis of arguments: sometimes, conclusions are not explicitly stated. Suppressed or implied conclusions should be supplied in the analysis of arguments, and then with care to apply the principle of charity in the statement of the conclusion. In this argument, it is reasonable to think that the suppressed conclusion is this: "Censorship is unjustified." The statements made in the quotation from *On Liberty* are intended to support this conclusion. Let's see how well the premises offered support the conclusion using a concept map illustrating the structure of the argument (Figure 4.11).

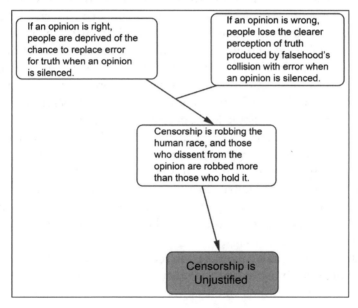

Figure 4.11

Has John Stuart Mill adequately supported his claim that censorship is unjustified? Remember that the three criteria of cogent reasoning are employed in the analysis of arguments. So ask yourself whether the information offered in support of the conclusion is true, whether it is relevant to the conclusion, and whether there is enough information provided to give you adequate reason to believe that the conclusion is true.

The first inference begins with two statements that are dependent upon each other to reach the conclusion. Note that the intermediate conclusion indicates that censorship robs the human race in general, and it robs dissenters more than those who agree with a position. To make this claim, the two separate premises regarding how those who disagree with the position are "robbed" and how those who agree with it are "robbed" are taken together. Are the premises true? Do they lead to the conclusion?

There is a sense in which the premises are true (in that, for example, people who are deprived of what they have a right or expectation to receive or to hold are "robbed" when the right is taken away or the expectation is not satisfied) and they appear to be relevant to the conclusion in that Mill has asserted that both sides (dissenters and those in agreement) are prevented from getting that to which they are entitled. On the other hand, is it true that truth is made clearer when it is compared with error? Is this a fact, or an assumption that Mill has made for which there is no evidence provided? If it is doubtful that truth is made clearer when it is compared with error, there is a weakness in the argument that may render this inference equally weak.

But what of the second inference? In this, from the intermediate conclusion to the main conclusion, Mill states that censorship robs the human race (and robs those who dissent from the opinion more than those who agree with it), and this information is provided to establish the conclusion that censorship is unjustified. Assuming that it is true that preventing people from having access to something to which they have a right (if there is indeed a right to information) is morally wrong, then censorship (at least in some instances) is unjustified. However, does the conclusion that censorship is unjustified hold true in all instances? If you can think of a case in which censorship might be justified, then the general statement made in the conclusion is rendered less likely to be true than what might initially appear to be the case.

In short, when you analyze the inferences in an argument by carefully setting them out in a concept map, you have provided a convenient and effective means by which to check the inferences to determine whether they satisfy the relevance and strength requirements. Further, you may identify aspects of the claims made in the argument that might need further justification or that indicate the need for additional research. For example, you may wonder whether there have been psychological studies done showing whether false information juxtaposed against true information makes truth more clear, and you may wonder whether there are conditions in which some information, whether false or true, might be justifiably censored. There could be such instances, say, in cases in which there are instructions on the Internet explaining how to create poisons or incendiary devices, or in cases of child pornography. It may, in other words, be that

Mill's conclusion regarding a prohibition against censorship is too strong (i.e., it is not warranted by the premises).

Now, it is clearly the case that the method of analyzing an argument presented in the past few paragraphs lends itself handily to written arguments, but what of those that are spoken and heard? Even here, concept mapping is useful as a note-taking device where you have the opportunity to arrange information presented verbally in notes arranged around the conclusion of the speaker's argument, and in which you then have a graphical representation of the claims and reasoning presented. It is no different from what you might do if you heard (rather than read) Mill's argument about censorship, and which could be represented alternately in the following way (Figure 4.12):

Notice again that it makes no difference whether you use a concept map with the conclusion at the bottom, in the center, or in any other position. What matters is that you arrange the information in the argument in a way that is convenient for you, that will help you to be able to see relationships between claims, and that may also give you room to add notes that will be helpful to you in using, analyzing, and replying to the argument. For example, you might add a note to the map above indicating where you think the argument has gone wrong. (see Figure 4.13)

So far, the application of principles and theories of ethics has not been a major element of the analysis of arguments. But in the next chapter on creative problem solving in ethics we expand the use of concept mapping and the creation of arguments about ethical case studies through the ap-

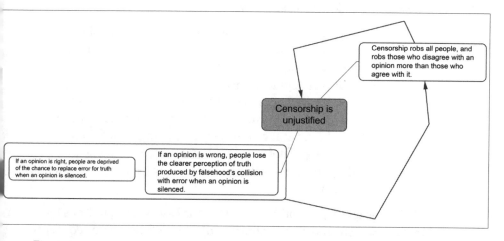

Figure 4.12

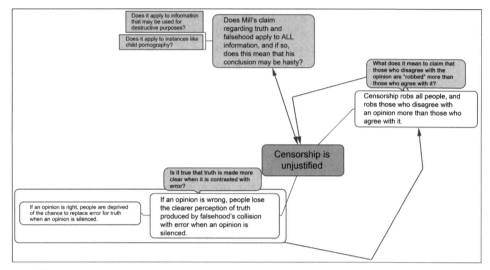

Figure 4.13

plication of creative thinking with ethical theories and principles. In chapter 6, we continue concept mapping for the creation of your own arguments on case studies.

Questions for Further Thinking and Discussion

1. Consider the following case study.

> Pete is a 13-year-old 8th-grader who spends a considerable amount of time playing first person shooter (FPS) video games. Since his mother bought one of the FPS games for him for his 12th birthday, Pete's grades have suffered, going from a solid B average overall to a C. Further, Pete rarely goes outside anymore after school, and instead turns on his computer and plays for five to six hours every evening before going to bed. Pete's mother has noticed lately that he is often sullen and angry as well as failing to be interested in activities with his friends and family members.

In a concept map, identify the facts of the case, some questions for further research, and a preliminary indication of theories or concepts in ethics you believe to be applicable to the case.

2. In a book, article, or editorial of your choice, choose an argument made by the author and, in a concept map, identify the facts of the case, some questions for further research, and a preliminary indication of theories or concepts in ethics you believe to be applicable to the case.

3. Using the concept map on the first person shooter video game case provided above, reorganize the map into a different format (e.g., main idea at the center with nodes moving out from the center, flow-chart format, or another of your choice). Which of these formats do you prefer, and why?

4. Mike claims that his performance on tests and examinations in school are enhanced by the fact that he takes medication for ADHD (Attention Deficit Hyperactivity Disorder) even though he does not have ADHD. He gets the medication from a friend who lives across the street and has been diagnosed with ADHD. Mike's roommate thinks that it is wrong for Mike to use the drugs for ADHD because it is cheating. Mike's girlfriend thinks that he should take the drugs because they give him a competitive edge that he needs to succeed.

   For this case, create a concept map identifying the main facts of the case and indicating what questions about the facts you need to ask and further research you need to do on the case.

5. Using the information from the ADHD medication case in #4 above, identify at least three ethical theory-based questions you believe are relevant and important for the case.

6. Return to the case of your friend, Cynthia, in the "Questions for Further Thinking and Discussion" at the end of Chapter 3. Create a concept map identifying the main facts of the case and the questions about the facts that you believe you need to answer to determine what your responsibilities are and what you should do.

References and Suggestions for Further Reading

Arthur, Ken. *Mind Maps: Improve Memory, Concentration, Communication, Organization, Creativity, and Time Management* (Kindle Edition). mindmap.us, 2012.

Buzan, Tony. *The Mind Map Book: How to Use Radiant Thinking to Maximize Your Brain's Untapped Potential*. Plume, 1996.

Buzan, Tony. *Mind Map Handbook: The Ultimate Thinking Tool*. Thorsons/HarperCollins, 2013.

There are numerous concept mapping software products available either free or at some cost. Ken Arthur's *Mind Maps* includes a list of various mindmapping tools.

MindMap is currently available free and has received a positive review (April 2013) from *PC World Magazine*. See http://www.pcworld.com/article/2032818/review-mindmup-is-a-free-effortless-way-to-create-mind-maps-in-moments.html. Retrieved 12/26/13.

MindJet has paid mind mapping software, MindManager, and downloads for purchasers to use mapping software on tablets. See http://www.mindjet.com.

Online app stores such as iTunes and Google Play have listings of mind mapping or concept mapping software also available, sometimes for a fee and sometimes at no charge.

5   Creative Case Analysis

Avoiding Moralism

Ethical cases abound for the person who has developed the practice of critical questioning presented in Chapters 1 and 3 above. There we explained the importance of John Dewey's work *How We Think* for the art of questioning and critical thinking, but we can find in Dewey's earlier work *Ethics* (written with James H. Tufts and originally published in 1908—the revised edition appeared in 1932) an expression of the importance of seeking out and confronting ethical issues in our lives. In other words, we find Dewey and Tufts suggesting that a case study approach to ethics cultivates critical questioning and blocks dogmatic moral theorizing or **moralism**. This is the first step in opening up the possibility of approaching ethical case studies creatively, which is the central focus of this chapter. In *Ethics* Dewey and Tufts write:

> Indeed, one of the chief values, from the standpoint of theory, of considering the moral bearing of social problems is that we are then confronted with live issues in which vital choices still have to be made, and with situations where principles are still in process of forming. We are thus saved from the "moralistic" narrowing down of morals to which reference has been made from time to time; we appreciate that morals are as wide as the area of everything which affects the values of human living. These values are involved on the widest scale in social issues. Hence critical questioning of existing institutions and critical discussion of changes, proposed on the theory that they will produce social betterment, are the best means of enforcing the fact that moral theory is more than a remote exercise in conceptual analysis or than a mere mode of preaching and exhortation. When we take the social point of view we are compelled to realize the extent to which our moral beliefs are a product of the social environment and also the extent to which *thinking*, new ideas, can change this environment.
>
> Study from this point of view forces, as nothing else can, a conclusion reached in our theoretical analysis. It discloses in a concrete fashion the limitation of moral theory and the positive office which it can perform. It shows that it is *not* the business of moral theory to provide a ready-made

solution to large moral perplexities. But it also makes it clear that while the solution has to be reached by *action* based on personal choice, theory can enlighten and guide choice and action by revealing alternatives, and by bringing to light what is entailed when we choose one alternative rather than another. It shows, in short, that the function of theory is not to furnish a substitute for personal reflective choice but to be an instrument for rendering deliberation more effective and hence choice more intelligent.

We have quoted this passage at length because there are several highly important points that can be drawn from it. First, the "social point of view" that Dewey and Tufts are developing here is basically an ethical point of view taken from a "case studies approach," rather than a "moral theory approach." In other words, it is the view that our critical questioning is initiated by a practical situation or "problem" that arises in our lives and leads us to wonder how we may live our lives better while facing this situation. Second, this first point does not imply a disparagement of moral theory, but rather a shifted understanding in which moral theory is not seen as the goal of ethical thinking, but rather as a means to the ultimate goal. The ultimate goal that Dewey and Tufts highlight is action, by which we understand enacting the results (although of course there is never a final result while we are living) of our critical questioning and ethical thinking through our engagement with the world (the environment) in which we find ourselves. Thus, moral theory is a stimulus to action and further thinking, and when viewed in this light it becomes a fundamental step in linking creativity and ethics. A third point that follows from the others is the need to avoid moralism, which we can understand as a narrowing of perspectives, such that one seeks a single correct moral theory as the final end of ethical thinking. Moralism hinders creativity, which in its most basic meaning involves increasing alternatives and possibilities, because it limits the alternatives that may be created and considered. Thus we find in Dewey and Tufts the rejection of a moralistic moral theory approach to ethics and instead the promotion of a case studies approach to ethics (i.e., the approach developed in this book).

Expanding Ethics

A related problematic approach to ethical thinking is the commonplace conception of "ethics" and "ethical decision-making" as the reflection on moral dilemmas and the attempt to distinguish two possible choices, namely the right one and the wrong one (and thus anyone who disagrees with one's evaluation is stuck on the wrong side of fence). But do all such sticky, striking ethical situations we find ourselves facing really lead to "di-lemmas" (i.e., "two assumptions or alternatives")? Should ethics be conceived primarily as the rational attempt to determine right from wrong, which would seemingly be the predominant view of philosophical ethicists, or should our conception of ethics be expanded to emphasize more practical concerns for the well-being of others and oneself and the creative attempt to further that well-being? Obviously, how we conceive ethics will be decisive for how we explore the subject, so let us consider this distinction more closely.

Consider the understanding of ethics found in the justifiably well-respected textbook *The Elements of Moral Philosophy* by James and Stuart Rachels. Here the authors explain that "the essence of morality" is to "let our feeling be guided as much as possible by reason," and morality is defined as "the effort to guide one's conduct by reason—that is, to do what there are the best reasons for doing while giving equal weight to the interests of each individual affected by one's decision." Easily a philosophical favorite, this view follows in the tradition of Socrates and Plato as commonly conceived, in which reason rules and emotion must be either subjugated or purged. Although rationality is certainly important for morality, it is interesting to note that quite a different emphasis can be found in the recent work of philosophy professor Anthony Weston, who has written on both rational argumentation and creative problem-solving. Perhaps surprisingly, Weston's definition of ethics in *Creative Problem-Solving in Ethics* makes no reference to reason; instead, he defines it as "a concern with the basic needs and legitimate expectations of others as well as our own." Although not necessarily opposed to the common view, it is clear that Weston's main emphases are different, for they fall on concern and creativity, while Rachels and Rachels focus on reason and judgment.

Are these different views of ethics compatible? And if so, is this always the case, or does a heightened sense of "rationality" sometimes obstruct the concern for the well-being of others? How, then, should we think about ethics, and how should we mediate between these different views to move beyond impasses in judgment and towards developing a consensus for action guided towards the furtherance of our well-being?

In order to begin to answer these questions we need to take "a more expansive view of ethics," one that according to Weston incorporates inventive ethical thinking and practical creativity. Weston provides us with a striking example that begins with this ethically charged situation:

A child in second grade underwent chemotherapy for leukemia. When she returned to school, she wore a scarf to hide the fact that she had lost all her hair. But some of the children pulled it off, and in their nervousness laughed and made fun of her. The child was mortified and that afternoon begged her parents not to make her go back to school. Her parents tried to encourage her, saying "The other children will get used to it, and anyway your hair will soon grow in again."

Now, what if you were the teacher of this class and had to determine how to handle the situation? Let's suppose that you are greatly bothered by it after school and throughout the evening. Maybe you toss and turn throughout the night. On the more common conception of ethics what to do the next day would be rather clear: sit the children down (perhaps in your anger or uneasiness with the situation you would raise your voice to get them in order) and lecture them about the wrongness of embarrassing and teasing others. You could provide thoughtful reasons and arguments about harm to others and appeal to the principle that one shouldn't treat others in a way that one would not want oneself to be treated. Perhaps you would want to make the lesson stick by punishing those responsible and of course you would also have provided the class with an account of responsible action in a way that a second grader can understand. Such an approach seems rather straightforward, but would it be the best way of increasing the well-being of the class? Can you think of other ways to deal with the situation? Here's what our teacher in the story did.

> The next morning, when their teacher walked into class, all the children were sitting in their seats, some still tittering about the girl who had no hair, while she shrank into her chair. "Good morning, children," the teacher said, smiling warmly in her familiar way of greeting them. She took off her coat and scarf. Her head was completely bald.
>
> After that, a rash of children begged their parents to let them cut their hair. And whenever a child came to class with short hair, newly bobbed, all the children laughed merrily, not out of fear but out of the joy of the game. And everybody's hair grew back at the same time.

As Weston explains this moving example of creative problem-solving in ethics, without lecturing or moralizing the teacher provided a key moral lesson in "ethical solidarity," the idea that "we are all in this together." As we reflect on this example, let us take Weston's point that "ethical problem-solving is not just a matter of finding a way out of a specific, practical fix. It is also an occasion to better live out our values and, indeed, to better the world itself. That is the very essence of ethics!"

A similar perspective is presented by David McNaughton in his recent paper, "Why Is So Much Philosophy So Tedious?" Here McNaughton explains how the conception of philosophy as a task "to find a cut-and-dried solution that will resolve as many as possible of the problems all at once" is not his own, because "especially in ethics it tended to feel like a game of skill rather than a real inquiry into the human condition."

What an interesting contrast this view provides to conceiving the application of reason as the essence of ethics, as cited in Rachels above. Of course, Weston's view does not reject reason, although it may be challenging to discover by which rational argument the teacher decided to shave her head, but reason is not the primary value to which everything else is subordinated. Instead, the primary focus is on living—on living well, of which reason most certainly is a part, but not the only, or necessarily most important, one. (Certainly the role of emotions in ethics is a significant one that should not be undervalued, although this topic is too broad to be pursued here.) We are not suggesting, however, that one must either adopt rationality in ethics or adopt creativity, for clearly that would create a false dilemma the likes of which we are trying to avoid. Instead, what we wish to suggest are possibilities for opening up ethical thinking to allow for the interplay of reason, emotion, and creativity.

More Mindsets to Avoid: Dogmatism, Relativism, and Subjectivism

If moralism is the narrowing of ethical perspectives, then applying creativity to ethical case studies involves the exact opposite. Creativity, then, can be understood as the broadening of perspectives, or a bringing forth of new possibilities. Before developing methods for stimulating creativity, let us briefly consider certain other mindsets that impede creative ethical thinking. In addition to moralism, these mindsets are **dogmatism, relativism,** and **subjectivism.** For each one of these broad "isms" there are subsets, but the point is that they all represent for the most part metaethical positions that serve as what Weston calls "ethics-avoidance disorders." For example, moralism is but an expression of dogmatism, and relativism and subjectivism can sometimes lead to "a kind of ethical laziness," which could be called "rationalizing" or "offhand self-justification" (e.g., one often hears excuses, such as "It's all relative" or "That's just what I think," which provide little opening for creative problem-solving methods). Let us comment briefly on these positions.

Although there are some important philosophers who may embrace a kind of qualified **relativism,** most have recognized the many significant problems involved in cultural relativism. First in significance, as Rachels and Rachels have shown in *The Elements of Moral Philosophy*, is that the conclusion that "there is no objective truth in morality" simply does not follow from the premise that "different cultures have different moral codes." Whether objective truth in ethics is achievable remains an open question in the face of cultural diversity, and one could think that it is towards this goal of objective truth that we practically strive through our fallible human efforts. Further, the cultural relativist seems to maintain that cultures are morally infallible, that they are all equally "right," and that we cannot blame other cultures for "wrong" or "evil" deeds. This position is hardly practicable and hinders the idea that we can make progress in ethics through creative thinking and dialogue with other cultures.

There are, however, points that we can learn from cultural relativism, for it teaches us to be cautious in our ethical thinking and to be open-minded, which is certainly a prerequisite for creativity. When one is not open to other possibilities of acting in certain situations one is likely to fall into dogmatism, the second major "ethics-avoidance disorder."

It is important to note that there are different kinds of dogmatism, one which can be called religious dogmatism and the other philosophical dogmatism. Religious dogmatism, as we see time and time again, can be very dangerous. Although we would not go as far as Christopher Hitchens (1949–2011) in *God Is Not Great* to claim that "religion poisons everything," to think that we can know with absolute certainty the will of God that only needs to be obeyed may very well lead us "to opt out of moral thinking altogether," as James Rachels (1941–2003) has argued in his article "God and Moral Autonomy." But ethics requires interpretation and thinking for oneself and it is clearly arguable, as Weston has shown in *A 21st Century Ethical Toolbox*, that these practices lie at the center of religious experience, thus making a more positive view of religion possible.

Although philosophers (such as Socrates) often oppose religious teachers (such as Euthyphro in Plato's classic dialogue), it would be a mistake to think that philosophers are exempt from slipping into dogmatism. After all, there is perhaps no small number of philosophers who take their theoretical stances as ethical verities, and this is why the expression of the "end of ethics" (see above) is instructive. All too often, especially in the college classroom, an ethical situation is said to be best understood as a dilemma between two specific ethical theories. For example, many students learn about the "Heinz dilemma" introduced by psychologist Lawrence Kohlberg. It goes like this:

A woman was near death from cancer. One drug might save her, a form of radium that a druggist in the same town had discovered. The druggist was charging $2000, ten times what the drug cost him to make. The sick woman's husband, Heinz, went to everyone he knew to borrow money, but he could only get together about half of what it cost. He told the druggist that his wife was dying and asked him to sell it cheaper or let him pay later. But the druggist said "no" . . .

What are Heinz's options here? For philosophers, this example serves nicely to illustrate two theories and two choices: either Heinz takes the utilitarian view and steals the drug to save his wife, or he takes the deontological view that one has a duty not to steal and watches his wife die. But are those really the only two options? Surely just a little imaginative thinking will lead to more than just these two possibilities.

Consider again the Student Loan Forgiveness case. This could also be presented as a straightforward dilemma between a deontological and utilitarian perspective, which are the easiest two ethical theories to contrast, since the latter is consequentialist (i.e., a consideration of the consequences matter), whereas the former is not. Thus, although neither Kant nor Mill had to deal with a mountain of student loan debt, one could reasonably argue from a Kantian, deontological point of view that student loan forgiveness is not morally justifiable, since it would involve breaking or rescinding a promise to repay a debt. For Kant promises must never be broken, just as lies must never be told. On the other hand, from a utilitarian point of view we could suggest that happiness would be increased by forgiving student loan debt for the many struggling graduates. Of course, how to work out the happiness calculation may be tricky, but one might plausibly suggest that considerable happiness will accrue to those students who are forgiven (e.g., they can move forward in their lives and perhaps much of their future happiness could be attributed to removing the burden of their student loans), while the unhappiness produced would be vague and seemingly negligible. After all, it is only persons, not institutions, that can experience happiness, and it is hard to see how loan forgiveness would lead to serious unhappiness—let alone pain—on the part of those who work for the institutions that grant the loans. Perhaps those students who did not need to take out a student loan to finance their education or those who repaid their student loans would be unhappy, but this unhappiness would hardly come close in comparison to the happiness of the others.

While these two perspectives represent plausible ways to consider the case, it seems disingenuous to think that they are the only ways it can be considered, and that the issue of student loan forgiveness is black and white. What other possibilities are there for reflecting on this case? We will return to this question below.

But please don't get us wrong. We are not suggesting that ethical cases should not be considered from contrasting theoretical perspectives. Some of our best friends are theoretical ethicists, and we both find theoretical speculation to be quite an enjoyable activity. The problem is rather a too limited consideration of moral theory, and the conception that a single moral theory can exhaust the framework for reflecting on a case. What we are arguing against is a dogmatic view of ethical theorizing that holds that a situation should only be thought of in terms of utility, or duty, or virtue, or care. We are certainly not arguing against doing or teaching ethical theory, as long as this approach to moral problems is rightly understood as one among others and doesn't entirely dominate the culture created in the classroom or in any other aspect of our lives. Instead, we are actually suggesting that students need to study more ethical theories, because they open up alternative ways of thinking about a situation, and as the experts in creativity suggest, opening up such possibilities is a first step towards applying creativity.

The third position that impedes creativity in ethics is **subjectivism**, and behind this position one finds the significant philosophical distinction between facts and values. As is well-known, this distinction originates in David Hume's *A Treatise of Human Nature*, which proposes that you cannot derive an "ought" from an "is." On the surface, the idea seems cogent. As many would suggest, the world consists of facts, not values, and there is a clear difference between saying "the book is heavy," which is quantifiable (e.g., it weighs five pounds) and the qualitative statement "the book is good." But is it really fallacious to presuppose that you can derive an "ought" from an "is?" Some prominent contemporary philosophers have rejected this view, including Hilary Putnam, who has argued against the fact/value dichotomy, and John Searle, who has demonstrated that one can derive an "ought" from an "is." In fact, the neuroscientist Sam Harris has defined values as "facts about the well-being of conscious creatures," and in his recent work titled *The Moral Landscape: How Science Can Determine Human Values*, he writes that "a clear boundary between facts and values simply does not exist." Even beyond considering the technical arguments, what is worrisome for practical ethical thinking is that if you seriously think that no "ought" can be derived from an "is," then it would not be a big step to suggest that research in ethics is impossible, because after all, what are you researching? This is certainly one practical reason to question Hume's view, and another is that, following Weston in his *Creative Problem-Solving in Ethics*, getting a fuller picture of a situation through collecting all the relevant facts is essential to the creative exploration of ethical possibilities, and it is where students need to start in their research on the case studies. Thus, this is the first step towards applying creativity to ethics.

Facts clearly do make a difference to a consideration of ethical possibilities. After all, the fact that anencephalic children (i.e., children born with only a brain stem and not the rest of the brain) die within two weeks (although often it is just a few days) after birth is highly significant when considering whether to transplant such a child's organs. It is especially important when researching to find "suggestive facts," which according to Weston are "those that open up new ways of approaching a problem." One example Weston discusses is this. "Did you know that of the 30,000 people killed by guns every year in the US nearly half of them are suicides?" This fact suggests that if we are only thinking about the pros and cons of gun control, we may miss the possibility of thinking about suicide-prevention and how by "giving people compelling reasons to live," we may actually improve the whole situation for us all.

Another example comes from a case used in the 2010 Intercollegiate Ethics Bowl called "Virgin Records," which involved the ethical issue of whether it would be morally justifiable for a young female college student, Natalie Dylan, to auction off her virginity in order to pay down her nearly $100,000 student loan debt. One student who researched this case highlighted key facts regarding prostitution. In his position paper he wrote:

> The fact of the matter is that most prostitution that occurs exhibits a great deal of risk. In the United States, 82% of prostitutes report having been raped at least once while 73% of prostitutes report having been raped more than five times. This alone is enough to conclude that prostitution, in the form it usually takes, entails a great deal of risk on the part of the prostitute. However, this may not even do justice to the plight of prostitutes, who are regularly controlled by means of drugs and violence by a pimp. Though there are exceptions, the vast majority of prostituted women are there by matter of circumstance, not choice, perhaps explaining a rate of 69% of prostitutes diagnosed with post-traumatic stress disorder at the same rate as combat war veterans.

The significance of these facts is that they served to broaden a discussion which had previously been focused on a consideration of an individual's right over her own body to include a look at the larger picture and the many risks involved in prostitution. Thus, research performed with careful attention to the facts of the situation and the goal of arriving at meaningful and useful interpretations already constitutes an expression of creativity, which should be understood as a practical activity available to all mindful individuals, rather than a mysterious process employed by only the very few.

The Concept of Creativity

Given that this chapter deals with a practical application of creativity in ethics, we must now consider the concept of creativity more specifically. We must first note, however, that a precise statement of what constitutes creativity is problematic—and may indeed be seen as a hindrance to creativity—and that a thorough discussion of creativity, which is currently the subject of much overdue research and debate, is beyond the scope of this work. Further, as the root word "create" originally meant to "make something out of nothing," this would seemingly make it impossible fully to understand the creative act, for how can one understand the paradoxical creation of something from nothing? Where do new ideas come from? It was the impossibility of answering this question that led Plato to deny that there are any new ideas, but few of us would find his view persuasive today. Instead, we now understand that all creation of new ideas is a product of prior processes—social, environmental, intellectual—and that the more dynamic the conditions underpinning these processes are, the more likely it is that new beneficial ideas will be generated. Thus, it is important that we pay attention to the processes and work to provide the interactive space for intersubjective creation.

When we look at the history of philosophy, we find that philosophers such as Aristotle and Kant related creativity to the concept of genius, but this does not capture the practical application that we believe all individuals can joyfully employ, not only those whom we might consider exceptionally gifted. Key notions that repeatedly occur in a discussion of creativity include freedom (i.e., possibility, and with it spontaneity), imagination, and originality, with the central idea of bringing into existence something new and unique. Thus, if you make a pencil that looks like any other pencil, we would hardly say that you have created a pencil. But if you make a pencil out of leaves or some new material, then we would appropriately say that you have created a "leaf-pencil." With regards to ethical case studies, our concern lies in coming up with new ideas and practices for dealing with ethically-charged situations. And if the situation in question is itself new and unique, then it may be a creative act to consider applying "old ideas" to new situations. So, reflecting on what Aristotle would say about the mountain of American Student Loan Debt would involve a new interpretation, and thus an expression of creativity; whereas reflecting on what Aristotle would say about slavery would not, since we can discover his view on slavery (it was favorable, unfortunately) without bringing any new application of his thought to bear. For this reason, an academic approach focused on combining contemporary case studies and theoretical ethics will naturally involve creativity and enhance the education process.

Play is also an important stimulant to creativity, and there has been research on the positive effects of play on the human brain and the significance of play for education. This is a good reason for students working with contemporary case studies to interact playfully by applying methods for enhancing the creative process or through engaging in ethics bowl activities which involve a playful competition. It is important to keep in mind, however, that taking play seriously involves a focus on the process, or what Gadamer calls the "to and fro movement" in his analysis of the concept of play, more than any final result, which puts an end to play as play.

In *Creativity: Ethics and Excellence in Science*, Mike Martin develops the conception of "moral creativity," which he defines as "the act or virtue of making new and morally valuable products," and such products are said to be morally valuable when they contribute "to human and environmental goods." As already suggested, the various ideas that help to define creativity are reflected in the "creative case analyses" that we develop here, but more importantly we are concerned with what could be called "collective moral creativity." In the context of ethical case studies our goal is not merely that an application of creativity leads to the production of something new and unique by one individual (e.g., we are not trying to stimulate the production of the most idiosyncratic or outrageous way of dealing with a case), and we find it difficult, if not impossible, to defend the view that a creative product is ever solely the work of one single, solitary individual without any regard to others. Rather, collective moral creativity involves the production of something new and unique by a consensus of individuals which contributes to the good life of all involved. This book is a product of collective moral creativity, as it could not have been brought into existence without the interplay with students, colleagues, editors, publishers, and family members, and we suggest that collective moral creativity should become not only the focus of one's academic study, but also of one's life. This is obviously a lofty goal, but it is reachable with serious play, sound research, right effort, thoughtful insight, and perhaps a little moral luck.

Now let us describe further some aspects of creativity and how they can best be achieved. First, consider freedom, which involves the ability to choose from a variety of possibilities. With this in mind we must work to generate possibilities, to multiply the perspectives and theoretical lenses from which a particular case may be viewed. This involves exploring more ethical theories, rather than fewer, and also not being constrained by one particular theory. For example, sometimes students, as well as instructors, develop a liking for one specific philosopher's views and wish to relate everything to that specific philosophy. For example, someone may be in deep agreement with Aristotle's virtue theory and thus already presuppose that Aristotle has the right answer to some particular case. Nevertheless, while it may be true that Aristotle was a brilliant mind who had insightful and far-reaching thoughts on many issues, already to begin with such a presupposition can be limiting in that it may shut off other possibilities. For however great a thinker Aristotle was, he did not, and does not, have the answer to every problem. No one does, which is why we must strive towards collective moral creativity and work to free ourselves from certain pre-judgments (another way of saying prejudices) that would limit our interpretations and creative imagination. This involves developing a heightened awareness of one's own patterns of thinking and the ability to control one's own thoughts, but it also involves relating to others in a way that optimizes the flow of new ideas. Thus, it is crucial that students (as well as instructors) listen well to others, respecting their independent abilities to contribute to the process. Nothing kills creativity more quickly than a refusal to listen to the ideas of others, and such an unwillingness to listen is also counterproductive to critical thinking, which calls for distancing oneself from one's own thoughts and careful reflection. Spinoza writes in his *Ethics* that "the world would be much happier, if men were as fully able to keep silence as they are able to speak," and the ever creative philosopher Friedrich Nietzsche (1844–1900) writes in his iconoclastic *Twilight of the Idols* the following words, which can be read as developing the conditions for becoming a creative spirit:

> Learning to see—accustoming the eye to calmness, to patience, to letting things come up to it; postponing judgment, learning to go around and grasp each individual case from all sides. That is the first preliminary schooling for spirituality: not to react at once to a stimulus, but to gain control of all the inhibiting, excluding instincts. Learning to see, as I understand it, is almost what, unphilosophically speaking, is called a strong will: the essential feature is precisely not to "will"—to be able to suspend decision.

Nietzsche's words point to the self-mastery necessary to fend off those forces that would inhibit creativity, and thus when we approach an ethical situation with the goal of creating an innovative and new solution, we must begin by recognizing that in our initial process no ideas should be censored. There are no bad ideas when embarking on a creative case analysis in search of good ideas.

Investigating the Facts

Knowing that the development of creativity involves a broadening of perspectives and an opening of possibilities, we can understand how the more research we conduct into a particular case the greater opportunity we will have for creativity to appear in our case analysis. Thus, we must begin by investigating the facts of each case and collecting the necessary background information, while also paying particular attention to those facts or aspects of the case that stand out as unusual or difficult to assimilate into a coherent statement. An interaction with one's peers is essential in stimulating creativity, and thus it is important initially for students to present the facts about their case either orally or in writing or both to their peers for feedback. Ideally, students will begin by presenting the details of their cases informally to other students in groups, and then later provide a formal presentation in writing. At the various stages when the case is presented to one's peers, the peers should ask themselves the following questions and respond appropriately to the presenter:

1. Have the most significant facts been identified?
2. Are all the facts presented relevant?
3. Is the factual information presented, including background information, complete, and if not, what facts do you need to get a fuller picture?
4. Are there any facts that stand out as particularly suggestive or just plain weird?

The back and forth between a presentation of the case and a far-reaching discussion of the facts will undoubtedly reveal particular ideas that need further research as well as alternative ways of conceiving the ethical situation. The more opportunities you have to practice presenting information to others, the more it will help build confidence, so that when it comes time for a formal presentation it will not seem as daunting a task.

As discussed in Chapter 3, we also need to begin our case analyses with a conception of the ethical questions involved, so following a discussion of the facts students will also need to discuss and work towards a consensus regarding these questions:

5. What are the major ethical issues raised by this case? What is the central ethical question?

Following a preliminary identification of the central issues and question(s), students can then work to apply particular methods that will further stimulate a creative flow of ideas. One methodological practice already suggested in discussing research on the cases involves listening without censor in an open discussion of the facts and ethical issues involved in the cases, and this practice should continue as students work to apply different methods to stimulate creativity.

Fortunately, there are some well-known methods for generating ideas and enhancing creativity, the most popular of which is probably "brainstorming." In effect, a group discussion involving listening without censor is already the beginning of brainstorming, but what would make it more clearly an expression of this technique is a rapid and spontaneous voicing of ideas. While spontaneity and serendipity are key elements of this process, it can still be performed in a structured way, such that each member of the group takes turns expressing his or her understanding of a key fact, question, or idea. We call this "structured brainstorming," and it may be performed in one of two ways. In the scenario in which students have already conducted some initial research on their cases, as we have discussed above, then working in groups of three to five students they should present the central facts and ethical issues of the case in three to five minutes, with the other group members then taking thirty seconds to one minute to respond to question (1) above, followed by a free discussion period of two to three minutes, and then repeat the same process for questions (2) to (5).

If, on the other hand, students are being presented with a case without anyone doing prior research, then the structured brainstorming could begin by having one student read the case to the others in a group of three to five students, and then students take turns to respond to each of the following questions in thirty seconds to one minute, with a two to three-minute open discussion after each student has presented his or her ideas.

(a) What are the most important facts in the case? Explain.

(b) What are the most unusual facts or aspects of the case? Explain.

(c) What are the major ethical issues and the central ethical question raised by this case? Explain.

(d) What aspects of the case require more research? Explain.

By considering how to explain their responses students will be led to discover reasons for their views, however obvious they may think these reasons are, and this may also reveal certain pre-judgments held by students. These discussions will undoubtedly produce many ideas that will require more careful thought and research, while it may also reveal less promising ideas that naturally fall by the wayside even with the students openly listening to each other without censor. Of course, it is possible to adjust the time limits of this process while also addressing different questions in subsequent group discussions.

Let us now consider a specific case to illustrate some of these ideas.

Case: Indian Family Law

India is among the world's largest nations, is home to the second largest population (over 1 billion people), and has incredible religious diversity. Article 44 of the Indian Constitution requires a uniform civil code throughout India, but at present much of Indian civil law is based on traditional case law.[1] A key element of Indian civil law includes the separation of some elements of personal or family law (marriage, divorce, child custody, inheritance, alimony, etc.) into three separate streams of jurisprudence: Hindu, Muslim, and Christian. The effect of this tradition is that Hindus, Muslims, and Christians are each governed by a distinct set of legal rules with respect to civil family institutions, though they share a criminal code which also affects family life.

During the English colonial period of India's history, Warren Hasting[s], a British legislator who helped mold India's civil justice system, attempted to integrate cultural sensitivity into India's family law system. Hasting[s] acknowledged that Hindu and Muslim traditions were integral to Indian identity and spearheaded the integration of traditional religious texts and leaders into the Western legal system. Arguably, Hasting[s'] aim was to acknowledge and respect the indigenous traditions of India. Similarly, feminist scholars in the West have argued that impartial justice is an inappropriate standard in the evaluation of family affairs, preferring more personal standards of care.

The Indian legal system's sensitivity to religious faith stands in stark contrast to the legal system of the United States, which is ostensibly religiously neutral. The U.S. system is inspired by a longstanding western

---

1. Indian Const. 1950. Art. 44. Online at: http://lawmin.nic.in/olwing/coi/coi-english/coi-indexenglish.htm; Anil and Ranjit Malhotra, "Family Law And Religion -The Indian Experience," *International Association of Matrimonial Lawyers Law Journal*, http://www.iaml.org/cms_media/files/family_law_and_religion_the_indian_experience.pdf?static=1

ideal of impartiality in the administration of justice represented by the Greek goddess, Themis, blindfolded and holding a sword in one hand and scales in the other. In this tradition, impartiality is thought to be the best method for reaching justice. As a result, in the United States personal legal disputes such as marriage and divorce are governed by a secular legal system insulated from the various religious traditions widely affiliated with personal and family matters.

For decades, women and women's groups in India and abroad have objected to the use of traditional religious laws such as Sharia and Dharmaśāstra. Under Sharia law, Muslim women have been denied divorce, child custody, and maintenance because of misogynistic gender norms within traditional Islam. For example Shah Bano, a 62-year-old Muslim woman, was divorced by her husband and was initially awarded maintenance or alimony payments available to women of other faiths under the Indian criminal code. However, subsequent legislation and courts held that as a Muslim woman, Bano was only eligible for three months of alimony after which it was expected that she would be cared for by relatives.[2]

If we imagine that this case is presented to us for the first time, then we will begin with the process of structured brainstorming in which students start by reflecting on the question of the most important facts. What are the most important facts of the case and why? What do you think? It is likely that a discussion of this question would highlight the facts in this concept map (see Figure 5.1).

This is not necessarily an exhaustive presentation of concepts, but it is likely that a discussion group would suggest most of these ideas. For example, some students might read the case and come away thinking that the most important fact is that men are favored and women are oppressed in India. Why and how would this be explained? In response, a student might reveal an understanding of traditional Sharia law practices and say that it is most important because of the "misogynistic gender norms" within traditional Islam. Other students may question this view and some may emphasize the importance of a common, impartial civil code. Still others may highlight another key fact, namely the great diversity of the population and the need for sensitivity, and perhaps explain how this appears to conflict with impartial justice. Even if there is some disagreement

---

2. *Mohd. Ahmed Khan vs Shah Bano Begum And Ors*, 1985 AIR 945, 1985 SCC (2) 556 (Indian Supreme Court, 1985), http://indiankanoon.org/doc/823221/.

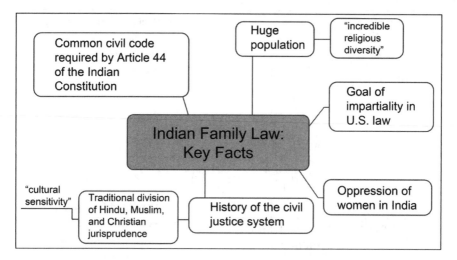

Figure 5.1

on an initial discussion of the facts of the case, it is more than likely that there will be some agreement as well, and students will be at once alerted to the multiple ways of conceiving of the case. By encountering various viewpoints while considering the goal of reaching consensus, which thus initially presents itself as a problem, students' minds will already be inclined towards a creative resolution of the case.

What are the most unusual facts or aspects of the case? Here again the answers will vary and may reflect individual differences among students. Possible responses are included in Figure 5.2.

In explaining these unusual facts the following explanations could be offered as examples. First, why is it unusual that a divorced Muslim woman is supposed to be cared for by relatives? Non-Muslims might find this unusual in the following ways: Why should it be the responsibility of relatives to care for a divorced woman? What if they have their own families to care for? What if she doesn't have any relatives? Second, that the British legislator Hasting[s] was sensitive to Indian diversity could be questioned as unusual because why should a British official show sensitivity and respect towards various groups within India when they showed little sensitivity when colonizing the country? Why shouldn't the legislator argue that the motherland knows best and that this is the way the civil justice system should be? Third, many students may find Themis, the Greek symbol of justice unusual in the following ways: Why is the symbol for the important

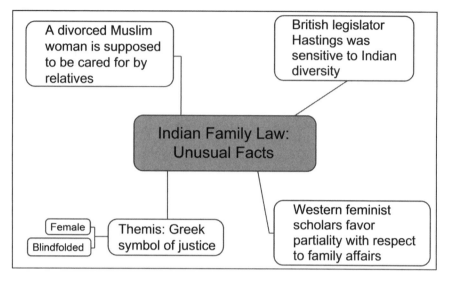

Figure 5.2

concept of justice female when men have dominated over women? Is this a suggestive fact? Is it meant to suggest that there is an important connection between justice and femininity? And why is justice blind? Isn't justice an ethical concept that should involve a very careful seeing of the particularities of a situation? Fourth, why is it unusual that Western feminist scholars suggest that partiality is appropriate with respect to family affairs? While this fact suggests that feminist ethical theory would be at least one appropriate lens to apply to this case, it is unusual because in arguing "that impartial justice is an inappropriate standard" in this case the feminists are agreeing with those who argue for separate standards of justice, even if some of them are based on misogynistic reasons.

This focus on unusual facts and aspects of the case can lead to many interesting questions, some of which may be considered when responding to the next question: What are the major ethical issues and the central ethical question that are raised by this case? The ethical concept of impartiality is central here, and we could ask how impartiality is related to respect for diversity, and perhaps also whether impartiality and fairness are identical concepts. Another ethical issue is the relationship between morality and religion, and we could ask the following question: Is it ethically justifiable for a legal system to be sensitive to different religious faiths? If so, why and under what conditions is this justifiable? If not, why not? We could also pose a different question: How should Article 44 of the Indian

Constitution be implemented in a way that best provides for the well-being of all citizens of India, regardless of age, gender, or religious faith? This is undoubtedly a tremendously challenging question, especially when we reflect that it has yet to be resolved by the Indian people.

A detailed discussion of these questions (a, b, c) will directly lend itself to answering the final question regarding what research is needed. Clearly, students will need to research the actual Indian laws involved, from the initial expression of Article 44 in the Indian Constitution to more recent laws such as the Hindu Marriage Act (1955), the Protection of Women Act (1986), and the Child Marriage Act (2006). The references given in the case are obviously important, as the article cited in the first reference raises the question of whether a uniform civil code is an aspiration or an illusion. It also exposes the fact that the Indian Constitution, like the U.S. Constitution, guarantees fundamental rights to equality, freedom, and protection of life and personal property. But what happens when different traditions with apparent religious connections can be seen as violating the constitution, such as the caste system effectively prohibiting inter-caste marriages? What happens when Islamic and Shariat courts issue *fatwas* (religious decrees) that contradict individuals' constitutional rights? Unfortunately, the Indian Supreme Court has not yet decided on whether having parallel legal systems is constitutional, and there is good reason to fear that any new system that seeks to change centuries of customs will be met with great resistance as well as much violence. On the other hand, in the article "Family Law And Religion: The Indian Experience" (see the first reference to the case above) Anil and Ranjit Malhotra suggest that if India can find a way through this great difficulty they could become a shining role model for the whole world.

Further research will also provide opportunities to explore the history of relevant Indian laws as well as actual cases that have resulted in the creation of such recent acts. While much research will thus involve legality, it will be important for students to keep the ethical questions front and center and to avoid confusing the law with ethics. Nevertheless, we would like to know whether Hastings or others provided an ethical justification for his view, and thus this historical research could prove ethically relevant.

As mentioned above, within the case itself we find an implicit suggestion to research feminist ethical theory with its focus on care over impartial justice, and this is a suggestion that should not go unheeded. Further, with the concept of justice being central here, it would be an oversight not to consider Rawls' *A Theory of Justice* (see Chapter 1) and how it may be applied to the case, as well as related theories. Also mentioned within the case is "the stark contrast to the legal system of the United States," and this suggests that we could also research the arguments for impartiality and the reasons for divorcing religious and legal systems. As always when conducting research, it is important for students to focus as much as possible on the information most relevant to their central questions. For, as you have probably already recognized, these are vast areas of research that will offer a wealth of ideas conducive to a creative case analysis.

Cultivating Creativity

A helpful technique for producing creative case analyses that arises naturally from the case on Indian Family Law specifically is what we call "Intercultural Comparison." Just as we have suggested that students should not consider moral problems from a single theoretical perspective, so too is it no longer enough in our ever-shrinking world to consider moral problems only from a single cultural perspective. Within this case we find clear opportunities to compare the Indian and American cultures and legal practices, and it is interesting to consider the differing viewpoints with regards to the relationship between a secular state and religion. In American culture we find a sharp divide between the state and religion, as expressed in the First Amendment to the U.S. Constitution, where we read that "Congress shall make no law respecting an establishment of religion." Whereas India embraces a form of secularism that rather than respecting no religions seeks to accommodate them all. Our intercultural comparison could also consider the cultural views of Muslims, Christians, and Hindus and how these views relate to ethical practices. Although some case studies may be narrowly situated within one specific culture (e.g., the Student Loan Forgiveness case), it is more than likely that by considering the issues from another cultural perspective that we will gain new insights into ways of thinking about the case. If students only know one culture's perspective on a case then they really do not know very much at all, an idea that is clearly explained by John Stuart Mill in *On Liberty*:

> He who knows only his own side of the case knows little of that. His reasons may be good, and no one may have been able to refute them. But if he is equally unable to refute the reasons on the opposite side, if he does not so much as know what they are, he has no ground for preferring either opinion ... Nor is it enough that he should hear the opinions of adversaries from his own teachers, presented as they state them, and accompanied by what

they offer as refutations. He must be able to hear them from persons who actually believe them . . .he must know them in their most plausible and persuasive form.

This is a powerful expression of the importance of seeking out ideas, reasons, and arguments that contrast with one's own, and one of the clearest ways of doing this is through considering a particular case from the point of view of another culture and then exploring the reasoning behind the other culture's view. For example, it seems difficult to imagine the Student Loan Forgiveness Case arising in another culture, but why is that? Is student loan debt unique to the United States and if so, why? How is higher education financed in the rest of the world and what are the reasons for these practices? If we begin by considering cultures close to us, such as the European cultures, then we may be surprised to find that most European countries have tuition-free higher education. How interesting! Obviously, much research would be needed to understand well the perspectives of other cultures on this case, and while such research will reveal more complexity rather than less, it is greater complexity that yields greater opportunities for creativity. On the other hand, when considering Indian Family Law in light of Mill's view we would most like to hear the separate civil family institutions defended by those who actually practice and believe in them (i.e., Muslims, Hindus, and Christians). This suggests the possibility of seeking out and conducting research interviews of, for example, Muslim Indians and Hindu Indians in order to try to learn and understand the reasons for their views. Clearly, a case analysis that incorporates such interviews into its argumentation will be more creative than one that does not.

Next, most students will be familiar with the psychological process of association, which is the mind's ability to join or rejoin ideas and emotions that have either been experienced together or are related to each other in some way. When students brainstorm together it is natural that they will express ideas that have been associated in some way, often based on their prior experiences. Weston takes this process a step further, however, by encouraging students to "invite exotic associations," by which he suggests a methodical practice of creating relationships between seemingly unrelated ideas. One way that this can be done is by choosing a random object (which, for example, could be determined by simply looking around one's environment and choosing something, or by randomly pointing a finger in a book to come up with the closest noun) and then trying to come up with (i.e., create) a way that this object could be used in an attempt to answer the ethical question. So, let's imagine again that we are considering the student loan forgiveness case and we look around the classroom and see a newspaper lying on the floor. How could a newspaper be used in dealing with the case? Here is where students could take turns coming up with multiple ideas using a newspaper. Perhaps students could deliver newspapers in order to lower their student loans, rather than having them forgiven, or perhaps all students who need student loans could be given some employment opportunity at the college newspaper instead. Or perhaps instead of being free, the school newspapers could be sold at a small cost with all earnings going to reducing student tuition. Or perhaps students who write for the school newspaper could earn college credit for their work, thus reducing the number of credits for which they have to pay. These are all interesting ideas, and we can also ask how this newspaper example might be applied to the Indian Family Law case. Think about it, or try to use another object as an example. Here again, the importance of listening to others' responses without censor, judgment, or criticism cannot be understated, and even when a response seems especially far-fetched it can nevertheless be valuable in opening one's mind to the ability to consider fresh, if also strange, ideas. And by doing this, as the neuroscientists will tell us, one establishes the mental conditions that are conducive to the creation of new thoughts.

Another method for cultivating creativity is one that Weston calls "go to extremes," which is closely related to what creativity expert Edward de Bono calls "the Intermediate Impossible." This method is highly valuable in approaching ethical case studies—it is one that we have found most valuable—for it asks students to imagine the best possible outcomes to a situation (this is what is considered the "extreme" or "impossible," although it could also be considered "the ideal") and then to try to think backwards from the extreme to find ways that it might actually be made to happen in reality. One raises extreme possibilities of a perfect solution by asking "What if?" questions. Thus, an obvious extreme with regards to the student loan forgiveness case would be that all student loan debt is eliminated and that all future students graduate college without any debt. What if there were no student loan debt? Wouldn't that be the ideal? Actually, with regards to college students graduating without any student debt, this is already a reality for students in many of the top schools in the U.S. Recognizing the severity of the student loan debt problem, in 2001 Princeton University was the first to offer financial aid packages to those students requiring it without including a burdensome student loan, and many other prestigious colleges and universities have initiated similar financial aid packages since then. Still, what are we to do with the mountain of student loan debt that already exists? Would it be morally justifiable and economically feasible to forgive it all? With this question we return again to the heart of that case study.

As for going to extremes in the case of Indian Family Law, would not the ideal be one in which all people were treated fairly regardless of their age, gender, or religion? What if Hindus, Muslims, and Christians could come to agree on a uniform civil code? Perhaps some will think that this would be impossible without changing traditional religious practices, and while this presents itself as a formidable objection, if we start from the extreme we will try to imagine a political state which allows for both a flourishing of religious beliefs while also expressing a determined respect and protection of the rights of individuals. How could this happen in a way that religious beliefs are not seen as being attacked, which would most surely result in adherents of those religions digging in their heels and fighting against any change? Perhaps we could imagine an extreme in which all Indians were well-educated about the prominent religions in their country and the philosophical ideas behind adopting a uniform civil code such that new interpretations of the religious beliefs arise in a way that they do not conflict with respecting the rights of all individuals. Surely all religious traditions undergo new interpretations leading to new practices, so this would not be as unusual as one might think. So, if we come to an agreement on this point, then the next step will be to imagine what specific changes will be needed in the education system in India to begin to advance towards this lofty goal.

Although the methods of creative ethical thinking presented here are admittedly modest, that does not detract from their significance. We are surely all familiar with "brainstorming" as a means of stimulating creativity in a group, but how often do we apply this method to ethical problems? As Weston tells us in *Creative Problem-Solving in Ethics*, "the key rule [of brainstorming] is to defer criticism," but how often do we really come together in groups or communities in the spirit of openness, ready to listen and reflect and slow to speak, to discuss possible ideas for dealing with an ethically charged situation? Instead, it seems more often to be the case that the "for" and "against" side of an issue is presented to us first; frequently it is forced upon us through the media in a way that inhibits the application of creativity.

Consider some additional examples. The first of the 2009 Regional Ethics Bowl cases concerned "Sexting" (i.e., sending nude photos in text messages with one's cellphone) and some of its consequences (e.g., teenage suicide), and in a creative exploration of this case our students attempted to move beyond a simple legalistic, right-or-wrong mindset and brainstorm on how this problem, which has come about through advances in technology and certain cultural perspectives, might be approached in the most satisfying way. Students who considered this case came to some valuable insights through an application of the "go to extremes" method. In their discussions, our students quickly asked: What if we had different attitudes toward nudity and sex such that sexting met with no embarrassment (and consequently did not lead to teenage suicide)? Or, what if students were better educated about sex, nudity, and respect of self and others such that sexting lost its provocative appeal? In ethical case studies thinking about the best case scenarios and reasoning backwards from these possibilities is an activity that nicely shows how creativity and reasoning can be combined. A few other examples include: What if we could legalize drugs and regulate them in a way that would eliminate violence and addiction? What if parental leave could be granted in a way that would benefit children, parents, and employers? What if we could satisfy both vegetarians and meat-eaters (and of course also non-human animals!) by producing a delicious cruelty-free synthetic meat?

By approaching cases in this creative way students cultivate a noticeably less dogmatic and more cooperative attitude towards developing positions that would best address the case, and this itself is a step forward in making ethical progress. As suggested above, however, none of this discussion is meant to imply that creativity trumps everything, for surely not every idea generated through the particular use of these methods is equally defensible. What is most important is the productive interplay between creativity and rational argumentation, for both activities have valuable roles to play in formulating insightful and intelligent ethical positions. In relation to critical questioning, creativity involves imagining many possibilities, and it is a valuable step in a process that opens up a space for careful ethical thinking which endeavors to find the way to enhance the well-being of us all.

Now that the importance of creativity for ethical thinking has been clearly seen and we have some practical strategies for bringing it into play in our case studies, it is time to return to a reflection on ethical theories. Unfortunately, most major ethicists have neglected to address creativity directly, even though it can be viewed as a key part in ethical reasoning. Nevertheless, there are some recent approaches in moral philosophy that lend themselves well to the pursuit of creativity in ethical case studies. One example can be found in *The Elements of Moral Philosophy* by James and Stuart Rachels where they respond to the question "What Would a Satisfactory Moral Theory Be Like?" Here they develop a view that shows an openness to multiplicity and a flexibility that provides opportune conditions for creative activity, even when not explicitly sought. They call this view "multiple strategies utilitarianism," for the central goal is to maximize the happiness or well-being of all beings, and even though there are surely many ethicists who would not call themselves "utilitarians," it is hard to imagine that they would seriously find this goal objectionable. In relation to the view Henry Sidgwick (1838–1900) promoted under the name "motive utilitarianism," Rachels and Rachels recognize that there can be multiple motives or strategies for achieving the general welfare of all. They therefore bring together all ethical theories under the umbrella of a broadly stated utilitarian goal in such a way that virtue theorists and Kantian deontologists will recognize parts of their own theories. Although they do not mention creativity as a factor in ethical thinking, their approach can nevertheless be seen as a morally creative one inasmuch as it opens up possibilities for new thinking while seeking a good end, and it also acknowledges that we should care about creating things with value. Their approach may be seen as a compromise of sorts (and contemporary ethicist James Sterba argues in *The Triumph of Practice over Theory in Ethics* for a view he calls "Morality as Compromise"), as it emphasizes the best parts of some theories over lesser parts of others. For example, some of the multiple strategies will involve showing partiality in caring for our family and friends (an Aristotelian and ethics of care virtue), while also considering deserts (a Kantian emphasis). For Rachels and Rachels we should all act according to our "best plan"—the optimal list to be happy and contribute to the general welfare—which includes virtues, motives, commitments, social roles, duties, everyday rules, and a strategy for dealing with conflicts. Obviously, balancing all the items on our optimal lists will require a great deal of creative and critical thinking, while also offering us one thoughtful way to conceive of applying ethical theories.

Questions for Further Thinking and Discussion

1. Explain which mindsets impede creative ethical thinking and how these mindsets can best be counteracted.
2. Who comes to mind when you think about a "creative person," and what sorts of personal traits does this person possess?
3. With regards to the "Heinz Dilemma", what other actions can you imagine Heinz performing to deal with the situation? What would you do?

4. What do you understand by "collective moral creativity" and which specific practices could be followed both in and out of the classroom to facilitate this?

5. Apply some of the methods for enhancing creativity discussed in this chapter to a consideration of the "Granny Cam" case presented in Chapter 4.

6. Consider the sample answers given above with regards to the Indian Family Law case. Can you think of any additional responses to these questions? If you specifically try to "invite exotic associations" with this case what do you learn? How do you think this case can be best resolved?

7. Are there any additional methods that you are aware of—or maybe already use—that stimulate creativity and can be applied to ethical case studies? Explain.

8. How does "multiple strategies utilitarianism" enhance moral creativity? Is it a cogent ethical theory?

9. One of the standard or common responses to the moral issue of gun control is that, at least in the United States, gun control or wholesale banning of guns is unjustified on the basis of the Second Amendment to the Constitution. Another common response is that people have a right to protect themselves, and to ban or control guns will deprive people of the right to the most basic of rights, that of self-defense. If, however, you are thinking creatively, what other considerations or what other arguments—not centered on the U.S. Constitution or the right to life or self-protection—can you develop to conceptualize the issue differently from these and other common positions?

References and Suggestions for Further Reading

Dewey, John and James H. Tufts. *Ethics*, Revised Edition. In *The Collected Works of John Dewey: The Later Works, 1925–1953*. Volume 7: 1932. Southern Illinois University Press, 2008. The lengthy quotation is from page 316 of this edition. The original version of this book is available at www.gutenberg.org.

De Bono, Edward. *Serious Creativity: Using the Power of Lateral Thinking to Create New Ideas*. HarperCollins, 1993.

Harris, Sam. *The Moral Landscape: How Science Can Determine Moral Values*. Free Press, 2010. The quotation is from page 11.

Harris, Sam. "Science Can Answer Moral Questions," TED Talk. Available at: http://www.ted.com/talks/sam_harris_science_can_show_what_s_ right.html.

Hitchens, Christopher. *God Is Not Great: How Religion Poisons Everything.* Twelve Books, 2009.

Hume, David. *A Treatise of Human Nature.* Oxford University Press, 2000. The famous "is-ought" distinction is found in Book III, Part I, Section 1.

"Indian Family Law." The Intercollegiate Ethics Bowl^SM cases are published by and may be used only with permission of The Association for Practical and Professional Ethics. (APPE, 618 East Third Street, Bloomington, Indiana 47405; Tel: (812) 855-6450; E-mail: appe@indiana.edu.)

"Intercollegiate Ethics Bowl." Association for Practical and Professional Ethics. Available at http://www.indiana.edu/~appe/ethicsbowl.html (Retrieved July 26, 2010).

Martin, Mike W. *Creativity: Ethics and Excellence in Science.* Lexington Books, 2007. The quotations above are from pages ix–x. As the title suggests, the central focus throughout this work is the relationship between scientific creativity and moral creativity. Nevertheless, the early chapters on "Creativity and Ethics" (Chapter One) and "What Is Creativity?" (Chapter Two) are particularly relevant.

McNaughton, David. "Why Is So Much Philosophy So Tedious?" *Florida Philosophical Review* IX.2 (Winter 2009): 1–13. The quotation is from page 8.

Nietzsche, Friedrich. *Twilight of the Idols.* In *The Portable Nietzsche.* Ed. & Trans. Walter Kaufman. Penguin Books, 1982. The quotation is from section 6 of "What the Germans Lack."

Putnam, Hilary. *The Collapse of the Fact/Value Dichotomy and Other Essays.* Harvard University Press, 2004.

Rachels, James, and Stuart Rachels. *The Elements of Moral Philosophy.* 6th ed. McGraw-Hill, 2010. The quotations on "reason" are from pages 11 and 13, and the quotation on "cultural relativism" is from page 18. For a discussion of "multiple-strategies utilitarianism" see section 13.4 on pages 177–180.

Rachels, James. "God and Moral Autonomy." In *Can Ethics Provide Answers? and Other Essays in Moral Philosophy.* Rowman & Littlefield, 1997. 109–124. The quotation is from page 118.

Searle, John R. "How to Derive 'Ought' from 'Is'." *The Philosophical Review.* Vol. 73, No. 1 (January 1964): 43–58.

Sterba, James P. *The Triumph of Practice over Theory in Ethics.* Oxford University Press, 2005. Sterba calls his defense of morality "Morality as Compromise," and this is explained on pages 28–31.

Sternberg, Robert J. and James C. Kaufman, eds. *The Cambridge Handbook of Creativity*. Cambridge University Press, 2010.

Stover, Dawn, ed. "The Mad Science of Creativity." *Scientific American Mind*. Special Collector's Edition. Winter 2014. This special issue presents several interesting articles that provide a general, up-to-date overview of creativity research and offers additional ideas on play, innovation, and techniques for stimulating creativity, among others.

Strawser, Michael. "Creative Case Studies in Ethics." *Teaching Ethics* (Fall 2010): 105–119. Parts of this chapter have previously appeared in this paper, and they are reprinted here with the author's and publisher's permission.

Weston, Anthony. *Creative Problem-Solving in Ethics*. Oxford University Press, 2007. See Weston's Preface for the suggestion to expand ethics. See Chapter 1, "Creativity's Promise in Ethics" for his presentation and discussion of the Heinz Dilemma and the story of the child with leukemia, as well as his understanding of the meaning of ethics. In Chapter 2, "Ethical Explorations," he presents his methods for creative-problem solving in ethics.

Weston, Anthony. *A 21st Century Ethical Toolbox*. 2nd ed. Oxford University Press, 2008. The quotations above are from Chapter 1, "Ethics as a Learning Experience." Chapter 2 deals with "Ethics-Avoidance Disorders."

6   Applying Ethical Theories

Traditional thinking regarding ethical theories is that once you know the theory, including its major principles or tenets and some of its theoretical nuances and problems, you are fully prepared to apply the theory to solve real-life, ordinary ethical problems and dilemmas. While traditional thinking about the application of ethical theories to cases is perhaps a worthwhile ideal goal, in practice it is not so simple. It is rarely the case that a moral problem lends itself to simple analysis of the application of the principle of utility or the categorical imperative or the development of the virtues from virtue ethics, and in fact as we noted in Chapter 5, trying to perform such simple analysis of a case impedes creativity and collaboration. Instead, real-life, practical problems are dynamic, complicated, and "messy." They are dynamic in that facts can sometimes change the ways in which people evaluate a moral problem and there are times when the problems identified in a case change or are augmented by the experiences, preferences, and moral sensibilities of those who are considering them. Moral problems are usually complicated, and in many instances the complications arise from the dynamic nature of human life and the particular contingencies of cases. And moral problems are "messy" in that their complications and the multiple points of view from which they may be analyzed, understood, categorized, and solved are as complex and multifarious as the people who consider and try to solve them.

It is perhaps instructive to think of our attempts to understand and solve moral problems in the way in which Ralph Waldo Emerson conceived of the notion of consistency. He noted in "Self-Reliance" (1841) that "a foolish consistency is the hobgoblin of little minds." There are multiple interpretations of what Emerson meant by this statement, but the one to which we will subscribe for our purposes is this: Each day is different from every other, and just as you don't prefer all the same things as an adult that you preferred as a child, and just as you don't rightly limit yourself to one point of view or one approach in attempting to solve other practical problems, it is equally unjustified to limit ourselves to one theory or to one principle to solve complex moral issues. If you take your car to a mechanic to determine the source of a noise that appears to be coming from the engine, you do not—nor should you—expect the mechanic to decide, prior to inspection of the car, that it must be a problem with the transmission. Your mechanic may specialize in transmissions, but the fact that your mechanic is a specialist in this area does not mean that every car problem arises from the transmission. Similarly, if you are not feeling well from a pain in your abdomen, consulting a podiatrist is not the proper avenue to take. While a podiatrist deals appropriately and adequately with part of the human anatomy, application of the methods and procedures of podiatry are not consistent with identifying and alleviating the pain in your abdomen. This does not mean that podiatry is irrelevant all together, and that no one may ever consult a podiatrist for anything at all. What it does mean is that podiatry is for human feet, not for abdominal pain, and no matter the level of expertise of the podiatrist, her or his area of expertise is not consistently or appropriately applied to abdominal pain.

On the other hand, the noise in your car may very well be present in the engine, but it is possible that the source of the noise is the transmission. In a case like this, you may need to secure the services of two mechanics, or a mechanic who specializes in two types of car problems, to deal adequately with the noise coming from under the hood of your car. No one calls you inconsistent for utilizing two mechanics or the dual expertise of one mechanic in attempting to solve the problem causing the noise in your car. In fact, it is often the right and sensible thing to do. It is important to note here that whether we are considering transmission problems or a pain in your abdomen, Emerson's attitude toward consistency does not mean that you should go in every conceivable direction looking for a solution to the problem. While *foolish* consistency is something to avoid, consistency itself is to be embraced, utilized, appreciated, and applied. So even though it is clear that utilitarian moral theory and Kantian deontology are very different theories and come from very different theoretical and moral points of view, there are times when the use of both theories to solve a practical problem is not only acceptable, it may also be useful and efficient in yielding a way to conceptualize and to attempt to solve a moral problem.

There may be other instances of ethical case presentation and analysis that lend themselves efficiently and usefully only to one sort of theoretical backdrop. The point is to find the route to a proposed solution to a moral problem that can work, that is consistent within itself, that is acceptable to reasonable people considering the case, and that does not violate important moral principles that any reasonable person would wish not to violate. The question remains, however, how to manage to satisfy such a variety of complicated requirements.

Case: Declawing Cats

A local pet rescue organization puts up cats and dogs for adoption, charging $100 to the person adopting the animal to cover the costs of food, vaccinations, and spay/neuter surgery on the animal. The pet rescue organization screens potential adopters, and once approved to adopt a cat or dog, the organization requires the new pet owner to sign a contract agreeing, among other things, that the cat or dog cannot be transferred to another owner without the consent of the pet rescue organization and that under no circumstances shall a cat be subject to declawing.

Mary adopted a male cat from the organization and has grown very attached to him. He is generally a very well-behaved cat, but he sharpens his claws on her furniture and has torn an entire section off the back of her very expensive couch. Mary is considering buying a new couch, but she doesn't want to spend the money on a couch just to have the cat tear it. Her veterinarian's office told her that there is no way that the pet rescue organization will know that she has had the cat declawed unless she tells them, and the vet's office is willing to declaw the cat. Mary has decided to have the cat declawed.

In addition to mapping out the facts and facets of the case and determining what sorts of information you may need for complete analysis of the case (background research), you also need to decide what theoretical point(s) of view you will use to formulate your position on the case and how you will use theory (principles and concepts from the theory or theories you believe is or are most applicable and appropriate to the case) to justify your position. A concept map may be helpful in achieving your goals for analysis of the case (see Figure 6.1).

Concept Map of the Case Facts

This map captures the primary features of the facts presented in the case. It is up to you how you wish to organize the information, but in the map above, the left side of the map contains three main ideas (information

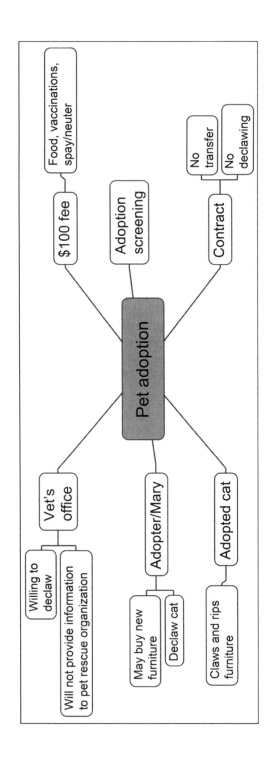

Figure 6.1

about the veterinarian's office, about Mary (the person who adopted the cat), and about the cat himself. The right side of the map contains three separate facets of facts regarding the pet rescue adoption organization, including the cost for adoption, screening of potential adopters, and the contract that the person adopting a pet must sign. It is clear that you already know all these facts simply from reading the case, but a good map of the facts of the case will serve as the background for determining what kinds of and how much information you may need or want in beginning to formulate your position on the issue.

It is important to note here that you may have already formed your opinion on the issue. That is certainly acceptable and may help to guide the direction of your research. But try not to let your preconceived notions cloud your judgment. You may find that you will change your mind either about the acceptability of having the cat declawed in general, or you may retain that general position while at the same time reconsidering some aspects of the case as you continue with your research.

Now that you have mapped the factual information embedded in the case, ask yourself questions about what you might need or want to know about the facts of the case as noted in the expanded concept map, below. You will also likely find, as indicated in the following map (Figure 6.2), that the questions you ask about the facts will also begin to lead you to questions about the right, the good, obligations, responsibilities, principles, concepts, and theories.

Concept Map of Needed Research and Moral Questions

You now have a good starting point. Remember, however, that the ideas presented in this map are those of the authors of this book and you are not limited to the format of this map. You may have ideas that you wish to add to this map, or some here might seem to you to be irrelevant or not particularly useful. What you put in a concept map is up to you. The main things to keep in mind and to include in your map are the facts of the case that you believe are relevant to making a decision on the presence of ethical issues in the case, identifying areas of the case that need further research so that you may make the best and most informed moral decision available to you, and to begin to ask related questions about the moral and social issues involved in the case.

As you can see from the map of the pet adoption case, questions begin to arise as you look more closely at the facts of the case. You know that Mary paid $100 to adopt the cat, and that the fee was to cover the costs of

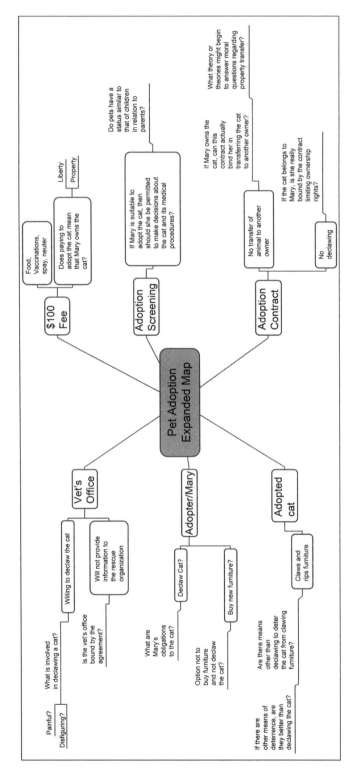

Figure 6.2

food, vaccinations, and neutering the cat. But does the fact that Mary paid to adopt the cat mean that Mary owns the cat? If she does own the cat, what does that imply?

Under some moral and social interpretations of the concept of ownership, owning something means that the person is free to do with that thing as she or he sees fit. Ask yourself, however, whether it is possible to "own" a living thing in the same way it is possible to own a computer, a house, or some other piece of real property. Your answer to this question (which is itself a moral and social question) will have equally weighty moral implications.

Further, we know that the pet rescue organization screens applicants to determine their suitability to adopt a pet. Even though we do not know from the facts of this case of what the screening process consists, it is possible that there is information available at pet rescue organizations in your local area, or that you might find on the Internet, explaining the screening process in general. In fact, you may find yourself researching pet rescue and adoption organizations and find that it is a general practice among many of them to perform screenings of potential adopters, and from the information you find, your background research and the questions you ask will enrich the development of your own position on the case.

One question you may wish to ask yourself is this: If Mary is suitable to adopt the cat, does that not also mean that she is suitable and capable of making decisions about the cat and its medical procedures? For example, assume that there is nothing in the contract that Mary signed about taking the cat for regular, routine visits to the vet's office and that there is nothing in the contract regarding the kind of food Mary chooses to buy for the cat. If such information is not included in the contract, then Mary is free to make these decisions for herself and for her cat. Suppose that on a routine visit to the vet, it is found that the cat has three bad teeth that need to be removed. It is certainly the case that tooth extraction for a cat (as for a human being) can be painful either during a procedure or after it, but that it may also be the case that the pain and discomfort of having teeth extracted is more than compensated for by the benefits to the cat in the long run, freeing it from additional health problems associated with decayed, infected, or otherwise unhealthy teeth.

In addition to considerations about health decisions that Mary may make for the cat she has adopted, an associated question may arise: Do pets have a status similar to that of children in relation to their parents? For example, parents have a responsibility to make decisions on behalf of and for the benefit of their children as they see fit. It is possible that other people may not agree with, say, the choice of religious orientation of the parents and they may believe that subjecting children to the tenets and lifestyles associated with a particular religion is unacceptable. Do you believe, however, that simply because your neighbor (or an adoption agency) believes that you ought not to subject your children to the teachings of a Fundamentalist Christian sect that the neighbor (or the adoption agency) has the right to interfere? If you decide not to have your male child circumcised, is it any business of the adoption agency (or your neighbors)?

Beyond these factors of the case, a related question is whether the contract that Mary signed regarding the cat she adopted actually binds her in ownership rights (if in fact she actually owns the cat)? That is, sometimes contracts are not enforceable because they are not legitimate. How would you go about determining whether the contract for the adoption of the cat is legitimate and enforceable? Even more importantly, was the contract morally enforceable from the outset even if it is not legally enforceable?

As you continue to think about the facts of the case and additional information you may need to form and justify your position, you may return to the question of whether Mary actually "owns" the cat at all. There is a movement to consider pet animals not as property, but as dependents, in a sense, where the person who adopts the pet is its "guardian" rather than its owner. You may not have known this as you have been reading and thinking about the pet adoption case, but your background research would be likely to reveal that fact. Revealing that fact may very well add another layer of reasoning and issues to the pet adoption case and may have some impact on the way in which you ultimately argue for a position on it.

Other issues involved in this case have to do specifically with the cat and what Mary is proposing be done to him. Do you know how cats are declawed and whether the procedure is very painful? If you find that it is a very painful procedure either during or for some time after the procedure (or at both times), does this have an impact on your attitude toward declawing the cat? Where would you look to find out relevant facts about the medical procedure of declawing?

Does Mary have an obligation to the cat? Whether she is the owner of the cat or its guardian, are there certain things that Mary has a moral obligation to do or to provide to the cat for its well-being? Is declawing something to be done that will promote the cat's well-being, or is it a selfish decision that Mary is making in thinking of buying a new couch and declawing the cat? If you knew whether Mary would not have the cat declawed if she did not buy a new couch, would this have an impact on your evaluation of the case? If you knew that Mary was likely to give the cat away or return him to the pet rescue organization rather than to have him declawed, would this have an impact on how you evaluate the case?

Notice, too, that the veterinarian's office told Mary that they are willing to declaw the cat and that the pet rescue organization will not know that Mary had him declawed unless she tells the organization that she has done so. But does the veterinarian's office knowing that Mary signed a contract agreeing not to declaw the cat have any binding effect on the veterinarian's office? Put differently, is what the vet's office told Mary relevant to the issue of declawing the cat?

Finally, we know that the cat claws the furniture and that Mary has grown fond of the cat. We know that she is considering declawing as a way to solve the problem of ruined furniture. But are there other effective means of deterring cats from tearing furniture? This is a point for further research. Perhaps you could go to a local pet store and ask about such products (they do exist), you could go to the Humane Society of the United States' website to see whether there is any information there, or you could visit a local vet's office for their advice, among other sources of information.

The point in carefully mapping out or conceptualizing in some other way the facts of the pet adoption case is to determine what information you need regarding the facts and to determine at least some of the questions that arise about the issues in the case that seem clearly to have moral import. Among those that seem to have moral import in this case are the concepts of ownership, paternalism (decisions made or actions taken on behalf of another person or being), the pain and/or benefit of the surgical procedure of declawing a cat (as well as long-lasting effects of the procedure), whether Mary or the vet's office are bound by the agreement that Mary signed, the obligations of an owner or guardian to an adopted pet (including being aware of and considering alternatives to declawing), whether having a pet is a matter of ownership or guardianship, and general obligations that a pet owner or pet guardian has to the pet.

The process in which you have been involved in mapping out the case should lead you to form good questions about the case, including some overriding question or questions that will guide your research into the moral aspects of it. Some questions that may come to mind regarding the pet adoption case are these:

- Is it morally justifiable for Mary to have her cat declawed?
- Should the contract with the pet rescue organization override Mary's rights as the owner or guardian of the cat, or the reverse?

- Is Mary morally justified in violating the contract with the pet rescue organization?

Let's say that your position on the issue—after you have done background research into factual issues, and assuming your familiarity with the major ethical theories and principles involved in theoretical and applied ethics— is that it is not morally justifiable for Mary to have the cat declawed.

How will you justify your position? The answer is that you will do so using a combination of the facts of the case and the additional information you have gathered about them, and principles and concepts of one or more ethical theories that you believe are appropriately applied to the case. A very important point regarding the development of your position is that the more general the moral question asked, the more dynamic and expansive will be the development of your position. Note, for example, that in the potential questions to be asked regarding this case that the most general one, whether it is morally justified for Mary to have the cat declawed, can be answered in part by answering other questions that arise as you engage in research and critical reasoning regarding moral justification.

Concept Mapping and Developing
Your Position on a Case Study

The map below represents the application of concept mapping to argument creation and analysis. Remember that there is no requirement that a concept map be constructed in a specific way. Your preference for construction of the map may be different from the one below. The creation and analysis of an argument may be done using a concept map in which one's own ideas and background research are combined with theories or principles from ethical theories to begin to fill out and express your own position.

In the map of the cat declawing case study, the central feature of the map is the answer to the question (which might, for this abstract representation, simply be something like "Is it morally permissible or justifiable to X?"). Your answer might be something like this: "It is not morally justifiable to X." Situated around this central concept are your reasons for reaching the conclusion, as illustrated below (Figure 6.3).

Notice that the elements of an argument represented in the map do not include reference to all the issues or facts presented in the case. You may believe that some of the facts presented in the case are not relevant to the

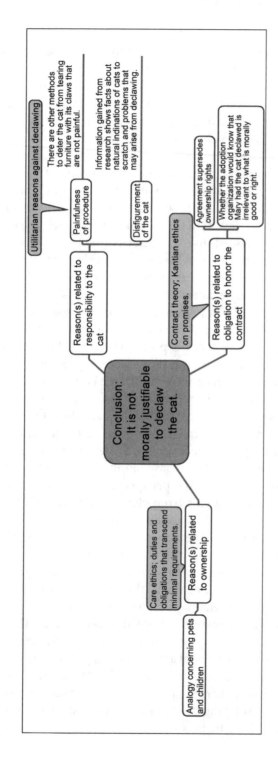

Figure 6.3

argument you are constructing; you may believe that some of the facts in the case have no relationship to moral issues; or it may simply be the case that the argument you are constructing is such that only some information presented in the case is relevant to your position. Whatever the case may be with respect to the facts included in your argument, make sure that you construct the strongest possible argument available to you from your background research. To ensure the quality of the argument that you construct, pay attention to the same criteria for cogent reasoning that you apply to analysis of the arguments of others. In other words, ensure that, to the best of your ability, you include information in your argument that is true and unambiguous, that is relevant to the conclusion for which you are arguing, and that you have provided sufficient information to justify your claim.

For this case, assume that you have done some background research on the facts related to declawing a cat—you visited a local veterinarian's office to ask about the procedure, how it is done, and any risks and problems associated with declawing a cat. Assume also that you took into account the claims made by Robert Nozick's theory of property acquisition and transfer and, while you believe that his position justifies the claim that Mary owns the cat (that is, that the cat is like a piece of property), you also recognize through the ethics of care and utilitarian considerations that the cat is a sentient being capable of feeling and suffering from pain. You also believe on the basis of your research that the pain the cat will suffer from declawing, including behavioral problems that are often associated with declawing, far outweigh the inconvenience Mary experiences from the cat ripping her furniture. In fact, you have found in your research both at the local veterinarian's office and at a pet specialty store that there are alternate methods of deterring cats from clawing furniture that are neither painful nor dangerous and that are not prohibitively expensive. Furthermore, you have considered the issues and think that even though you believe the cat to be Mary's property, there is a sense in which Mary's adoption of the cat has the same kind of implications that parents having children will experience. For example, there are children who ruin furniture by spilling liquids on them, ripping them with sharp instruments, or writing on them, but reasonable parents find creative and effective means to keep children from damaging furniture without harming the children or depriving them of recreational activity or things they need. So if Mary's adoption of the cat makes her like a "parent" to the cat, she owes it to the cat (and perhaps even to herself) to find a creative and effective means to keep the cat from damaging the furniture that does not harm the cat or deprive him of anything he needs.

Notice that in this hypothetical presentation of conditions for an argument regarding declawing a cat that more than one ethical theory has been used to justify the position. As we noted before, we take Emerson's position seriously to avoid foolish consistency. Even though Kantian deontology is a completely different type of theory from utilitarianism, you can see in the rough sketch of a possible argument regarding declawing a cat that the incompatibility of the theories (one is non-consequentialist and the other is consequentialist, for example) does not mean that the theories cannot be used to reach the same conclusion. Furthermore, the ethics of care (in which you might note that Mary has obligations to the cat that transcend minimal requirements, taking into account that Mary loves the cat, that she is attached to the cat, and so on) is probably incompatible in many ways with Kantian ethics, but this does not keep you from using one theory to inform the analogy between children and pets and another theory to justify your claim that keeping the promise made not to declaw the cat has stronger moral import than ownership rights provided in a rights-based theory like that of Nozick. The point is to make the strongest case, not to limit yourself to a favorite theory or principle the application of which would not be conducive to justification of your position.

Noting that there may be a theory that is not helpful in making your case does not mean that your case is weak. It simply means that there may be some other theory or principle that is more appropriately applicable to the case.

The creative aspects of the conclusion reached should not be underestimated, nor should the abilities of those who disagree with you. For example, in a context such as Ethics Bowl competition, the team you face may have a completely different view on the issue and they may have thought of avenues of research and application of theories that never crossed your mind. When they present their ideas to you, you have then to take them into account in continuing to justify your position as well as, if appropriate, showing your opponent's position to be wrong in some way. There are also instances in which your opponents provide information and arguments that will strengthen your position.

While there are people who believe that the most important factor in any competitive environment is "winning," we take the position that the most important consideration in ethics is finding good answers to good questions. We all win when complex and important moral questions are answered in ways that are rational and well-structured, justifiable and acceptable to people who consider, in a reasonable fashion, potential solutions and conclusions offered in the attempt to address ethical problems.

We believe that concept mapping for facts, theories, and argument construction is one of the ways in which reasonable approaches to complex and important moral issues is achieved. The notion to "map" a case or argument may well be likened to mapping out the directions to reach a particular destination. Creating a map of a case is like finding one's position with a GPS (global positioning system). It shows you where you are and what landmarks are nearby. The parts of the case are different landmarks with roads leading both to and from the main idea of the case, as well as sometimes to and from each other.

Once the map of the case has been created, along with indicators giving you a guide to what information needs to be gathered, the next task is to do the background research to find the answers to the good questions you have asked about the facts of the case. Once you have done background research to compile additional information and you have formulated a primary ethical question to ask about the case, the next step is to apply creative and critical thinking to formulate your own argument. The conclusion is your destination, and the facts and inferences constituting your argument are the roads you take to reach it.

But because taking a road filled with potholes would make your trip unpleasant, slow, and problematic, your task is to build a sturdy, high quality road that leads to the destination in the most efficient manner possible. Doing this requires high quality materials and workmanship, and it sometimes means that there are obstacles in the way that need to be removed or, where they cannot be removed, the road you create needs to be modified to fit the terrain. In other words, to reach the conclusion, you need to find the best possible information (satisfying the "truth" requirement) and organize it in a way that leads to the conclusion in a manner that does not stray from the issues (irrelevance, the avoidance of which satisfies the "relevance" requirement), and that contains the proper information in sufficient quantities (satisfying the "strength" requirement) to justify your conclusion.

Identifying and Writing Ethics Cases

One of the most effective and creative ways to apply the methods, principles, and theories you have learned so far in this book is to write your own ethical case study. To experience moral reasoning and theorizing from a different point of view, writing cases of your own is useful. Writing a case also requires the use of your creative abilities in presenting the facts of the case. Case studies should be written to provide a guide to additional research and the process of asking good questions while at the same time not providing either the questions or their answers. In other words, writing a case study requires that you check your opinions at the door as much as possible so that you can write the case study without "**poisoning the well**," so to speak, with indications of your own position on the issue or issues. For example, suppose that you have just finished reading an article in a local newspaper about students being encouraged to apply to an unaccredited local college by television advertisements indicating that graduates of the college are immediately employable upon graduation. In the article, five graduates of the college were interviewed and all of them reported that they had been unable to find jobs in their degree fields and all had graduated within the past two years. At the end of the article, the author/journalist noted that the state in which the college is located is investigating the college for fraudulent and misleading advertising. State regulators have found that over 60% of the graduates of the college fail to find employment in their degree fields within one year of graduation and 45% fail to find employment after five years. Further, 100% of the students of the college who apply for admission to regionally accredited colleges find that none of the credits earned at the unaccredited college are transferable.

How would you go about writing up the article as a case study designed to elicit questions having moral import? First, you need to gather the facts of the case. Second, it may be helpful to check other news sources to determine whether other news items about the college have been published and what kinds of news stories have been reported. Third, you should go to the college's catalog to determine the facts about their accreditation status and check their website to determine whether there are published statements of placement rates of graduates. Doing these things, and perhaps others, are necessary to write the case so that you are not subjected to the possibility that the news source in which you first read the article about the college has gotten all the facts—or some essential facts—wrong! For example, it may be that the news article you read contained the name of a different college that is in fact accredited; the graduation rates reported might be erroneous, and checking other reliable sources of information will aid you in being able to write the case study with the best information at your disposal.

Another way to put it is that writing a case study is attended with some of the same potential pitfalls and problems that are associated with analyzing and evaluating, or writing and constructing, an argument of your own. Care must therefore be taken in writing them to avoid irrelevance, to ensure that you provide your readers with accurate information, and that you recognize the potential for moral issues embedded in the facts and conditions of the case.

It is also possible that a case does not immediately or obviously lend itself to the generation of good ethical questions to ask, and therefore not to ethical analysis. Consider, for example, the case of the 13-year old boy and FPS video games. It might at first appear simply to be an obvious case of a young boy playing video games instead of doing well in school, and perhaps you think that the reason his grades have gone down is his immersion in playing games. But look more closely at it, and questions arise having moral import. For example,

- Is it morally justifiable for FPS video games to be used or played by children?
- Would the child's mother be justified in not allowing her son to play FPS games?

You can probably think of several more questions with ethical import. Remember, too, that ethical questions are about what ought to be or should be the case in the sense that what ought to be or should be is a condition or state of affairs leading to the right or to the good in an ethical sense such as that having to do with rights, with conditions leading to a good life, and so on.

Another example that generates ethical questions (in addition to legal, social, and political ones) is the recent (December 2013) lack of action on the part of the United States Congress to extend emergency unemployment benefits. Regardless of one's political leanings, and notwithstanding questions about the economic impact of the action of Congress, there are moral questions to ask, such as what is the moral justification for unemployment benefits in general, and whether it is morally justifiable in times of recession, when there are three applicants for every single job opening in the United States, to fail to extend emergency unemployment benefits, among others.

Perhaps it is reasonable to believe that in almost every condition or situation in which we find ourselves personally, socially, politically, and interpersonally, there are embedded ethical issues, problems, and dilemmas. Some of the questions having ethical content may seem trivial on first glance, but there is someone, somewhere, for whom the questions to be asked are matters of importance having implications that are simply not immediately recognized by those who are not directly affected. Take, for example, television commercials for St. Jude's Children's Research Hospital, the Humane Society of the United States (HSUS), and other charitable organizations. In many of the HSUS commercials, images are shown of dogs, cats, horses, cows, and other non-human animals that have been abused or neglected; and in the case of the children's hospital, images of children undergoing cancer testing and treatment are prominently displayed. In all these cases, a voice-over in the commercial asks you to donate funds to help to alleviate the suffering of the animals and the children. We, the authors of this book, have recently seen the commercials for St. Jude's and for the HSUS on the same television station played within an hour of each other.

Supposing that you would like to contribute to both organizations but your finances will allow you to contribute only to one of them, which do you choose and how do you decide? After making your decision, have you done the right and the good thing? How do you know? Is one of the organizations more deserving of your contribution than another? And what if you saw another commercial for PETA (People for the Ethical Treatment of Animals) but you do not agree with the political position of the organization, while at the same time being concerned for the welfare of the animals that PETA intends to help? These considerations—and many more—are factors that may have an effect on the ethical issues engendered and the questions that may be asked. In sum, ethical issues are everywhere and not only in obvious cases or in ways apparent at a first glance. To be a responsible moral agent—and to be responsible in and for asking and answering good questions about ethics—creative and critical thinking are essential.

Questions for Further Thinking and Discussion

1. Can you think of instances in which it would not be advisable to use more than one ethical theory in formulating a position on a case?
2. In your considered view, should consistency in arguing for a position be considered more important than persuasive methods of argument such as appeals to emotion and appeals to fear?
3. Go back to the "Granny Cam" case study presented in Chapter 4 and argue for your position regarding the primary question(s) of the case that you have identified. Use a concept map to identify issues and questions and to argue for your position.
4. Write a case study from your own experience, from your imagination, or from trusted news sources. Ask a friend, relative, or someone in your class to identify the major facts of the case and to propose a primary ethical question arising from the case study. On the basis of this question, develop and defend your position on the issue.

5. Return to the ADHD medication case presented earlier, and argue for your position regarding the primary question(s) of the case you have identified. Use a concept map to identify issues and questions and to argue for your position.

References and Suggestions for Further Reading

The Critical Thinking Community. See http://www.criticalthinking.org.

Emerson, Ralph Waldo. "Self-Reliance." 1841. In *Essays: First Series*. Available online at http://www.emersoncentral.com/selfreliance.htm and other Web sources.

Richardson, Henry S. "Moral Reasoning." *The Stanford Encyclopedia of Philosophy*. Spring 2013 ed. Available at http://plato.stanford.edu/entries/reasoning-moral/.

7 Conclusion

Throughout this book we have repeatedly emphasized the importance of asking good questions, but we would not want you to infer from this that the answers are not just as important. One does not rightly ask a question about ethical issues without proposing at least a possible answer, and when dealing with ethical questions, as Dewey and Tufts suggest, the ultimate end of our questioning is action. Thus, in the end, practice triumphs over theory in ethics, a view which has also been defended recently by philosophy professor James Sterba. In the Conclusion to *The Triumph of Practice over Theory in Ethics*, Sterba distinguishes between a "warmaking way of doing philosophy" and a "peacemaking way of doing philosophy." He writes:

> Those who engage in a peacemaking way of doing philosophy are committed to:
>
> 1. a fair-mindedness which, among other things, puts the more favorable interpretation on the views of one's opponents,
> 2. an openness which reaches out to understand challenging new views,
> 3. a self-criticalness that requires modifying or abandoning one's views should the weight of available evidence require it.

Not only do these valuable commitments make peace, but they are especially important for the cases studies approach to ethics that we have developed in this book, as they facilitate the kind of dialogue and collective moral creativity that leads to good actions for the benefit of us all.

In earlier chapters, you have had the opportunity to engage in critical and creative thinking about several ethics case studies. These have been introduced for suggested methods of information gathering and research, for developing questions about case studies, for thinking creatively about solutions to ethics questions, and for creating and evaluating arguments about cases. In this chapter, the goal is to synthesize the information presented in previous chapters so that you can engage in sustained analysis and evaluation of a single case from start to finish. For this process, we offer hypothetical elements of analysis and suggestions that you may use as a partial guide to answering the questions on the case study at the end of the chapter.

So, consider the following case study and follow along with the processes that might be involved in attempting to determine the good questions to ask and the good thing or the right thing to do regarding it. The processes are those you have seen in previous chapters; you must understand and take into account the factual issues and features of the case and determine whether more information is needed regarding claims made in the case. Once you understand the nature of the moral case presented, you need to determine what questions to ask about it. You then need to deal with concepts and principles from ethical theories to begin to try to answer the moral questions you have posed, and you also need the tools of basic logical analysis to be able to formulate and justify your own position on the case. Further, you will need to take into account potential objections to your position—they should be interpreted as favorably as possible—and be prepared to answer counter-arguments and perhaps even to change your mind when your own position is shown to be weak or when another position is more compelling than your own. To see the full complexity of moral reasoning think of the following case as an introduction to ethical case analysis, from a beginning appraisal of factual elements of the case to the development of your own moral position concerning the issues.

Case: Medical Marijuana

David is a registered nurse at a local hospital who works in a critical care oncology unit. In the state in which David lives, medical marijuana is illegal even though studies have shown that it is helpful in many cases for cancer patients. One of David's patients, a 68-year old woman in the last stages of advanced cancer whose life expectancy is less than one year, asked David to help her to obtain a significant amount of marijuana so that she would have it at home to alleviate some of the symptoms of her condition and the treatments for it. The patient's physician told the woman that medical marijuana would be appropriate for her condition, but that he was unable to prescribe it or help her to obtain it. Her physician is active in the local medical community and is part of a state-wide effort to legalize the use of marijuana as an adjunct to medical treatments. David is also a member of an activist group working to legalize medical marijuana.

You should read the case critically and carefully to ensure that you have identified the relevant facts and initial questions. It is at this point that you begin to engage in factual background research on the case from the questions you have asked regarding it. It is also here that the use of a concept map will be helpful to you in organizing the facts you have identified (see Figure 7.1).

In the next concept map (see Figure 7.2 below), we have added some questions that may arise about the case, including what may be a primary question for case analysis. Questions such as the following are included: You probably wonder from what kind of cancer the patient is suffering, why the physician told her about the use of medical marijuana when it is illegal to obtain or to use it in the state in which the patient lives, whether David (or the physician) should help the patient obtain some quantity of medical marijuana, whether it is morally appropriate for the woman to ask David to help her to obtain a substance that is illegal, whether she ought to use an illegal substance at all, and so on. There are many more questions that can and perhaps should be asked. Some of them involve the factual issues of the case and others are moral questions to which factual issues will have some relevance. For example, perhaps you believe you should know something about the types of cancer and the types of cancer treatments for which medical marijuana is effective. Perhaps you should know in which states medical marijuana is legal and in which states it is illegal, and what are the relevant arguments on each side of the issue regarding its legal or illegal uses. You probably considered the distinction between what is illegal and what is immoral, and you may have asked yourself, even if you believe that marijuana use is immoral under ordinary circumstances, whether there are moral reasons that the woman ought to have access to it. Let's say that from your point of view, the main or primary question regarding the medical marijuana case this: Should a cancer patient have access to medical marijuana when it will be helpful in treatment? Once you ask yourself whether the cancer patient ought to have access to medical marijuana, you have begun the process of moral reasoning about the issue because you have identified what you believe is a main or major moral question—that is, the good question—to ask about the case. Remember, however, that there are other questions that may arise as you begin to conceptualize the issues revolving around the use of medical marijuana for cancer patients.

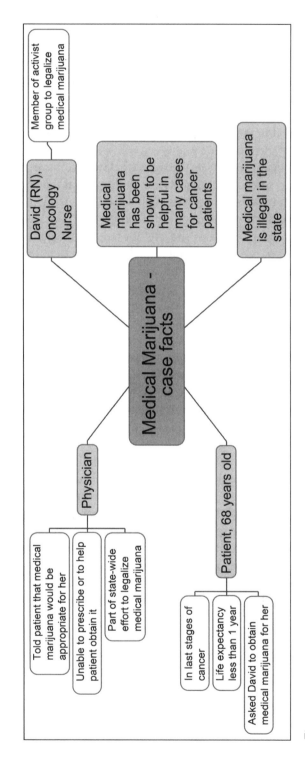

Figure 7.1

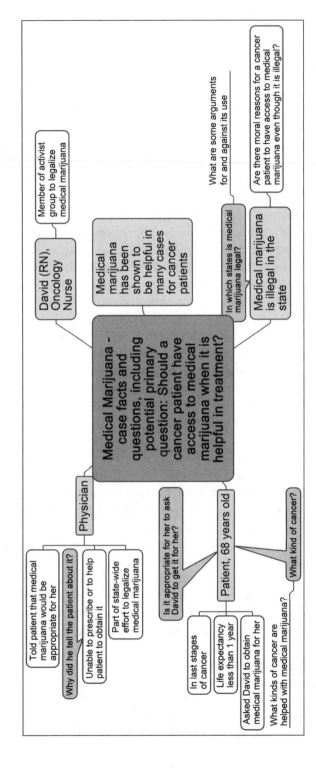

Figure 7.2

Creative Case Analysis

As you begin to conceptualize the case and apply creative thinking to it, additional questions and possibilities for research and analysis may arise, and if possible, brainstorming with others will lead to new ideas for consideration. For example, perhaps you wonder whether there are other diseases and conditions for which medical marijuana is effective. You may then begin to wonder whether it might be that your primary question regarding whether cancer patients ought to have access to medical marijuana should be stated more generally for any disease or condition. You might ask yourself whether it would be helpful or necessary to know the kind of cancer from which the woman in the case study is suffering, and your answer to this question may affect the way in which you evaluate and analyze the case. Assume you believe that without knowing the kind of cancer from which the woman in the case study suffers, you cannot make an informed decision about whether she, in particular, ought to have access to medical marijuana. Your thoughts in this instance do not lead you properly to believe that it is not possible to evaluate this case, or to believe you cannot construct arguments and make a decision about the moral issues embedded in it, since your thoughts may instead turn more generally to the use of medical marijuana for *any* disease, condition, or treatment for which it has been shown to be helpful.

Further, in light of the fact that medical marijuana is legal in some states and illegal in others, you propose to do an "intercultural comparison" of the different states—as each state may be seen to have its own distinct culture—and this naturally leads you to want to consider other countries and conduct research on those that support the use of medical marijuana. Also, a creative case analysis includes at least a preliminary application of ethical theories or concepts. Remember that you will need to do research on the background information on the case, including the diseases and treatments for which medical marijuana is effective and arguments from credible sources about states' decisions to legalize or not to legalize marijuana. Where such arguments include moral reasons, you will have valuable information to consider in forming and justifying your own position on the case study. There may, in addition, be other questions you thought to include that we have not included in Figure 7.2 above.

For now, let's take a look at some potential uses of ethical theories, principles, or concepts with respect to the case. Start with the facts and questions in the 1 o'clock position in the concept map in Figure 7.2. David is an oncology nurse, an RN who is a member of an activist group to legalize medical marijuana. One of the activities in which activists often engage is civil disobedience, where "civil disobedience" is not a matter of flaunting laws, rules, and procedures, but instead acting in ways that challenge such legal or moral requirements where they are justifiably thought not to apply. A historical example may be instructive here.

In his essay, "Civil Disobedience" (1849), Henry David Thoreau recounts the reasons for his incarceration for refusing to pay taxes. His position was that the Mexican-American War was unjust, and to pay taxes is to support an unjust war. Thoreau therefore decided that the appropriate course of action was to violate the law to make his point because acquiescing in the current and expected social course of events was tantamount to injustice and immorality. Perhaps David in our case about the use of medical marijuana would, given his activism on the issue, try to honor his patient's request as a matter of principle as well as to attempt to alleviate her suffering. On the other hand, case analysis in this context is not to try to second-guess David, but to try to determine for yourself what considerations might apply in making your decision on whether people who are ill and who would be helped by the use of medical marijuana morally ought to have access to it. So instead of trying to figure out whether David might decide to violate the law and procure some amount of medical marijuana for the patient, it is up to you to try to decide whether it is right and good for him to do so. You may be able to justify the position that it is right and good to do so by looking further into the moral dimensions of civil disobedience in works such as those of Martin Luther King, Jr., and John Rawls, for example, and deciding, based on what you have learned from that research, whether civil disobedience as a moral concept applies in this case.

Moving through the concept map in Figure 7.2, at the 3 o'clock and 5 o'clock positions are the factual statements that medical marijuana has been shown to be helpful in many cases for cancer patients, but that it is illegal in the state in which the patient in the case lives. Now, depending on the type and amount of background research in which you may have engaged, you may have looked beyond the use of medical marijuana for cancer patients and found that it has been shown in at least some scientific and medical studies to be helpful for other diseases, conditions, and the side effects of medical treatments as well. Perhaps due to that research, you have thought that considerations such as the alleviation of pain and suffering are morally significant, and taking a utilitarian stance on the issue, you believe that utilitarian concerns to create the greatest happiness for the greatest number, or in this case to alleviate or to eliminate pain and suffering, are applicable. On the other hand, you may have also thought about the obligations people have to honor and follow laws, and since the legal system in the state in which the cancer patient lives does not allow the use of medical marijuana, it may very well also be the case that it is immoral to permit its use. You may reach this conclusion on the basis of your conviction that the general civil and social fabric of society would be in peril if everyone simply violated laws whenever they saw fit and for whatever reason, and due to your concern for social order and the agreements that people make, explicitly or implicitly, by living in any given society or social system, it is incumbent upon them not to break the law. That is, you believe that it is not simply illegal to obtain medical marijuana, you may also believe, based on contractarian factors applied to the case, that it is immoral to obtain and use medical marijuana regardless of the benefits to patients.

You may believe it necessary and pertinent to consider the elements of the case having to do specifically with the conditions surrounding the 68-year old cancer patient. We know, for example, that she is in the last stages of cancer, that her life expectancy is less than one year, and that she has asked David, the RN, to obtain medical marijuana for her. While we do not know from this case study the type of cancer from which the woman is suffering, it may be irrelevant since there are, as you would find from your background research, types of cancer for which medical marijuana is helpful and effective. So even though it is conceivable that medical marijuana may not be helpful to this particular patient for her particular cancer (that is, perhaps her physician is wrong), it is impossible to know whether it will be helpful to her without the woman having had access to it. On the other hand, your background research probably yielded information on the rates of success in alleviating symptoms among cancer patients for whom medical marijuana has been deemed helpful or efficacious, in which case you can use that information even without knowing the type of cancer from which the woman suffers.

But what kind of theory should you apply? That is, do you take into account the ethics of care, the ethics of character (virtue ethics), contractarianism, utilitarianism, deontology, or some other? The answer to this question is up to you, but for our explanatory purpose here, let's assume that you believe the ethics of care to be most applicable, because you believe, in addition, that since David has chosen to work as an RN and that nursing is a caring profession, David ought to be moved by the plight of his patient. On the other hand, you consider that the patient has asked David to do something illegal for her benefit, and you wonder whether it is morally justifiable for her to have done so on the basis of Kantian ethics where, for example, we might assume that David has an obligation not only to his patients, but also to the standards of the profession of which he is a practitioner, and doing something illegal is contrary to his professional obligations.

Moving to the 11 o'clock position on the concept map in Figure 7.2, we come to the physician, his efforts to legalize medical marijuana, and what he has told his patient regarding the appropriateness in her case of medical marijuana, but that he is unable to prescribe or to obtain it for her. It may be at this point that our original question—Should a cancer patient have access to medical marijuana when it will be helpful in treatment?— which has been transformed into a more general question about the moral acceptability of the use of medical marijuana for any medical condition, now branches out into the question whether there is anyone in particular who has an obligation to provide the patient with medical marijuana even if it is illegal. Earlier in the discussion, we skirted that issue, pointing out that it is your position that matters here, but this case brings to the forefront of discussion a very important point about ethical cases and ethical reasoning: it is part of the very nature of ethics, its social and dynamic dimensions, that decisions and arguments made about ethical issues are not the concern of a single, isolated moral agent making a general decision that applies to everyone, but that it may sometimes also be the case that our arguments turn toward what ought to be done by some specific person in some specific condition. This case therefore illustrates both the importance and centrality of a major question to be asked about a case and the fact that it may very well turn out that subsidiary moral questions about what some person ought to do are relevant and important as well.

If you believe that there are such subsidiary moral questions concerning the physician, what are they? Perhaps you wonder whether the physician should have told the woman about medical marijuana being efficacious for her condition and treatment at all, especially since she is apparently very ill and is most likely not in any condition to obtain the substance on her own. On the other hand, perhaps the physician is behaving in a civilly disobedient way, telling her about the use of medical marijuana for her condition so that she will know that, medically speaking, it is in his professional opinion good for her to try to obtain it in some way on her own. Our thoughts about the nurse, David, who is a member of an activist group to legalize marijuana, are also applicable to the physician in similar ways. But there may be even more to the case with respect to the physician since the physician is bound by the Hippocratic Oath. Perhaps it is relevant and important in your evaluation of the case to familiarize yourself with the Hippocratic

Oath, with any statements of physicians' obligations from the American Medical Association, and other relevant organizations. These facts may help you to determine how to evaluate any part of the case having to do with the physician and his actions.

Suppose for this case that you have read the Hippocratic Oath, and on the basis of what you understand of that aspect of the medical profession combined with your understanding of ethical theory, you have noted the same sort of conflict in the case of the physician that you noted with respect to the nurse. That is, the physician has an obligation in a caring profession to look out for the best good of those for whom he is responsible for care, but he also has obligations to the professional organizations that in some ways govern his behavior in that profession.

Let's say at this point that you have completed your background research and you have formed a position on the issue of whether medical marijuana ought to be available to a patient when it is helpful in that person's treatment. Assume that your conclusion is that it is not morally justifiable for any patient to have access to medical marijuana. In the next section, we will construct an argument for this conclusion based on hypothetical background research and the use of ethical theories and principles.

Formulating and Arguing for Your Position

Your reasoning about the issue and how you reach the conclusion constitute your argument, and your argument, to be both persuasive and acceptable from a logical as well as a moral point of view, must contain good reasoning (that is, it must be composed of true, factual information; it must satisfy requirements of relevance; and it must have sufficient information to make the case you wish to put forward). Your position will become well-formed and your argument will be expanded with: (a) the tools of logical analysis, especially the application of the conditions or criteria for cogent reasoning from Chapter 2, (b) methodical and careful reading of the case as in Chapter 3, (c) identification of facts and questions for research as discussed in Chapter 4, (d) identification of creative solutions to help to guide and sharpen the construction of your position, as explored in Chapter 5, and (e) careful formulation and argumentation for your position as indicated in Chapters 4 and 6.

For the medical marijuana case study, "your" argument appears in the following concept map (Figure 7.3). Note that for explanatory purposes, we have intentionally formulated "your" argument with some weaknesses. Remember, too, that in reading a concept map for argument construction

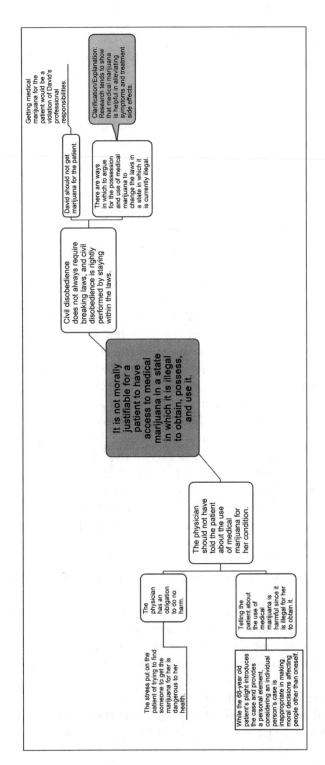

Figure 7.3

and visualization, read the map from the outside to the inside. For the format of the map below, where any information appearing at the outer edges of the map is a premise, information appearing between the premises and the main conclusion is either an intermediate conclusion or a clarification of a statement, and the statement in the middle of the map is the conclusion to which all the reasons are intended to lead.

The map in Figure 7.3 shows the structure of an argument in which the author contends that it is not morally justifiable for a patient to have access to medical marijuana in a state in which it is illegal to obtain, possess, and use it. On the right side of the map the reasons are given, moving from the outer edge of the map to the main conclusion.

Assume that you are the author of this argument and you hold the position, based on your background research about the obligations of oncology nurses, that it would be a violation of David's professional responsibilities to obtain medical marijuana for the 68-year old patient in the case study, which leads you to the conclusion that David should not get medical marijuana for the patient. Further, however, you agree that medical marijuana is shown to tend to be helpful in alleviating symptoms and treatment side effects, but also that there are ways in which to argue for possession and use of medical marijuana to change the laws. So while you agree that it tends to be helpful, medical marijuana is, from your point of view, an issue that might properly be the subject of legal argument to change the laws. By combining your intermediate conclusion that David should not get medical marijuana for the patient with your claim that there are ways to change the laws through argument, you conclude that civil disobedience does not always require breaking laws. From this, you claim in a suppressed or implied statement that obtaining medical marijuana for the patient would be an act of disobedience, but since getting medical marijuana for her is illegal, and because you have concluded that civil disobedience is rightly performed only by staying within the laws, you conclude that it is unjustified for the patient to have access to medical marijuana in a state in which it is illegal.

Further, on the left side of the map, you take into account the position or situation of the physician in the medical marijuana case. Here, you reach the intermediate conclusion that the physician should not have told the patient about the use of medical marijuana for her condition. Your reasons for this are that the primary obligation of the physician is to do no harm. You believe, however, that it would be stressful for the patient to try to obtain medical marijuana when it is illegal in her state to possess or use it, so the physician telling her that it would be helpful to her actually creates a condition in which the patient is put under undue stress. In addition, you believe that, as a matter of clarification in the argument, it is inappropriate to consider the condition or plight of any individual patient in making a decision on the moral rightness or wrongness of the use of medical marijuana for people other than oneself.

The previous claims are, in short, your position on the case. Let's say that you believe that you have argued sufficiently for your position. The fact that you believe this is the case does not mean that other people will think the same.

Engaging in Dialogue and Considering the Viewpoints of Others

Let's assume that you have constructed the argument represented in part by Figure 7.3 and that you present your argument in writing or verbally to one or more people. Remember that your concept map will not contain every word or element of your reasoning. A concept map is a visual representation of the major points of your argument. It is necessary to fill in the details, sources, and clarify inferences verbally or in writing when presenting your position to others. Your audience may agree with your conclusion without at the same time agreeing that your reasoning leading to that conclusion is as good as it should be. Or, your audience may disagree with your conclusion while recognizing that some of your reasoning contains partially justifiable but largely insufficient reasoning. Of course, your audience may take any number of stances regarding your position and argument. In fact, your audience may have its or their own different way of conceiving of the case. For now, we turn to a potential audience (reader or hearer) member's analysis of your overall argument and its particular inferences.

Looking at the right side of the map in Figure 7.3, your argument is that David would violate his professional responsibilities by obtaining medical marijuana for the patient, so he should not obtain it for her. In this inference, have you made a clear distinction between types of obligations that David may have? For example, have you shown that David's professional obligations are moral obligations, and even if you have done so, does the fact (if it is a fact) that he has such a professional responsibility or obligation clash with what might be argued from a different point of view to be an obligation to obtain medical marijuana for the patient? In other words, is there a conflict of moral obligations shown in your first inference at the top right of the map in Figure 7.3? If so, you need to clarify the nature of the conflict and attempt to show how the conflict can be resolved (if in fact it can be resolved). Further, what is the source of your information on

David's professional obligations? Is it a reliable source? Is there a code of ethics for RNs who work in oncology, or is there a specific statement of the obligations of RNs at the hospital in which David works? In other words, when you present your argument, you need to make it clear in your prose (written argumentation) or in speech the source(s) of your information so that those who are attending to your argument will know whether the information you are presenting is accurate, current, reliable, and so on.

Moving inward from the right side of the concept-mapped argument, you claim that there are "ways" to argue for the possession and use of medical marijuana to change the laws of the state in which it is now illegal. What ways are they? Suppose that you assert in a written form of your argument that people might engage in a drive to sign a petition to send to the state capitol. From this premise, you conclude that civil disobedience does not always require breaking laws and that it is rightly performed by staying within the laws. Your audience may wonder at this point whether you understand the nature of civil disobedience. You have, in this hypothetical inference, given the example of a way to change the laws through petitions and signature drives. There is nothing civilly disobedient in doing so, so the inference to claims regarding civil disobedience in your intermediate conclusion suffers from irrelevance in two ways: first, a non-civilly disobedient action does not lead to a conclusion about civilly disobedient actions; second, your argument exhibits a misunderstanding about the nature of civil disobedience, leading to your intermediate conclusion's weakness. Since the intermediate conclusion about the nature of civil disobedience is claimed to follow from an irrelevant premise, and it is itself either highly questionable or false, you have not sufficiently established the conclusion.

Now turn to the left side of the concept map in Figure 7.3. Here, you claim that since it is stressful for the patient to engage in the process of trying to obtain medical marijuana, the physician has created conditions that may harm the patient. You add to this notion that the physician also has a moral obligation to do no harm, from which it follows that the physician should not have told the patient about the use of medical marijuana. Your audience, however, may note here that there may be a distinction between what is good for a patient to know and what a patient has a right or a reasonable expectation to know from her or his physician. So, even though the physician may have a moral obligation arising from the Hippocratic Oath not to harm his patient, it does not necessarily follow that he should not have told her about it. There may, for example, be other obligations to which the physician is bound that override the arguably minor harm that would come to the patient from the "stress" of trying to obtain medical marijuana. In fact, there is nothing in the case stating or indicating that the physician told the woman that she should go about trying to obtain it; the physician told his patient that it would be helpful, but that he could not get it for her. It is an unjustified stretch of the imagination to go from what a physician tells a patient will be helpful to claiming that the physician has told the patient to obtain that thing. But more, even if it were true that the physician should not have told the patient about the use of medical marijuana, it does not follow from that fact that it is not morally justifiable for a patient to have access to it. You may be able to think of analogous cases showing that there are reasons that some particular person ought not to have been told or informed of a particular fact that do not lead to the claim that *no one* ought to have access to or know about the fact. This is a clear case of hasty conclusion, a violation of the strength requirement in that what may be true of one person does not imply or lead us reasonably to believe that the claim is true about *all* people.

The Significance of Dialogue

Going through all of these steps in analyzing a moral issue or case takes time and care in gathering facts and assessing the moral impact and reasoning involved in justifying your position. In addition, similar processes are involved in evaluating the reasoning put forth by others regarding a case study.

For example, suppose that you and your brother are debating the issue of the use of medical marijuana by the cancer patient and you both agree that it is acceptable for her to have access to it and to use it, but you have different reasons for holding that position. You may both have good arguments to offer in support of your claims, and in fact it may be possible for you to combine your independent reasons and facts to create a more complete and persuasive position than either of you might have derived by yourselves. On the other hand, you and your brother may disagree vehemently about the moral status of the use of medical marijuana, where you believe that it is justified for the use of cancer patients, but your brother believes that the use of medical marijuana is not justified in any case at all. Before you reject your brother's position out of hand—and before he rejects yours—it is essential to determine the quality and veracity of the claims made for each position and the quality of the argument or arguments put forward for both of your positions. It will not do simply to assert that you are right and your brother is wrong and believe that in doing so you have settled the issue. He is not likely to be moved simply by the strength of your conviction, and you are not likely to be moved simply by the forcefulness of his tone of voice. Instead, you both need to take the time and effort to investigate the matter fully so that you can make the best decision regarding the moral issue(s) in the case.

Disagreeing with your brother, and evaluating his claims, is best and most appropriately approached not by simply stating your position again, but instead by looking into the nature of his argument, and by your brother looking into your argument, and trying to determine whether there are errors in reasoning or factual problems in the presentation of your individual cases. Simply showing that your argument is stronger than that of your brother does not mean that his argument is weak in and of itself, nor does his showing that his argument is stronger than yours in some particular way indicate that your argument is to be rejected. There may be points in both of your arguments that deserve and require further investigation to make the best decision regarding the case of which you are both capable.

What we are saying about a hypothetical disagreement between you and your brother can also be said about disagreements between you and your fellow citizens, who may charitably be considered brothers and sisters in an extended sense. Thinking in this way leads us to the field of "deliberative democracy," which emphasizes the need for people of different backgrounds and perspectives to come together in civil dialogue. If done well, people may better understand one another and come to see options that were not seen before.

Remember what was said earlier in this book about the importance of openness—a necessary condition of genuine questioning—and listening, and add to that Sterba's related points on fair-mindedness and self-criticalness at the beginning this chapter. Applied together, these concepts lead to genuine dialogue, which is essentially ethical in that it seeks to encounter and engage with the other where she or he is in her or his understanding, rather than seeking to dominate or master her or him by trying to find as many faults in the understanding as possible. In *Truth and Method* Gadamer explains the special experience of relating to another person or a "Thou." He writes:

> It is clear that the *experience of the Thou* must be special because the Thou is not an object but is in relationship with us. . . . Since here the object of experience is a person, this kind of experience is a moral phenomenon—as is the knowledge acquired through experience, the understanding of the other person. . . . In human relations the important thing is, as we have

seen, to experience the Thou truly as a Thou—i.e., not to overlook his claim but to let him really say something to us. . . . Here is where openness belongs. . . . Without such openness to one another there is no genuine human bond. . . . Openness to the other, then, involves recognizing that I myself must accept some things that are against me, even though no one else forces me to do so.

For Gadamer the essence of philosophy is such dialogue, and this suggests that philosophy is essentially ethical in nature.

Concluding Comments on Processes in Case Study Analysis

Remembering that moral issues are almost always public issues is important in the analysis of arguments and in the associated decision-making in which you and others engage. It is possible that a bill to allow the use of medical marijuana in your state will appear on a ballot for your vote.While you may find it easy simply to vote based on what you feel at some given moment, keep in mind that the lives and welfare of others—and perhaps someday your own welfare—are affected by your vote on the issue, which should be incentive for you to look more deeply into it and make a decision based on good information and sound reasoning.

Formulating positions and making decisions on moral issues is what this book is about. It is about ethics and reasoning; it is about asking good questions (questions that are in themselves good to ask and questions that are about what is good); it is about answering those questions using the best information and the best reasoning at your disposal, and it is about making decisions based on the answers to the questions you have asked that are also focused on the good.

As you can see from the medical marijuana case, there are several steps involved in trying to solve moral problems or answer moral questions. The process begins with (1) a careful identification and assessment of the facts of the case. It proceeds with (2) engaging in background research on the facts and in asking questions about the facts. Further, your research and reasoning activity moves forward through (3) asking questions about the moral issue(s) in the case, and it proceeds through (4) using ethical theories and principles, combined with the facts you have from the case and that you have derived through your research, to answer the question or questions about the good (and the right) that your research has led you to develop. You will use moral theories, principles, concepts, and arguments to (5) formulate a position, but in addition you will also engage in critical and creative thinking to (6) propose potential solutions to problems and answers to the moral questions you have asked. Of course, engaging in this six-step process takes time, as you will be immersed in careful research, critical questioning, ethical reasoning, and philosophical dialogue. But more, this process highlights and teaches the importance of teamwork and collaboration, and it allows for the chance to discover, appreciate, and use a wide variety of approaches to solve moral problems and answer moral questions. We are confident that by engaging in this six-step process involving asking good questions, you will ultimately succeed in formulating the best possible answers.

Questions for Further Thinking and Discussion

1. Consider the concept map of the facts and questions for further research for the medical marijuana case. Are there other facts about the case that need to be added to the map? Are there additional questions that should be asked regarding the medical marijuana case? Explain.

2. Even though there is a primary question for the case identified in the medical marijuana case, what are at least three other important and potential primary questions that could be asked about it? Explain.

3. Research some sources that discuss the issue of medical marijuana that are both philosophical (use the *Philosopher's Index*) and popular (e.g., news and media). What source(s) do you find that are most significant for understanding the issue?

4. Do you agree with the conclusion of the argument provided for the case in which an attempted justification of the position that medical marijuana use is unjustified is offered? If you do not agree with the conclusion, why is that the case? Explain. If you do agree with the conclusion, but you have a different way to argue for it, what is that argument? How is it better than—or how does it enhance—the argument provided in the discussion in the chapter?

5. In concept-mapped form, provide additional evaluation of the reasoning contained in the argument regarding the medical marijuana case. Are there any instances of violation of the criteria for cogent reasoning (truth, relevance, and sufficient information) in the argument? What are they? How might they be corrected? How do they affect the overall quality of the argument?

6. Is civil disobedience ever morally justified? If so, why, and under what conditions? If not, why not?

7. Are there alternative ways to conceptualize and analyze cases that are different from the 6-step process of reasoning involved in case study analysis? Explain.

References and Suggestions for Further Reading

Cavalier, Robert, ed. *Approaching Deliberative Democracy: Theory and Practice*. Carnegie Mellon University Press, 2011.

Gadamer, Hans-Georg. *Truth and Method*. 2nd ed. Trans. Joel Weinsheimer and Donald G. Marshall. Continuum, 2004. The quotation above is from pages 352 and 355.

Hippocrates. "The Oath" (400 BCE). The Internet Classics Archive. Trans. Francis Adams. Available at http://classics.mit.edu/Hippocrates/hippooath.html.

King, Martin Luther Jr. *Letter from the Birmingham Jail*. HarperCollins, 1st ed., 1994.

Sterba, James P. *The Triumph of Practice over Theory in Ethics*. Oxford University Press, 2005. The quotation on the peacemaking way of doing philosophy is from page 156.

Thoreau, Henry David. "Civil Disobedience" in *Civil Disobedience and Other Essays*. Dover Publications, 1993.

Appendix

SAMPLE CASES

Case 1: Crime Deterrence

In July of 2013, the City of Cincinnati, Ohio, police department embarked on a program to attempt to reduce the number of juvenile shooting victims. Over the last five years, according to the report from WCPO in Cincinnati, there has been a 200% increase in juvenile shooting victims. The program will invite or require teenagers who are involved in gangs and drugs to attend meetings at a local school in which the "teens will see gruesome photos of gunshot survivors" in an attempt to "make some at-risk teens think about their lifestyle."

Lt. Joe Richardson commented that "You're not killed, but you're walking around with a colostomy bag and that's just not the way to get a girl's attention by limping down Warsaw Avenue with a colostomy bag." In addition, the TV news station provided a link in the text associated with their video report to the Robert Wood Johnson Foundation's article, "For Gunshot Survivors, Wounds that Don't Heal," in which one victim's story revolved around the revulsion and shame associated with having a colostomy.

The response from the Ostomy community was quick. The President of the United Ostomy Associations of America, David B. Rudzin, wrote a letter to Jay Warren, a WCPO-TV reporter on the story, who then forwarded the letter to the Vice President and General Manager of WCPO. The Cincinnati Police Department's Interim Chief, Paul Humphries, wrote a letter of apology to representatives of the United Ostomy Associations of America in which he stated that there was no "ill will intended" but "the results were hurtful to some in the ostomy community." He indicated that it was "a mistake on the part of well-meaning individuals and not a deliberate attempt to offend anyone."

Some members of the www.ostomy.org discussion forum commented on the issue, with some believing that the use of the colostomy example would be effective in reducing gun violence and injuries and was not offensive to ostomists while others took a more negative approach. Further, however, the representative and spokesperson for uncoverostomy.org, Jessica Grossman, posted a comment on July 31, 2013, on Uncover Ostomy's blog that she is "beside (herself) with anger. Anger towards the Cincinnati Police Department." Jessica notes that "the point of this campaign, while a noble cause, is extremely misguided and ignorant. It's just another example of the negative stigma still out there." She closes with this: "By the way, Joe? I can guarantee that if you saw me on Warsaw Avenue—I'd get your attention."

REFERENCES:

Grossman, Jessica. IDEAS (Intestinal Disease Education and Awareness Society) Uncover Ostomy Awareness Campaign: http://uncoverostomy .org/blog/.

Multiple Authors, United Ostomy Associations of America website and discussion board: https://www.ostomy.org/forum/viewtopic.php?f= 2&t=23134.

Robert Wood Johnson Foundation. "For Gunshot Survivors, Wounds that Don't Heal," http://www.rwjf.org/en/about-rwjf/newsroom/newsroom -content/2012/07/for-gunshot-survivors--wounds-that-don-t-heal.html.

Warren, Jay. "Cincinnati Police Hope to Sway Teens with Photos of Colostomy Bags, Paralyzed Shooting Victims," (video and text) http://www .wcpo.com/news/cincinnati-police-hope-to-sway-teens-with-photos-of-colostomy-bags-paralyzed-shooting-victims.

Case 2: Child Custody

Over the past decade, there has been a significant increase in the numbers of grandparents who take over care of their grandchildren when the parents are unemployed, incarcerated, drug-addicted, or otherwise unable or unwilling to care for their children. Some grandparents seek temporary or permanent legal custody of the grandchildren for whom they provide care so that they will become eligible for foodstamps, medicaid, and other aid to families with dependent children, which is especially important for elderly grandparents living on fixed incomes and for whom care of grandchildren is a significant financial commitment. That grandparents seek custody of grandchildren is often a point of contention for the parents, who do not want to lose the ability to claim their children on income tax returns and in many cases receive earned income credit as an additional benefit. Many parents wish someday to be able to regain custody of their children once their living conditions improve, and fear that they will be unable to get their children back.

Robert and Fiona, the parents of two children under the age of 8, are both unemployed. Robert has recently completed a 12-step program and is actively seeking employment. Fiona, however, is both drug-addicted and an alcoholic who has been arrested several times in the past for neglecting her children. Fiona's parents, Edna and Roy, have filed for permanent custody of Robert and Fiona's children. Robert's parents also want custody of the children, claiming that Edna and Roy are unfit guardians because they allow their daughter to live in their home where the children also live, and since Fiona is an alcoholic and drug addicted, it is an environment unfit for the children to live in.

Case 3: Baseball Ethics I

Baseball is generally considered to be a non-contact sport. Unlike the other major team sports, it is possible, if not a frequent occurrence, for a baseball game to end without any direct contact between opposing players. Of course, runners may be tagged by defensive players, and they may occasionally try to slide into an opposing player (usually a shortstop or a catcher), but there is very limited opportunity to inflict direct harm unto another player, unlike in football or hockey. Major League Baseball has even started a process to eliminate home plate collisions from the game because of the threat of dangerous injury that it brings. However, it is still possible for a pitcher to throw a baseball directly at a batter in order to intentionally hit him. This practice has long been considered to be an accepted part of the game, and today the majority of pitchers are capable of throwing balls at speeds around 100 mph and thus able to cause permanent, even fatal, injury.

On August 19, 2013, in a game between the arch-rival New York Yankees and the Boston Red Sox, the Boston pitcher Ryan Dempster faced Alex Rodriguez, who had recently returned to play following the appeal of an unprecedented 211–game suspension issued to Rodriguez (or "A-Rod") for his alleged use of performance-enhancing drugs acquired from the Florida clinic Biogenesis of America. (While the ethical question of whether the use of performance-enhancing substances by professional athletes should be permitted can also be considered, that is not the issue here.) What happened during Rodriguez's first at-bat against Dempster in the second inning shocked many in the baseball world. The first pitched delivered sailed behind Rodriguez's back, obviously communicating that Dempster wasn't happy with A-Rod's return to play. Dempster continued with two close, inside fastballs that brushed Rodriguez back off the plate, and then with a 3-0 count against the Yankee slugger, the fourth pitch that was thrown directly to hit Rodriguez in the back as he tried to turn away from the pitch.

The home plate umpire immediately issued a warning to both benches and the Yankee manager Joe Girardi stormed furiously out of the dugout to argue with the umpire. Girardi was ejected from the game and afterwards said this in an interview: "That baseball is a weapon. It's not a tennis ball. Or it's not an Incrediball that's soft. It's a weapon, and it can do a lot of damage to someone's life. And that's why I was so upset about it. You can express your opinion and be upset with someone, but you just can't start throwing baseballs at people. I mean, it's scary." Girardi also communicated to the press what he told his 6-year-old son, Dante: "Part of pitching is pitching inside, that's all part of it, but I don't ever want you to hit anyone on purpose."

As expected, most reactions to the incident seemed to depend upon which side of the rivalry one is on. Both Dempster and the Red Sox manager John Farrell denied that hitting Rodriguez was intentional, but ESPN analyst and former World Series Champion pitcher for the Boston Red Sox, Curt Schilling, said, "It was as intentional as it gets. Umpires are given the leeway to eject on their own call. That was intentional and that's what you were supposed to do, is eject the pitcher and the manager together." Regarding Rodriguez still being allowed to play major league baseball, Boston pitcher John Lackey said, "I've got a problem with it. You bet I do. How is he still playing? He obviously did something and he's playing. I'm not sure that's right . . . It's pretty evident he's been doing stuff for a lot of years I've been facing him." On the other side of the dugout Yankees pitcher C.C. Sabathia said, "You don't throw at a guy four times. He [Dempster] violated every code in every way."

Girardi offered perhaps the most passionate statement: "You can't start throwing at people. I mean lives, I mean people have had concussions, I mean lives are changed by people getting hit by pitches. You know, whether I agree about everything that is going on, you do not throw at people. You don't take the law into your own hands. You don't do that. . . . What is wrong with people? You cheer when someone gets hit? You know, I'm going to say it again, what if that was your son? You know, what if, what if your son got hit? Breaks an arm, gets hit in the head, has a concussion? . . . Man, I'd be embarrassed. I see little kids in the stands, wonder what's wrong with our world today."

Rodriguez had little to say afterward, but let his bat do the talking on the field by hitting a home run off Dempster on his second at-bat of the game. Although the Yankees went on to win the game, they failed to make the playoffs, and the Boston Red Sox went on to win the 2013 World Series.

REFERENCES:

Blum, Ronald. "Red Sox pitch hits A-Rod, Yankees manager cries 'foul'," *Komo*
     news.com, August 20, 2013. Available at: http://www.komonews.com/
     sports/Red-Sox-pitch-hits-A-Rod-Yankees-call-for-suspension—2203
     72481.html.
Dubow, Josh. "Dempster suspended five games for hitting A-Rod with
     pitch," *The Norman Transcript*, August 21, 2013. Available at: http://
     www.huffingtonpost.com/2013/08/18/a-rod-hit-pitch-ryan-dempster-
     girardi-ejected-video_n_3777365.htmlhttp://normantranscript.com/
     sports/x312411645/Dempster-suspended-five-games-for-hitting-A-Rod
     -with-pitch.
"Girardi on A-Rod getting hit," Video at *MLB.com*, August 18, 2013. Avail-
     able at: http://normantranscript.com/sports/x312411645/Dempster-
     suspended-five-games-for-hitting-A-Rod-with-pitchhttp://wapc.mlb
     .com/nyy/play/?content_id=29850797&query=girardi%2Bon%2Barod
     %2Band%2Bdempster.
Klopman, Michael. "A-Rod Hit By Ryan Dempster, Joe Girardi Ejected In
     Yankees-Red Sox Game," *The Huffington Post*, August 18, 2013. Avail-
     able at: http://www.komonews.com/sports/Red-Sox-pitch-hits-A-Rod-
     Yankees-call-for-suspension—220372481.htmlhttp://www.huffington
     post.com/2013/08/18/a-rod-hit-pitch-ryan-dempster-girardi-ejected
     -video_n_3777365.html.

Case 4: Baseball Ethics II

As suggested in Baseball Ethics I, a related case for consideration involves the actual use of performance-enhancing substances in baseball in particular, and even in professional sports in general. Should such substances (note that to call them "drugs" already seems to suggest something bad) be allowed? And if so, under what conditions could they be ethically justifiable? For a discussion of the question "Should Steroids Be Banned?" see Michael J. McGrath (Yes) and Simon Eassom (No) in *Baseball and Philosophy: Thinking Outside the Batter's Box*, edited by Eric Bronson (Chicago, IL: Open Court, 2004), pp. 313–318.

Case 5: DisenCHANted?

Charlie Chan is a fictional Chinese-Hawaiian detective, created by novelist Earl Derr Biggers. Biggers published six enormously successful Charlie Chan novels between 1925 and 1931. Two silent Charlie Chan movies were made in the 1920s, followed by about four dozen more films, several radio programs, two television shows, and numerous comic book series over the next decades.

While cleaning out old files at Warner Brothers-Seven Arts Studios, vice president Harvey Chertok discovered a forgotten 1968 Charlie Chan documentary. Controversy erupted when the documentary was screened at the New York Chapter of the National Academy of Television Arts and Sciences in February 2010. While some film aficionados consider Charlie Chan to be an international entertainment icon who challenged many negative perceptions about the Chinese, detractors charge that the depiction of the Chinese-American detective is offensive racial stereotyping.

Critics call the portrayal of Chan by non-Asian actors in yellowface degrading. Chan's mangled singsong English and kitschy pseudo-Confucian aphorisms provoked ridicule: some older Asian Americans report that growing up they were mocked by Charlie Chan-inspired racial taunts. Chan's sons' flippant attitude toward their father's methodical investigations undermined the traditional value of respect for elders. Critics charged that Chan's apparent subservience to whites and his failure to respond to racial slurs encouraged offensive treatment and the perception of inferiority of Asian Americans.

Supporters counter that the first Chan films using Asian actors were commercially unsuccessful, and only when popular Caucasian movie stars played the detective did the movies become commercially viable. It was not racial bias, but rather business interests that dictated the choice of actors. The novelist Earl Derr Biggers' sympathetic treatment of Charlie Chan had a positive impact on interracial relations, shattering an offensive ethnic stereotype. Charlie Chan was created during a time when federal miscegenation laws were still determinative, and the American Immigration Act of 1924 prohibited immigration of Asians as an undesirable race. There was widespread fear among Americans of the "Yellow Peril": fear that Chinese overpopulation would lead to attempts to colonize and take over the world.

Biggers based his Charlie Chan character on the Chinese-Hawaiian detective, Chang Apana, after reading about Apana in a Honolulu newspaper. Apana joined the Honolulu Police Department in 1898. An astute and scrupulous investigator, fluent in several languages, with an intimate familiarity with the city and possessing a wide network of contacts, Apana was a respected and successful detective. His single-handed arrest of 70 criminals at one time is legendary. Biggers deliberately created the Apana-based character to counter the prevalent depiction of the Chinese as menacing and inscrutably evil. Charlie Chan was wise, shrewd, honorable, benevolent, and modest. He did not react to offensive stereotyping, but used these false perceptions to his advantage to thwart evildoers.

Nearly a century later, Charlie Chan remains a beloved hero to some, and an invidious stereotype to others.

REFERENCE:

"DisenCHANted" was used in the final round of the 2011 National Intercollegiate Ethics Bowl℠ when our team from the University of Central Florida won the competition. Our student team members were Kevin Dupree, Jessica Fears, Alexander Kaplan, Ramon Lopez, Catherine Perrault, and Stephen Oldham, and the team was coached by the authors and Dr. Madi Dogariu. The Intercollegiate Ethics Bowl℠ cases are published by and may be used only with permission of The Association for Practical and Professional Ethics. (APPE, 618 East Third Street, Bloomington, Indiana 47405; Tel: (812) 855-6450; E-mail: appe@indiana.edu.)

Glossary of Key Terms

Absolutism: the view that ethical values exist independently of human perspectives, particular cultures, and time periods.

Aporia: literally "no passage," which is to say lacking an answer or solution, such that the philosophical problem remains.

Applied Ethics: see **Ethics**.

Argument: in philosophy this refers to a series of statements, in which one statement, called the "conclusion," is said to follow from the other statements, called "premises."

Autonomy: the state or condition of being self-directed.

Biconditional: in logic, statements using the phrase "if and only if" between two atomic sentences are biconditionals. More specifically, biconditional statements are composed of two ("bi") conditional statements in which the antecedent and consequent of the first conditional reverse position in the second such that the first conditonal as "if p then q" is combined with the second conditional, "if q then p," that is more economically stated as "p if and only if q."

Care: see **Ethics of Care**.

Categorical Imperative: a key concept in Kant's deontological ethical theory which refers to an absolute command or commands (there are several formulations in Kant's writings) based on reason alone and not on personal ends. Kant's main formulation is this: "Act only on that maxim whereby thou canst at the same time will that it should become a universal law."

Cogency: a characteristic of a well-formulated argument that satisfies three criteria of cogent reasoning (relevant information, sufficient information, and information that is well-justified and likely to be true).

Compassion: feeling or participating in the suffering of another.

Conjunction: the combination of two atomic statements into one compound with the use of the word "and" or any of its equivalents and which is true only when all of its individual atomic statements are true.

Consequentialism: the view that the moral value of an action is determined by its consequences or objective results.

Contractarianism: the view that morality is based on the agreement of individuals. See also **Social Contract Theory**.

Contraposition: a form of immediate inference involving a combination of conversion and obversion.

Conversion: in logic, the equivalent converse of a statement is one in which the placement of subject and predicate terms is reversed, retaining the truth value of the original. Only E and I form statements undergo equivalent conversion.

Corollary: a statement that follows logically from another one.

Deductive Argument: an argument formulated such that the truth of the premises guarantees the truth of the conclusion. See also **Valid/Validity**.

Deontology: literally "the study of duty," this refers to an ethical theory, such as Kantian ethics, centered on the intention or motive to do the right thing specifically because it is one's duty or obligation to do so.

Difference Principle: in John Rawls' theory of justice, this is the notion that every rationally self-interested person would agree that social and economic inequalities are to be arranged so that they are to the advantage of the least advantaged members of society.

Disjunctive Syllogism: a valid deductive argument of this form: Either A or B. Not A. Therefore, B.

Disjunction: a compound statement formed using "or" or any of its equivalents which is true when either of the disjuncts comprising the disjunction is true. It is important to note that weak, inclusive disjunctive statements have this characteristic while strong, exclusive disjunctions do not. Strong, exclusive disjunctions are often clarified with the addition of the phrase "but not both" added to the standard "A or B."

Divine Command Theory: the view that moral values come from the command of a God or gods and that we have a duty to follow these commandments. The Divine Command Theory is closely related to the "Euthyphro Problem" which questions whether X is good because God commands it, or whether God commands X because it is good. See **Euthyphro Problem**.

Dogmatism: holding certain beliefs or opinions to be unquestionably true without considering the arguments or reasoning of others.

Equal Liberty Principle: in John Rawls' theory of justice, this is the idea that every person would recognize that everyone should have the same basic right to participate in the social and political process and to have an equal voice in the arrangements and decisions made on a social level.

Ethical Egoism: the normative view that human beings ought to be self-interested (cf. **Psychological Egoism**).

Ethical Relativism: the view that all ethical values lack a solid foundation and are "relative" to and therefore variable based on particular individuals or groups such that no one view can be seen as better than another.

Ethics: a branch of philosophy devoted to questions of value (e.g., good and evil) with regards to human actions and character (note that "ethics" come from the Greek word *ethos*, which means "character"). There are two sub-branches: **Applied Ethics,** which is devoted to using ethical theories within specific areas (e.g., business, healthcare, etc.), and **Theoretical Ethics.** Theoretical ethics can then be divided into two sub-categories: **Normative Ethics,** which deals with questions about what we should or should not do and what is the best way to live, and **Metaethics,** second-order level of questioning the nature of ethical language and the status of normative ethical claims.

Ethics of Care: a moral theory that emphasizes the significance of caring relationships in contrast to a theoretical emphasis on justice. The ethics of care is a major development of feminist ethics.

Eudaimonia: from the Greek word literally meaning "good spirits" and commonly translated as "happiness" or more recently "flourishing." This is the central goal of Aristotle's ethical theory and refers to an activity of the soul in accord with perfect virtue.

Euthyphro Problem: As originally formulated in Plato's dialogue, *Euthyphro*—"Is the pious loved by the gods because it is pious, or is it pious because it is loved?"—this problem concerns whether the value of an action is independent of or derived from the will of a (divine) being or beings. See also **Divine Command Theory.**

Existentialism: commonly said to have begun with Kierkegaard in the 19th century and made prominent by Sartre in the 20th century, this umbrella term refers to a movement in philosophy that focuses on questions of human existence and emphasizes the significance of individual responsibility for creating meaningful lives.

Fallacy: an error in argumentation or reasoning.

Feminist Ethics: this refers to a variety of ethical positions informed by the view that traditional ethical theories have neglected the moral views of women (cf. **Ethics of Care**).

Formal Logic: see **Logic.**

Golden Mean: in Aristotle's ethics this refers to the intermediate between extremes (where extremes are vices), which may be understood as the perfect or most excellent way (the virtuous way) to act in any given situation.

Good: this is obviously one of the most important ethical terms and thus also one of the most difficult to define. For Plato, the Good is the highest abstract idea and can only be realized after protracted philosophizing. In general, the good refers to that which promotes human learning, happiness, well-being, or the kind of life worth living.

Goodwill: in Kant's ethical theory this refers to the rational faculty for acting according to principles and is, according to Kant, the only thing good without qualification (i.e., good in itself).

Harm Principle: the notion, important in Mill's social theory, that a person is free to do as she or he sees fit as long as that person's actions do not harm others.

Happiness: this is the central goal of Aristotle's ethical theory and refers to an activity of the soul in accord with perfect virtue. In Utilitarianism, happiness is defined much more simply as "pleasure." See also **Eudaimonia**.

Hermeneutics: the art of interpretation.

Hypothetical Syllogism: a valid deductive argument of this form: If A, then B. If B, then C. Therefore, if A, then C.

Individualism: the view that persons should be free to develop their talents and to engage in activities as they see fit, provided that they do not harm to other persons. Individualism is usually contrasted with the interests of the community and of other individuals. Individualism is historically associated with the notion that human beings are not necessarily or naturally social or political beings.

Inductive Argument: an argument formulated such that its conclusion is likely to be true if the information provided in support of the conclusion is true.

Inference: in argumentation this is the intellectual process moving from premises to the establishment of a conclusion.

Informal Logic: see **Logic**.

Loaded Language: words used to provoke an emotional effect.

Logic: a branch of philosophy devoted to the rules and principles of good reasoning. **Informal Logic** deals with arguments that occur in ordinary language, whereas **Formal Logic** deals primarily with symbolically constructed arguments of purely deductive form.

Love: a fundamental human emotion and activity directed at the well-being of the other.

Metaethics: see **Ethics**.

Modus Ponens: a valid deductive argument of this form: If A, then B. A. Therefore, B.

Modus Tollens: a valid deductive argument of this form: If A, then B. Not B. Therefore, not A.

Moralism: a dogmatic view of ethical theorizing, in which one often seeks a single correct moral theory as the final end of ethical thinking.

Natural Law Theory: in general this refers to a view that holds that objective ethical values are derived from natural human reasoning.

Normative Ethics: see **Ethics**.

Obversion: a form of immediate inference and transformation of statements in Traditional Logic in which the quality of a statement (i.e., affirmative or negative) is changed and the prefix "non-" or its equivalent is added to the predicate term of the statement.

Opinion: in general this refers to an accepted belief that is not acquired through conscious reasoning.

Paternalism: a view of moral thinking which involves making decisions or taking actions on behalf of another person or being, usually including the belief that the person for whom decisions or made or actions are taken is not capable of acting wisely or well on her or his own.

Perfectionism: a view which holds that the central goal of human beings is to act continually and completely in every situation in the best way possible.

Philosophy: from a Greek word literally translated as "the love of wisdom," this is the academic and practical discipline of raising fundamental questions and seeking to answer them through critical reasoning.

Poisoning the Well: an informal logical fallacy in which one discredits a position from the start, usually through **Loaded Language**.

Premise: a reason offered in support of a conclusion.

Principle of Charity: this involves giving the strongest possible reading and rendering of the positions of others to provide the strongest possible evaluations of them.

Psychological Egoism: a descriptive view essentially meaning that human beings are self-interested and will do whatever they believe is in their own best interest (cf. **Ethical Egoism**).

Rationality: in its most basic sense this involves acting according to reasons.

Reflective Thinking: according to Dewey this is the kind of thinking that involves "turning a subject over in the mind and giving it serious and consecutive consideration."

Relativism: see **Ethical Relativism**.

Rhetoric: the art of speaking and writing persuasively.

Social Contract Theory: the view that governments exist by the consent and agreement of the governed.

Sophists: in ancient times these were paid itinerant teachers of rhetoric.

Sound/Soundness: the characteristic of a valid deductive argument in which all the statements comprising the argument are true. It is impossible for a sound argument to be invalid; but it is possible for a valid argument to be unsound.

Straw Man: an informal logical fallacy in which one misleadingly represents in a weak or weakened form the argument of another person with the express purpose of discrediting the argument.

Subjectivism: the view that ethical values are merely an individual's personal, subjective preferences, such that what is right for me need not be right for you.

Teleological/Teleology: tending towards a goal or purpose; purposive.

Theoretical Ethics: see **Ethics**.

Universalizable: capable of becoming a universal law.

Utilitarianism: an ethical theory that bases the value of an action on its "utility" or usefulness in promoting happiness. Jeremy Bentham (1748–1832) and John Stuart Mill (1806–1873) are the first major proponents of Utilitarianism.

Valid/Validity: an argument following the appropriate form such that if the premises are true, the conclusion must also be true, or better, the falsehood of the conclusion is inconsistent with the truth of the premises. Not to be confused with **Soundness**.

Veil of Ignorance: in Rawls' social theory this involves reasoning from the assumption that we do not possess knowledge of the contingent features of our lives, so that in a decision-making context we are not likely to formulate principles of justice that are unfair and unjust.

Virtue Ethics: an ethical theory developed from Aristotle (384–322 BCE) that focuses on cultivating virtues of moderation by habitually acting in accordance with "the golden mean."

Index